BROTHERS IN ARMS
BIKIE WARS
SIMPSON & HARVEY
FREEMASON LIES

TAURUS RISING

AUSTRALIA

ABRIDGED

I

NATIONAL
LIBRARY
OF AUSTRALIA

A catalogue record for this
book is available from the
National Library of Australia

II

Brothers in Arms
Bikie Wars
Simpson & Harvey
Freemason Lies

Taurus Rising
Australia
Abridged

J.G. FRANCIS

Cover Design: ©*2024 Janette Gail Francis, Australia.*
Front: Headstone (unknown photographer) James McLachlan & Jane McGregor immigrated to Australia as 'boatpeople' from Kilmarnock Scotland, in 1864 aged 20 and 21, married with 2 little girls, 3yo Jane & 1yo MaryAnne (named after James twin sister) MaryAnne died onboard EarlRussel from epidemic. Jane McGregor is my 3rd Great Grandmother, daughter of Margaret Adams & Thomas McGregor who is 2nd Great Grandson of **Scotland's folk hero Rob Roy MacGregor (1671–1734)**
I've same MtDNA as Jane McGregor McLachlan. Back cover: Janette c1982 aged 26, married & mother of three beautiful little boys.

Brothers in Arms Bikie Wars Simpson & Harvey Freemason Lies: Taurus Rising Australia Wildfire Abridged
NONFICTION—SELF-EVIDENT TERRORIST GOVERNMENT
ISBN **9781923287006** paperback grayscale
©2024 Janette Gail Francis, Australia.
For associated (available) full colour images see the associated publication (also ©2024) Taurus Rising: Fake democracy proved by one person & many true secret FREEMASON government crime. Wildfire volume 1&2 EBOOK ISBN 9780645597523 — Au$4.00 on Amazon.com.au priced for almost everyone to afford, to know truth about the global fraud named constitutional democracy.
My website https://janetteGailFrancis.com
www.Facebook.com/JanetteGailFrancis
www.youtube.com/@CallToArmsFromAustralia
Out of print
   ©*2018 JanetteFrancis Child In Time justice out of reach is justice denied.*
   ©*2024 Wildfire Volume 1 (eBook)*
   ©*2024 Wildfire Volume 2 (eBook)*
   ©*2024 Taurus Rising: Fake democracy proved by one person & many true secret FREEMASON government crime. Wildfire volume 1&2 ebook isbn 9780645597523*
   ©*2024 Brothers in Arms Bikie Wars Simpson & Harvey Freemason Lies: Taurus Rising Australia Wildfire Abridged isbn 9780645597578 - hardcover grayscale image.*

So much of our day to day life is fake without us even realizing. How many medical research papers are fake AI written? How many modern acclaimed literary genius novels are fake AI written? How many politicians speeches, award winning songs and film scripts are also fake AI generated? If it has errors like mine unashamedly does, then its fair chance its been written by a human until they start to include human errors in artificial intelligence text editors because barbaric people have no taboos.

"there's no defense against the wildfire of a mob"

"When you are right, you cannot be too radical; when you are wrong, you cannot be too conservative"

Martin Luther King jnr

Don't get angry, get evidence.

1: Arrows point to obvious evidence of abnormal & significant vibration.

INSANE SADISTIC BASTARDS

Their actions prove their criminal intent.

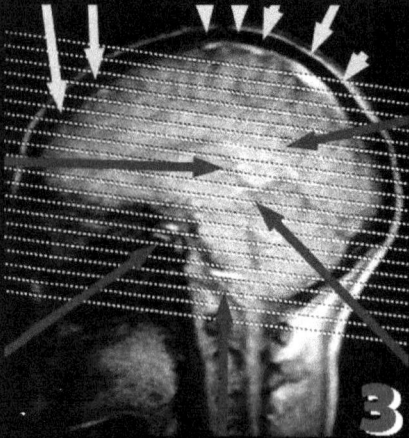

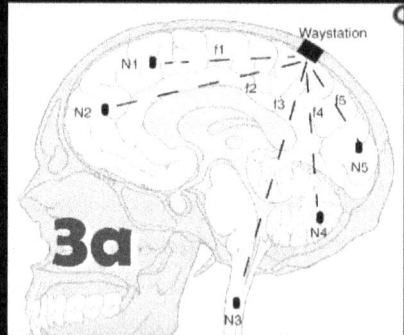

3

(3) MRI 2006 Janette head. NONE of these abnormal items were noted in the report despite that Janette asked for the MRI to identify the cause of abnormal vibrations and electrical sparking on her skin at locations of these abnormal items are and send abnormal electrical current (shock waves) into Janette's brain - along with specialist refusal to ID

3a

(3a) This USA government internet website image labels wireless phone network controlled experimental implant item as WAYSTATION.

www.ncbi.nlm.nih.gov/pmc/articles/PMC4156009/

Looking at image (3) MRI Janette's head, any reasonable person can see the unidentified item is in the same location on Janette's head.

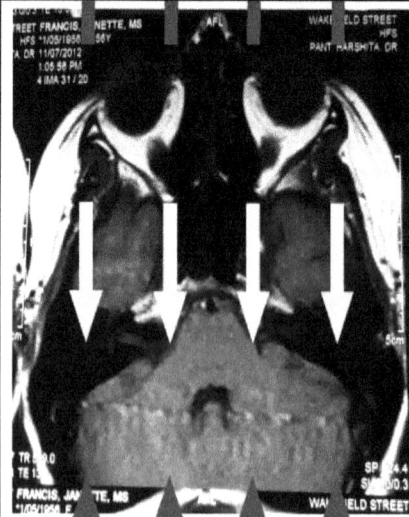

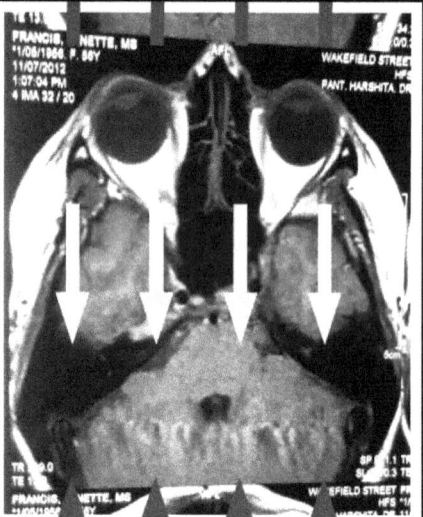

MRI: Slice 29 to 32 inclusive, (false "20" total).
Patient: Janette Gail Francis.
By: PERRETT JONES Medical Imaging, radiology partners with State of South Australia in hospitals across Adelaide.
Date: 11 July 2012.
At: Calvery Wakefield Hospital private hospital.

www.2-dogs.club

WHAT ELSE DID THEY 'FORGET'?
During the MRI Janette's head was significantly abnormally vibrating, (since 17 November 2005 unexplained energy strike). Janette says she *"That was positive as the vibration should show up in the image."* They did, but the radiologist decided not to report on them, (at arrows). They're similar to the mobile phone vibration identified on first page by the Kaunas Hospital Dept of Radiology USA.

© 2024 JANETTE GAIL FRANCIS

Call To Arms From Australia

Call to arms here means I'm seeking action from lawyers to help me sue the tortfeasors, and physicians whose prime concern is my safety in removal of very painfully located illegal implants.

The foreign items inside me are located literally from head to toe, they appear to have encircled me with cables not sure if they did that under belief that encircling me with cables would generate enough electricity to run their implants. The inordinate strength of the internal vibrations from the implanted cables indicate my entire structure has been used as frame material to mount their long-distance antenna.

Their silicone is partially seen in MRI of my head – criminal intent of radiologists is derived from fact the image of my full profile (front cover) was darkened by radiologists, obviously to make it hard to see the silicone clearly, as you can plainly see some of the (white) cables are very visible due to the darkness. Silicone is in pockets in my back around my armpits over my chest, on my leg bends at my hip and in my elbow bends. Other smaller pockets may exist. As I recall I was informed (when drugged) they had or were injecting the pockets then filling them up. No idea myself if they were just spinning me that to mess with me psychologically. I only know where they are (everywhere) and recall having mystery stitches where now, the most painful implants are in my spine and shoulder.

- They injected silicone in my fingers and toes.

- They implanted cables and other apparatus in the palms of my hands and soles of my feet, encasing their cables with silicone or other matter.

- Cables cross over my elbow (funny bone) making my elbow hurt to lean my head in my hand and elbow on a hard surface. Cables cross over my knees so they twang or roll over top on my kneecap as I walk or pedal a bicycle.

- I can't be certain what silicone is free floating and what's in pockets I'd like to be able to walk without the pain under the soles of my feet and front of my ankles where those cables scrape as I flex my foot walking.

- I'd like to sleep without cables tapping in my groin and around my pubic bone and anus, me keeping me half awake in a status of perpetual indecent violation.

- I'd like to sit in peaceful status of motionless without my head vibrating from the implants in the back of my neck, my throat and over top of my skull down my spine to my tailbone.

- I'd like to not have to pack my ears with toilet paper to soak up the liquid skin caused by constant vibrations on my head. I know its skin as it dries hard on the paper, ripping when I remove the wet or dry paper.

- I'd like to rest my ear on a pillow without waking in pain due to implants in my outer ear.

- I'd like to rest my ear on a pillow without hearing the constant digital pulse in my head and the squishing of liquid skin in my ear canal.

- I'd like to lay on my side or back in bed without waking in pain due to implants cable over my hip and tailbone inserted 1991 when pregnant.

- I'd like to sit without the sharp repetitive stabbing between my shoulder blades linked to the sparking and vibrating cables in my neck, left cochlear region, crown of my head, forehead, nose, lips, chin and jaw.

- I'd like to look down and up again without foreign matter catching at the back of my neck at base of my brain.

- I'd like to eat warm food and drink warm fluids without burning inside my mouth because there's so much silicone keeping my skin temperature inside my mouth very cool.

- I'd like to yawn without silicone herniating under my tongue.

- I'd like to pinch my index finger and thumb without silicone herniating under my little finger.

- I'd like full use of my dislocated thumbs again.

- I'd like to put on footware and tie laces without silicone herniating through my ribs.

- I'd like to twist sideways without silicone herniating through my ribs.

- I'd like to put my feet up without silicone herniating around the side of my knee and upper leg muscles.

- I'd like to sit in a kitchen chair without silicone herniating through muscles under the back of my upper leg above back of my knee

- I'd like to be naturally warm in winter again giving the sensation that my shins and sides of my knees radiating painful frosty cold despite that they're warm to touch.

- I'd like to be naturally naturally cool in summer again without the silicone encasing me like a bed-covering, refusing to let me naturally cool causing me to break out in an icy cold sweat from face to legs and everywhere in between with the minimalist amount of activity.

- I'd like to know exactly how much I naturally weigh as the extra silicone and scar tissue has masked my biological weight, this is important as when I'm close to malnutrition under 50kg, or have lower than my normal, low blood pressure - I suffer moderate dizzy spells as my male parent used to. He lived to 95. Now with the excess artificial weight I'm 70kg and suffer moderate dizzy spells as if I'm only 50kg, necessitating weight gain but I've no clue what my weight should be to not be malnourished because of all the silicone and 30 years of fuking scar tissue.

- I'd like to see these medical terrorists in an Australian prison for life.

- I'd like to have the silicone excavated from my poor nose (below) when they desired to make me look like a clown and resemplke the many names Camilla UNWIN, they injected silicone to broaden my naturally thin nose until it was oozing from the pores of my skin under my eyes, they injected silicone to enbulb the tip causing my poor nose to droop down with gravity like a limp penis and collapse inwards narrowing my nostrils. I refuse to mouth breathe as I know it'll alter my jaw shape.

- The cable (nose mouth photo) is engulfed in silicone. I have to work at it to evacuate silicone from the regin to expose the cable. There's another the same in my lower lip both inserted 1997. They're connected to my nose

2: Below: I'm pointing to *(c1997 secretly & illegally inserted)* vibrating cable implanted in my top lip, from video on Youtube titled **"See illegal implant cables inserted bt Australia's Freemason Organized Government Funded Terrorists"** uploaded one year ago, in 2023. My nose is full of hardened silicone that've caused my nostrils to collapse inwards giving my nose a permanent artificial 'flared nostrils' appearance & hindering nose breathing.

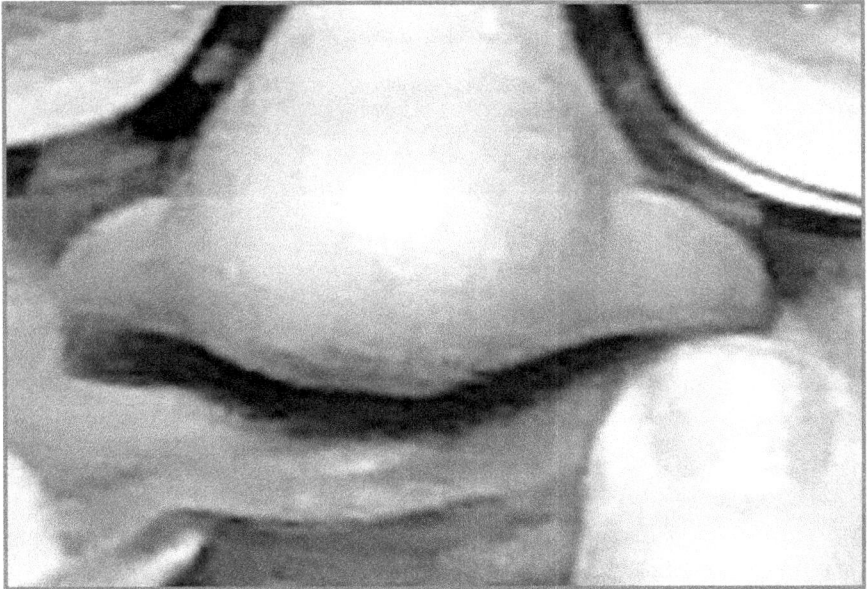

and chin with more cable. Vibrations are sound that makes heat.

My informative channel youtube have refused to advertise despite my paid requests:, which indicates government officials are illegally stalking my online presence to illegally censure me online by making my presence invisible in search engine searches.

@Call To Arms From Australia https://www.youtube.com/channel/UC12h0Ms3AT aUrUEDZTYOMXg

☓

3: To better read elongated text, tilt top of the page away from you.

These Details Omitted from Bikie Wars TV Mini Series

Preview this book **Brothers in Arms** by David Harvey, Lindsay Simpson

Page 266

On 23 November 1988, a full bench of the Court of Criminal Appeal overturned the six mens' convictions and sentences. The judges found that Justice Roden had erred in his directions to the jury and the full bench substituted manslaughter convictions for the standing murder convictions.

Hennessey, Heeney, Annakin and Melville had their non-parole period reduced to seven years; Ross received nine years non-parole and Kucler eight years.

Comancheros Ian White and Glen Eaves are also appealing against their murder convictions and sentences. Their hearing is listed for March 1989.

Kezra Lorenz is divorced from Rick (Chewy) Lorenz and now lives in London where she has written a film script about her life with a Comanchero.

Chief Superintendent Ronald Harry Stephenson was awarded the Commissioner's commendation at the Goulburn Police Academy in NSW on 7 August 1987, in recognition of outstanding leadership and command of police resources concerned with the investigation of the Father's Day Massacre at Milperra on 2 September 1984. Detective Superintendent Stephenson showed ability in controlling and co-ordinating this inquiry, greatly contributing to the successful outcome of this matter which brought considerable merit to the NSW police force, the Commissioner said.

On 26 January 1988, Chief Superintendent Stephenson was listed in the Bicentennial Australia Day Honours List and awarded the Australian Police Medal for distinguished service.

Detective John Garvey received the Commissioner's recommendation for bravery on 7 August 1987, in recognition of outstanding courage and devotion to duty in confronting Kucler and disarming him, and in negotiations and the disarming of the bikies thus enabling medical treatment for a number of injured people.

Detectives: All of the detectives who took part in Operation Hardwalk were invited to buy a Father's Day Massacre tie. The police ran a competition for the best design. On the second anniversary of the massacre, they held A Viking Tie night, entry being by wearing one of the ties. About 80 people turned up for a smorgasbord and a few drinks. One police officer described it as "a few postmortems on the whole thing." A comedian was hired for entertainment.

The Harris Park Clubhouse was converted into a doctor's surgery. The bullet holes were still in the garage roller door at the time the doctors moved in.

No. 150 Louisa Road, Birchgrove was bought by a member of the

266

janettefraNCIS.com

TABLE OF FIGURES

℺

CONTENTS

☿

UTTER BULLSHIT

Right Australia's Prime Minister 2024 photographer unknown. I added the crown jewels from wherever that was, it wasn't well described.

Below with written adaptation of (only names have been changed) SIMPSON & HARVEY's *'Brothers In Arms Inside Story of two* (political) *Gangs"* are some of the many sets of criminally defamatory fiction' words maliciously and intentionally falsely describing my biometric identity (face) my personality, my associates and me generally when I was 14-years-old as published or approved by NSW police department 's hundreds of police officers and other officials since 1989 funded by Australia's Federal government *pedophiles* in 2011-2012 as television miniseries BIKIE WARS.

"14-year-old **Joanne Slowman's** teenage memorabilia was his tattered sex license, his criminal record for shoplifting, and his expulsion from Catholic school for stealing beer from a delivery truck while on a school walkathon and kicking a nun while spitting & swearing profusely.

Adulthood came early for **Joanne**, who sought approval and love from the supposedly worldly characters he met at the regular haunts of bikers and other misguided souls in after slipping out his bedroom window in the dead of night aged (what was it) 12-years-old looking for underage sex with Freemason police in Liverpool New South Wales Australia

By July 1984 **Joanne** weighed more than seven stone. He had had his hair restyled, cut short around his face and left long at the back. He had his photograph taken at a booth that advertised four instant black and white photographs for $2. He pasted one of the photos on to a **"sex licence card"** someone had given him from a sex shop. In the black and white photo he kept in her wallet, his lips were pursed, his eyes flirted with the hidden camera.

"**This is to certify that the person named and described on the reverse side has been licensed to enjoy sex anytime, anywhere, anyway.**"

Joanne was not sure what "erogenous zones" meant, so he left that space blank. Underneath "turn-ons" he wrote "spunks" in green biro her mum Elaine Slowman stole from Tony Featherstone's office at Visyboard in Scrivener Street, Warrick Farm.. He thought about the word "restrictions", then wrote "none". His "turn-offs" he listed as "nifty, orry, **pigs**." They were terms he often heard his friend Misfeasance use. He had a stainless steel stud inserted in his left nostril as part of the new image. One day he bumped into his sister Chernobyl in Macquarie Street. **"You look like a cheap little slut!"** yelled Chernobyl, wrenching the stud from his nostril and throwing it down. "**I thought after all this time, you would get your act together a bit—get yourself a job. Pull your socks up and stop being a bloody little desperate!**" Chernobyl, now in her late teens, had a steady job at Paul Keating's electorate office as a secretary, and a man to settle down with. Not so Joanne. If the Las Vegas cafe was empty he and Misfeasance would wander down to the end of the street and hang around the Commercial Hotel in the concrete beer garden looking for anyone they knew. The Liverpool-based Rebels bikies used to drink there in the afternoons. **Joanne** would look for Shifty's bike, the black Harley, painted red, the petrol tank encased in gold pin striping, flames leaping out from the shiny sides. The word "Rebels" proclaimed his club allegiance. If his machine wasn't parked up the long driveway at the side of the pub with the other **Harley Davidsons, Joanne** would wait and listen"

Yes, Government paedophiles called me a *"child slut"* in 1989 and in writing — then funded TV miniseries to celebrate their premeditated criminal mutilations and defamations of me for their political or ideological causes (terrorism) which includes illegal removal of my legal right to sue them for damages, as multi-generation born citizen — these (above) false claims of me were repeated to others and my face many times in 1990s by *many Wollondilly Shire Councillors, staff and police pointing guns at me.* Aided by immigrant surgeons for my very extensive surgical rape and face mutilations. As my recent DNA is bright white their racial discrimination is now '*equality driven*' and *undeniably terrorism*. BUSTED. ꙮ

Back Cover **Simpson & Harvey's Brothers In Arms since 1984** being the 'theme' of their paperback which contradicts the coroner's records and 1984 press stories that stated the girl was 14, the used 15 so they could label my face as "cheap little slut" because I was raped when 15, so I suspect they wanted to leave me thinking it was those police children who organized my 1971 rape as being behind the SIMPSON & HARVEY trash — not Freemasons who murdered Jack BASSET in cold blood on 24 April 1988 before my eyes. The age of consent in NSW Australia in 1984 was 16, still is, should be 18.

"Among the dead, a fifteen-year-old girl caught in the crossfire when two heavily-armed bikie gangs, the Comancheros and the Bandidos, clash."

That's utter bullshit, its the main theme of the billions of words for the thousands of lies to conceal organized crime in Australia as told by hundreds of Freemasons and their police, their politicians, their physicians and the Freemason publishing families who've infiltrated the publishing industry to falsify many true facts not limited to the Monday 3 September 1984 front page Sydney Australia cover (right) criminally falsified globally since the Sunday before. Falsified in their 1989 paperback using my stolen biometric identity. Falsified for Government's funded 2012 television miniseries all sarcastically titled 'Brothers In Arms' with cloaked reference to Freemason Brotherhood psychopaths & sycophants in the 100s singing same song way out of tune to conceal truth in evidence of Freemason orchestrated murders on Sunday 2 September 1984 in drab car park of just another seedy pub, Viking Tavern, located in the industrial area of southern Sydney that chilly Spring afternoon simply impossible to forget because its peppered with so many blatant lied spun by Freemason terrorist police and their Freemason terrorist supporters.

First photo story says the only killed 'she' as 16 years old. Every subsequent police statement and television and radio news story on the matter stated 'she' was 14. The fake grave in Leppington's Lawn cemetery has headstone with no birth date and no body underneath no doubt. Naturally as we all know now 'she' only ever existed on paper. Despite the Attorney-General's coroner's records the NSW and Federal Australia's politically deluded Freemason centric government funded television miniseries and news documentaries to insist 'she' is 15 on death and had my 20 something adult face. In 21st century Australia your biometric facial features are well established as your lawful identity with same status as your name and signature your face is your own copyright identity that you own and no other.

Everything about the SIMPSON & HARVEY Brothers in Arms story is a liw therefore everything about the 1984 shooting deaths is also a lie to pervert the course of justice and due administration of law in the factual violent deaths of at least six male persons, they're all someone's much loved son. They deserve the truth to be told about their deaths. ♉

UTTER BULLSHIT

ORGANIZED CHAOS

SMH 3/9/1984

LATE EDITION

6 The girl was just standing

The Milperra massacre: police quiz hundreds

PAGE ONE

By RICHARD MACEY and DAVID MONAGHAN

More than 30 men were arrested last night as police questioned at least 500 witnesses after seven people were shot dead in a bikie brawl at the carpark of the Viking Tavern in the south-western suburb of Milperra.

No charges had been laid by 1 am

Among the dead was a 14-year-old girl who was selling raffle tickets at a family barbecue market day when she took a shotgun blast full in the face. The other dead were men.

One of the 20 injured had his arm chopped off by a machete as two rival bikie gangs, the Bandidos and the Commancheros, invaded the carpark in Beaconsfield Road at 1.55 pm.

Fourteen ambulances ferried the wounded, including one policeman, to Liverpool, Westmead and Bankstown hospitals. Armed guards were placed on the casualty wards last night.

One witness said the girl was standing beside him. The two of them were about seven metres from one of the gunmen.

"It was out with a gun and into it, he seemed to be firing in all directions," the man said.

"When I saw him he was pointing the gun our way, and then the little girl fell. She copped it in the chin. She must have died instantly.

"He must have fired eight shots. I hit the ground and then got up and ran — like everybody else."

A member of the British Motorcycle Association, a social club, was close to tears as he told of seeing the mutilated body of the girl.

"People took off in all directions. As I ran I was worried I was going to get a bullet in the back," he said.

The carpark that became a battleground had been the peaceful scene since 8 am yesterday of a barbecue and motorcycle parts market day organised by the BMA.

The venue had been widely advertised in the press, motorcycle shops and on power poles.

It was very much a family

Bystanders ran screaming from the carpark and people started falling beside cars.

One of the gang members, apparently shot dead as he charged toward his opponents, still clutched a baseball bat in his fist.

Three more bodies fell close together near a line of motorcycles, shot within metres of the gunmen.

The crowd scattered when at first two shots were fired from near a car at the back fence of the hotel grounds.

One of the gunmen paused to drink beer with friends during a lull in the battle. He was watched by Wayne McTighe, 12, from his home on the other side of Beaconsfield Road.

"He had blood pouring from the side of his head when he started shooting," Wayne said.

For about 15 minutes this gunmen laid siege to the hotel. About 40 people were trapped inside the Norseman Bar when the shooting started. They hid under tables as the shots rang out.

The first ambulance arrived while the firing continued. The gunmen lowered rifles to allow the ambulancemen to take away the wounded.

About 30 shots were fired in 10 minutes, with a pause while the two sides reloaded.

"I was standing in the driveway with my bike when I saw eight or nine Bandidos ride up," said a member of the British Motorcycle Association, "A couple of minutes later I heard gunshots and screaming. I hid behind a bike for a while and when the shooting stopped I took off without looking back".

Wes Graham, 23, who was on the hotel verandah when the shooting started, said he saw two shots fired in the air and then one man shot in the head.

"I saw another guy shoot someone in the guts, and he just keeled over and then the girl was shot. She wasn't even doing anything," he said.

One woman said: "I was in the carpark when I heard what I thought were firecrackers going off.

near the driveway of the bo shop.

Within two hours, more th 100 police from 19 divisions, Tactical Response Group, Special Weapons and Operati team and homicide detectives)

ORGANIZED CHAOS

South Australia 21st century Australian Labor Party Health Minister John David HILL, also known as New South Wales 20th century convicted killer Lance WELLINGTON member of Bandidos Outlaw Motorcycle Club, according to Penrith District Criminal Court records & all their NSW police Ministers & police Commissioners & entire police departments, since 1984.

THE Sun

BEST SPORT

No.23,685   30 cents

Telephone 202 2833. Letters to Box 506, GPO, Sydney, 2001.

TUESDAY, SEPTEMBER 4, 1984

CITY FINAL   SUPER VALUE

Shootout: Comanchero leader tells of the agony and the orphans

'BIKIE COP' QUIZZED!

POLICE OFFICER IN GANG PARTY PHOTO

LEANNE KILLING GUN CLUE: P2

POLICE investigators have a photograph they believe is of a young constable dressed in bikie gear at a Comanchero gang party.

The police officer, stationed in the inner city, is to be questioned on his alleged association with the Comancheros over a number of years.

By STEVE BARRETT and STEVE BRIEN

The picture is in the hands of senior police investigating the allegations.

The photograph was allegedly seized by police at the Comancheros' headquarters following Sunday's massacre which resulted in seven people being murdered.

The policeman is believed to have told detectives that he has socialised on several occasions with both

Continued on page 2

UTTER BULLSHIT

The Sun Tue 4 Sept 1984

LEANNE SLAYING: NEW RIFLE CLUE

DEAD DEAD DEAD

THE DEAD: Phil Jeski (left), Mario Cianter and Bob Lane.

● From Page 1

members of the Comancheros and Bandidos gangs but was not a member himself.

Police Minister Anderson has instructed Deputy Commissioner Barney Ross to hold a full Internal Affairs Branch inquiry into the photograph, and allegations regarding the police officer's involvement with the Comancheros.

The acting leader of the Comanchero bikie gang said today his four mates who were killed had left seven children fatherless.

And one of the bikie widows was expecting twins, he said.

Speaking from the Comancheros' head-

● Bikie boss Jock Ross... still in a critical condition with gunshot wounds.

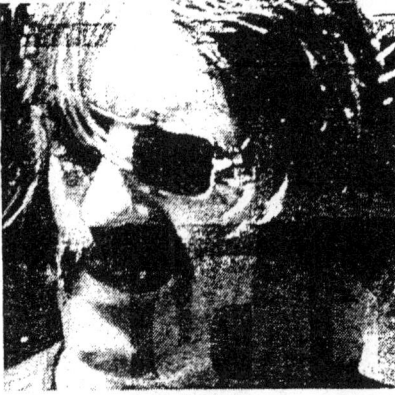

quarters at West Pennant Hills, leader Jay Jay, as he is known among fellow bikies, said: "All we can think about now is getting the families together to discuss their futures.

"We will make 100 per cent sure that all the women and kids left behind will receive some form of help and financial assistance from the club."

Meanwhile, police investigating the massacre say they have made a major breakthrough in their search for the killer of 15-year-old Leanne Walters.

They have been able to identify the type of weapon used.

Police say it was a heavy gauge rifle and not a shotgun as believed earlier.

The discovery makes the weapon far easier

CHARGED MAN DOESN'T SHOW

A MAN believed to be involved in Sunday's Milperra shoot-out failed to appear at Parramatta Court today.

Robert Alan Richardson, 30, unemployed, of Wentworth Avenue, Wentworthville, was charged with using a firearm on August 26.

Police Prosecutor Sgt Peter Horton told the court Richardson was "believed to be involved in the bikie incident which had appeared in the papers recently". The case was adjourned for a week.

● Leanne Walters

to trace, police say.

Leanne was standing in the car park of the Viking Tavern when

she was shot in the face.

Detectives today are checking the cache of arms they seized at the hotel at Milperra in an effort to find the weapon used.

Today the leader of the Comancheros gang, William George "Jock" Ross, 41, remains in a serious condition in the intensive care ward at Liverpool Hospital, suffering from multiple shotgun wounds.

The news that Leanne had died after being hit by a rifle shot and not a shotgun blast stemmed from the

results of a post-mortem examination yesterday.

Initial medical reports have revealed that all six bikies killed in the massacre died from shotgun blasts.

Police said that the three members of the Comancheros gang who fell almost side by side in the carpark of the hotel appeared to have been hit by separate shotgun volleys fired almost simultaneously as they rushed towards their attackers.

Ten bikies are still under police guard in Bankstown and Liverpool Hospitals.

LOTTO

THE winning numbers for Week 36 Lotto 1984 are: 33, 30, 27, 36, 35, 14 and the supplementary is 11.

Provisional prize pools are:

Division 1 — $2,000,000
Division 2 — $677,209
Division 3 — $677,209
Division 4 — $507,908
The total prize pool is: $3,862,326

ORGANIZED CHAOS

FATHER'S DAY MASSACRE

VICTIM'S DAD

Friends to start fund for Leanne

FRIENDS of Leanne Walters, 14, the youngest victim of the Father's Day massacre, have started a fund to raise money for her funeral.

Leanne's life had just taken a turn for the better when she was gunned down in Sunday's bikie bloodbath.

Friends say she was thrilled at recently finding work as a machinist in a factory in Liverpool's Hoxton Park Rd and had been happily settled in a foster home for four months.

"Things hadn't always been that good for Leanne, but all that was beginning to change," said one of her friends today.

"She had been expelled from school in Liverpool and had a series of foster homes," he said.

Last year she was in hospital for six months.

"Recently she had settled down quite a bit and was overjoyed at having found work."

Leanne became an innocent victim of Sunday's shoot-out as she sold raffle tickets in the Viking Tavern car park.

DEAD — Innocent bystander Leanne Walters

DEAD — Comanchero member Ivan Romcek

DEAD — Comanchero member Gregory Campbell

BIKIE FIRES SHOTS AT TERRIFIED MUM

● From Page 1

car window and just froze to the ground.

"That's when he started shooting and I hid behind the car."

Police said they were investigating the incident but were sure the gunman wasn't connected with the blood-

bath at the Viking Tavern.

Police found six .22-calibre bullets around Mrs McCarthy's home.

One bullet lodged in the front of the car behind which Mrs McCarthy had been hiding.

Another shot shattered the kitchen window and fell at the feet of the

friend as he sat there.

Mrs McCarthy said: "Thank God my 10-year-old son Jason is away or else he could have been killed."

She said she had never had any trouble in the street before and didn't know any bikies.

Jeffrey McCarthy rides a motorbike only on weekends and was never invol-

ved with bikies.

"I'm so frightened I just can't stay here. I'm going to go away for a few days because you never know what they'll decide to do," Mrs McCarthy said.

Jeffrey said he would sleep with a gun. "I'll use it if there's any trouble," he said.

DAILY MIRROR, TUESDAY, SEPTEMBER

& UTTER BULLSHIT

BRING MY LEANNE'S KILLERS TO JUSTICE!

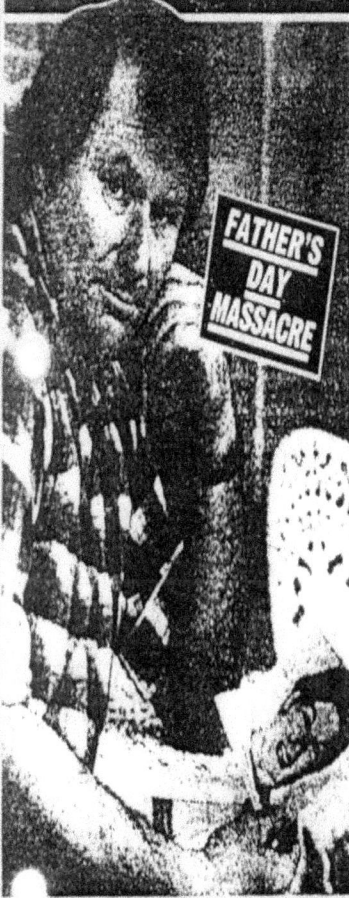

Heartbroken dad wants truth known

THE father of teenager Leanne Walters today broke his silence about his daughter who was killed in the Father's Day Massacre.

Mr Rex Walters said he wanted to see her killer brought to justice.

EXCLUSIVE by
MARK MORRI

"I want to see justice done — but more importantly I want the truth about my daughter to be known.

"The last time I saw her she came running up to me at a shop and said 'Dad I have your Father's Day present. I'll drop it around.'

"I can still hear those words," he said.

She was going to visit me on the Monday before came I was away on the weekend. On the Sunday at midnight I found out what happened.

"I was heartbroken."

Leanne died instantly when she was shot in the head during the bikie gun war which claimed seven lives at a Milperra hotel.

Brave

Mr Walters said he had accepted his daughter's death and wanted the public to know the truth.

She was just a bikie bye was a normal. I'm being told

Leanne was a brave 15-year-old girl who had fought off death twice before.

Last September Leanne was struck down by a disease which paralysed her from the neck down.

She was clinically dead twice but survived to spend months in a hospital bed.

She had a tube in her neck to breathe and after her release she had to teach herself to eat, dress and speak all over again.

"When I visited her in hospital I thought 'She's

not going to live,' my daughter is dying," Mr Walters said.

"Then I watched as she fought to live again and I was so proud of her.

"When she was released from hospital after four months she was in a wheelchair, but she had tremendous will power.

"Then after all that she dies in such a useless way," he said.

Mr Walters last saw his daughter two weeks before she was killed.

"She told me about the Father's Day present and how happy she was. She loved her job and was over the depression she had when she was ill."

Mr Walters and his wife are separated and Leanne lived with her mother until six weeks ago.

When the family home was sold, Mrs Walters moved to the central coast and Leanne asked her mother if she could stay in Sydney with the family of a friend.

She had never been in a foster home. She was only staying with a friend.

"I have none of Leanne's possessions because they are all at the home of where she was staying."

Leanne's father said he knew very little about the circumstances of her death.

'Nice fellow'

"I work for a touring coach company and was away on the Sunday. That's why Leanne was going to see me after Father's Day."

Mr Walters said he knew of his daughter's association with "Stretch" from the bikie gang the Rebels, who Leanne was with at the time of the massacre.

"I knew him as John, not Stretch. He was a nice fellow who never carried weapons, but just loved

FATHER'S DAY MASSACRE

…ENCE BROKEN: Rex Walters with a cherished photo of Leanne

WORLD SHOCKED BY MASSACRE

The Father's Day Massacre

7: Group of images various dates falsely claimed as the same dead Leanne Gaye WALTERS, Australia's fake dead, fake child shooting victim.

EXPOSING Rex Walters' LIES

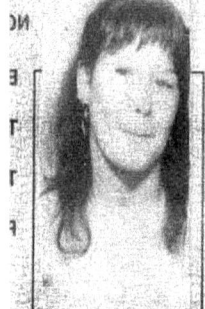

Janette Francis age 28

©2018

EARS NEVER LIE

Sydney news in first 24 hours: 100s police question 100s witnesses *as grieving family of only female and child killed* hand their photo to police who immediately released it for publishing *somehow* all of 1984 Sydney's many avid daily newspaper readers, funeral fund doners, police, press and television news researchers and reporters, 1989 book authors and researchers, politicians, government and private funders for 2012 TV series *all mysteriously missed poorly doctored ear* in "first photo"? that's Utter bullshit, **complements**[1] of New South Wales police department's terrorist gang, no doubt.

Ivan Romcek's Redacted Leg & Feet

Curiously, every time after I've been editing the Chapter with Ivan ROMCEK's deceased photos, having saved the chapter as a separate file, when I went back having opened the file three images were mysteriously deleted. Its as if someone is/was remotely shadowing my computer on their own computer. Which is preocular as I've never been on the internet at same time as I've been writing my book. All I can think of is that offenders came into my house when I wasn't home to plant a backdoor virus — or planted the routine (virus) when I was online — or most probably, a bit of both. Something like a keylogging so they can fiddle with my documents — remotely — when I'm editing them. There are number of other images that've similarly vanished from documents after printing to PDF. My habit is to save the document, then print to PDF, then close the document. I've noticed that sometimes after I print to PDF the word processor asks me to save the document again, but other times it doesn't — I suggest that second save is when the images are deleted.

The three documents missing in this chapter are:

1.   2014, Elaine SLOWMAN as Lynette STYLES, the photograph of her in a library and published in Wollondilly Advertiser online newspaper.

2.   1995, newly elected Wollondilly Shire Councillors from newsletter./

3.   2014, Ivan ROMCEK's disappearing leg and foot in the Queensland Courier Mail online photo. Following showing the centre person killed in 1984, whose leg was visible when published many times before 2014 mysteriously it was 'redacted' in 'Courier Mail' with a story about retired senior New South Wales police officer who was also in charge of the murder investigations pinned on another Ivan — Ivan MILAT, I'm

---

[1] Complements *means adds something,* compliments *means a politeness.*

8: Queensland online website perverting justice by redacting Ivan's leg & feet. I've lightened the original image from Internet so you can more easily see its been artificially darkened to redact Ivan ROMCEK's leg and feet. Why would someone do that 30 years after the event? Its absurd.

2:34pm Saturday, March 25th, 2023

The Courier Mail

Milperra Massacre: 30 years on, Father's Day will forever be a symbol of death and terror

https://www.couriermail.com.au/news/milperra-massacre-30-years-on-fathers-day-will-forever-be-a-symbol-of-death-and-terror/news-story/6e071eab762d414faefc27fe5718053e

The deep-rooted rivalry and feuding between the clubs exploded into violence on September 2, 1984, claiming seven lives and thrusting bikie gangs into the national spotlight.

Six bikies and 14-year-old bystander Leanne Walters were killed when the two warring clubs engaged in gunfire at a swap meet in the carpark at the Viking Tavern in Milperra.

The Comancheros suffered the greatest casualties, losing four members while the Bandidos lost two of their brothers.

referring to a prince of NSW Freemason police terrorism Clive SMALL another in a long list of police officer 'true crime' authors.

Incase you don't buy the companion color image book, I've included a grayscale copy of the same photo from inside every publication of the SIMPSON & HARVEY book.

10:1984 Ivan ROMCEK's leg & feet visible SIMPSON & HARVEY SIMPSON & HARVEY's 'Brothers In Arms' with my finger.

9: 1984 Ivan ROMCEK's leg & feet visible SIMPSON & HARVEY SIMPSON & HARVEY's 'Brothers In Arms' with my four fingers.

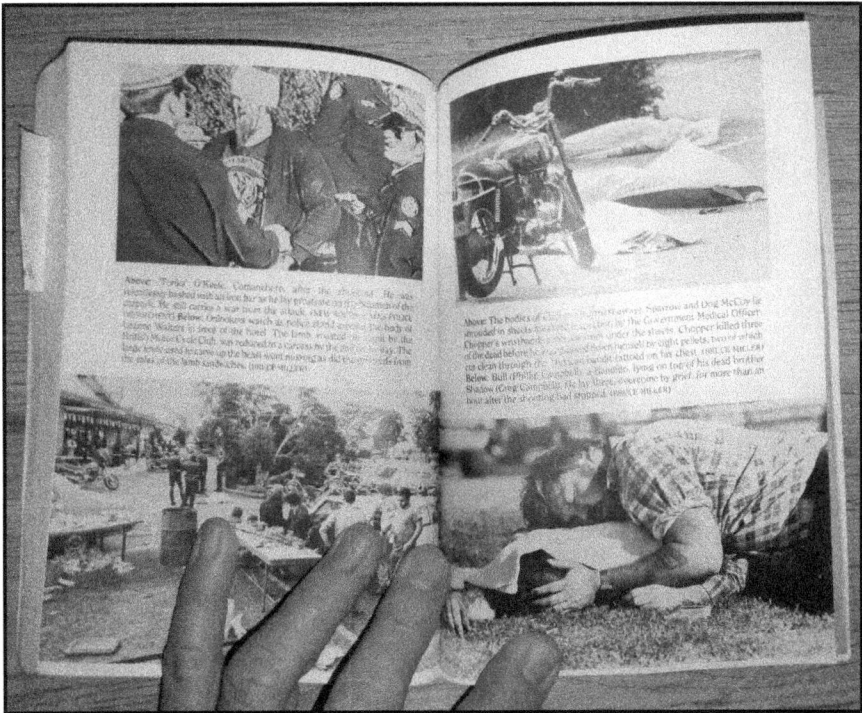

JOHN DAVID HILL ELECTION FRAUD

Interestingly in the same SIMPSON & HARVEY's 'Brothers In Arms' the last person to have a conflict with Ivan ROMCEK was stated as Lance

11: Lance WELLINGTON from SIMPSON & HARVEY's 'Brothers In Arms' - I'm guessing on orientation. Being a glasses wearer myself, the marks on his nose'd probably be from glasses. He's same bent nose as John HILL. Same tuft of hair on crown. Same head shape, same eye shape, same eye distance apart, same eye to nose to mouth ratio, same straight mouth, same ear alignment taking into account the angle of the camera & head tilt each time, same shoulders shape. Considering age, they look same person to me.

Lance later.

WELLINGTON. In the back of that publication Lance WELLINGTON was stated as being 36 when sentenced, the sentence was stated as ***"manslaughter 12 years, affray 6 years, non-parole period 7 years."*** Some 20 years later, the same Lance WELLINGTON was elected as a ***Labor Party*** member onto State parliament in South Australia, according to the SIMPSON & HARVEY stated true "true crime" facts that include all material they included in their (gutter trash) publication, which includes photos.

12: Australia's literal killer parliamentarian illegally nominated to parliament by Australian Labor Party, illegally anointed as Minister for Health by comrade terrorist, Jay Wilson WEATHERILL — John David HILL from website of University of South Australia. This is original orientation of this photo as copied from their website c2023.

Fact is that a person, like **Lance WELLINGOTN by any name**, whose been sentenced as stated in SIMPSON & HARVEY's 'Brothers In Arms' they're not qualified to stand for parliament. Therefore John David HILL committed fraud by his nomination and election.

As some twisted Labor Party joke, Premier Jay Wilson WEATHERILL appointed convicted killer John David HILL as the health Minister. More on that in chapter, Lancelot's Evil Twin. ♉

13: SIMPSON & HARVEY's 'Brothers In Arms' page "XV" or 15.

Glen Anthony Eaves after the battle.

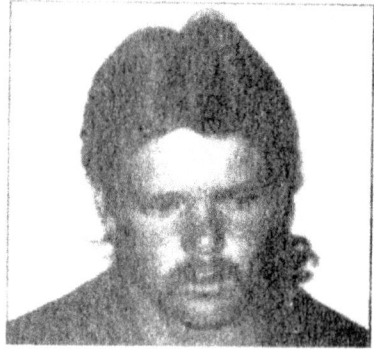

Eaves later.

Roo (Rua) Rophia after the battle.

Roo later.

Lance Wellington after the battle.

Lance later.

XV

14: Top left, me c1982, next to me c1984 as stolen for BIA, below 2 books.

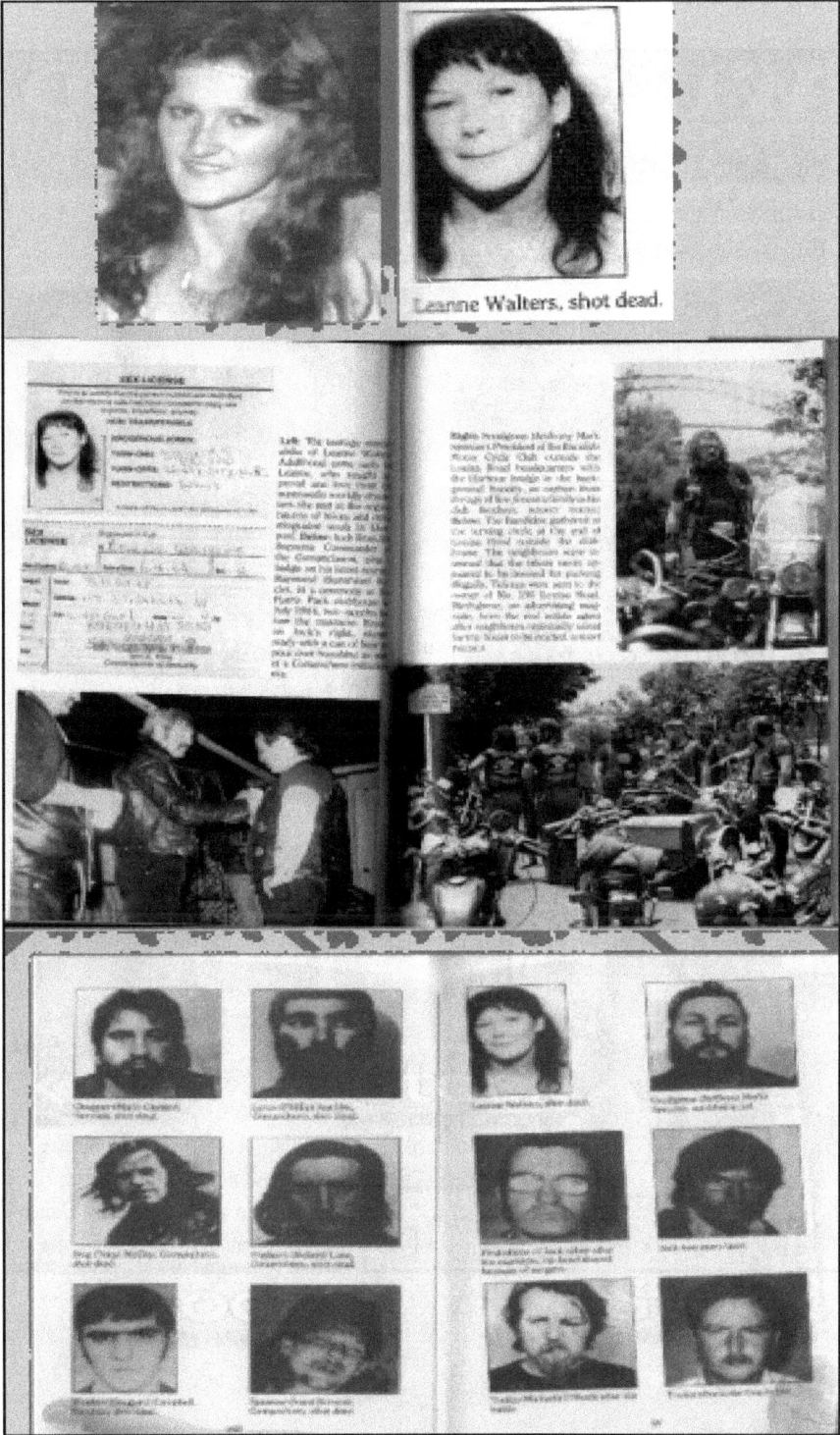

Leanne Walters, shot dead.

WITCH HUNTED
INCONVENIENT TRUTH
of GOVERNMENT CRIME

Leanne Walters, shot dead.
DailyMirror, Sydney Australia

Are you
Tamara Unwin
Lindsay?

Leanne Walters, shot dead.
The Sun, Sydney Australia

THE Sun
BINGO CARD!
VICTIM!
BIKIE
WAR:
REVENGE
FEARS
TRIUMPH

BROTHERS
IN ARMS

Sandra Harvey
Unwin Hyman
Ltd author of
Brothers In Arms
sister to Jennifer

Lindsay Simpson
Unwin Hyman
Limited author of
Brothers In Arms

Sharon Unwin
Bartrim
twin sister of
Tamara Unwin

Leanne Walters, shot dead

Cammilla Unwin
oldest sister of
Tamara & Sharon

Lynette Styles
author of
Kangaroo Court
mother to
Jennifer & Sandra

Jennifer Cooke
author of
Done Like a Dinner
sister to Sandra

Leanne Walters, shot dead.

Janette Gail Francis

GENOCIDE

Words hide secrets. What is a mocracy? Its government you pretend to have when you don't have lawful government. 'Democracy' a secret word for 'the mocracy'. Most criminals think sneaky. Political terrorists think cruel.

We live in an era where 'wicked' *is no longer* evil its sexy, where a sick or sicko *is no longer* sex predator its really good, and despicable *is no longer* the most disgusting thing you can think of its a children's story. We as adults are being brainwashed to groom our own children and grandchildren to accept sex predators as normal part of life. We've been so well brainwashed we don't even complain when the Government allow adverts prominently featuring *women and men proudly sitting with bare bottom on toilet* as they look into the camera grinning or talking to us like its what everyone does to strangers.

When channel flipping I stumbled on one such advertisement for Sorbent toilet paper during a ***Pokémon cartoon*** with a man walking to an outside toilet pulling his pants down and sitting on the loo as the camera panned back to make it perfectly clear he was (waist down) naked on the toilet, as children would see a sex predator talking calmly to them to normalize nakedness of strangers and adults in the presence of children.

Who are we is we don't care to protect our children by preserving decency so they get to live their childhood free of sex predators?

We're barbarians. That's the alternative and that's what people have been since the dawn of time. Civilized people don't virtually sell their children off to increase their income or strengthen their social status by not complaining about depravity in our day to day lives. Which is precisely what you dear reader are doing by remaining stoically calm in your submissive silence.

You may as well erect a shingle on your front lawn that reads

"PEDOPHILES WELCOME HERE".

Rarely stated historical facts prove that democratic countries are the enemy of peace as much as the religious ones, only the democratic ones war against peace in secret.

- Freemasons are global secret political party whose mostly unwilling patron is head of United Kingdom's Royal family.

- Freemasons globally are secret political terrorist predators protected by all police departments in every democratic country.

- Nazi Germany was a democracy where Freemasons were banned from Party membership.

- **Edward VIII King of England abdicated** on 11 December 1936 because agreed with Germans who opposed Freemason secret domination of governments across this warring planet.

- Poor Mrs Wallis Simpson was his unwilling ruse to ensure he remained living after denouncing his position as patron of Freemasons in his dominion, as his Russian Royal Romonov uncle-cousin probably had before he and his family were secretly slaughtered 16 July 1918.

- Shortly before his death when I was 23, I'd personally witnessed him scoff at mention of Freemasons in Australia televised interaction with British news industry, assassinated Lord Louis Mountbatten 1900—1979 was a huge influence on the young King Charles III. Irish Republic Army (IRA) had Freemasons too. Just because IRA took responsibility for this murder doesn't prove they did it.

• *Democracy is the secret enemy not a Grand hero.*

In Australia:

☞   You live because attempts to kill you have failed. You're employed because no one has created a defamation campaign to defame you.

☞   You own property or personal possessions because Freemasons & government public officers haven't stolen them from you.

☞   You enjoy good health only if you're wealthy or have perfect genes.

☞   You have access to legal rights only when it suits the political parties, Labor Liberal and Freemason.

☞   In Australia there's only government organized chaos and anarchy.

Earth's people history is maintained in perpetual repeat cycle. Our English ancestor Oliver Cromwell 1599—1658 murdered England's King Charles I to steal take control as *"the Government"* then he ruled *as if he was King* by birth. Seeing the error of their ways the English restored the monarchy after Cromwell's death because in a community there must be someone maintaining legal peace and order.

In Australia both houses in Canberra's federal parliament unconstitutionally enacted the *Australia Act 1986* to illegally alter the protections of the Australian Constitution removing the Crown in England as the last say in legal matters. Effectively killing off the power of the monarchy in Australia and our white Australian ancestors had in England. Each State in Australia continue like **CROMWELL** to call themselves *"the Crown"* in legal matters and courts of law to this day in 2024 exactly as *Oliver CROMWELL had 400 years ago.* Same scenario has played out in every country across our planet in Russia Romanov Royals, in Gaza they believe *they individually own* their God's land.

In Australia, government refer to voter's owned land as *"Crown Land".* Government public officers individually call themselves *"the"* Government or *"the"* police *"the"* parliament etcetera, as if they are singularly as a person that entity when they are *only servants of the voters* in any Government and immigrants not eligible to vote are guests of the voters.

We're told not even the King has the right to trespass on our land in Australia. Yet public officers calling themselves *"The Crown"* do trespass on our land and our person, do illegally convert our possessions to their use to criminally defame, harass or injure us with intent to murder us *with 100% impunity* — like this Celtic Trilogy with clipboard and files illegally manufactured.

Very little on planet Earth is as simplistic as it appears at first glance. The matters of trespass to my residence in 2018 above left, involves a Freemason as a mental health 'nurse or social worker' in Adelaide South Australia, who had been a senior police officer in New South Wales involved with the attempt on my life in 1987 above right. In the matter of above left the State criminal laws below apply to all three seen and identified in the associated State health department documents where this male and his accomplices write he "*found an opening*" to legally enter the property. I was born on first day of May 1956 therefore in 2018 I was well over 60 years old. ☿

CRIMINAL LAW CONSOLIDATION ACT 1935

section 5AA—Aggravated offences

*(1) Subject to this section, an aggravated offence is an offence committed in (**one**) 1 or more of the following circumstances:*

(a) the offender committed the offence in the course of deliberately and systematically inflicting severe pain on the victim;

(b) the offender used, or threatened to use, an offensive weapon to commit, or when committing, the offence; ...

(d) the offender committed the offence—

(i) intending to prevent or dissuade the victim from taking legal proceedings or from pursuing a particular course in legal proceedings; or

(ii) in connection with the victim's conduct or future conduct (as party, witness or in any other capacity) in legal proceedings; or

(iii) in retribution against the victim for taking legal proceedings or for the victim's conduct (as party, witness or in any other capacity) in legal proceedings;

(e) the offender committed the offence knowing that the victim of the offence was, at the time of the offence—

... (f) the offender committed the offence knowing that the victim of the offence was, at the time of the offence, over the age of 60 years;

section 15C—3) **home invasion means** *a serious criminal trespass committed in a place of residence;*

section 168—Serious criminal trespass

(1) For the purposes of this Act, a person commits a serious criminal trespass if the person enters or remains in a place (other than a place that is open to the public) as a trespasser with the intention of committing an offence to which this section applies

(2) A place is to be regarded as open to the public if the public is admitted even though—

(a) a charge is made for admission; or

(b) the occupier limits the purposes for which a person may enter or remain in the place by express or implied terms of a public invitation.

(3) A person who enters or remains in a place with the consent of the occupier is not to be regarded as a trespasser unless that consent was obtained by—

*(a) **force**; or*

*(b) **a threat**; or*

*(c) **an act of deception**.*

(4) A reference in this section to the occupier of a place extends to any person entitled to control access to the place. "

The "*deadly weapon*" is the Mental Health Act that allows forced drugging and forced electric shock to brain of a victim. The "*deception*" was that they used the fact I was a public housing resident to illegally claim they had legal right to be at my residence to enforce an government "policy" which isn't enforceable in any court of law. There was no "innocence" on their part, these persons reasonably knew they were acting criminally effectively impersonating police without any lawful evidence I'd committed any offense of any kind whatsoever. They wanted to "*assess*" my mental health. Not that a physician would have that right either, but none were qualified physicians. All three are self-proved by their actions as criminally dangerous psychopathic sycophants. Had they decided I was mentally ill they'd have caused my imprisonment and forced drugging. Indeed their entire mental department had already decided I was "*antisocial*" and "*schizophrenic paranoid and delusional*" about government public officers wanting to harm me. Think on that for a second.

At State election time in 2014 I was illegally imprisoned under Mental Health Act 2009 (SA) and forcibly drugged like the Nazi Party did to Jewish persons they illegally experimented on, without any lawful grounds whatsoever in 2014 Australia I was drugged and imprisioned for several months to dissuade me from suing them for defaming me, before I managed to get their illegal mental orders revoked.

The lunatics control the mental asylum in Australia.

Despite the prima facie evidence of crime, the security camera footage and their documents State police refused to charge them. Despite my my successful District Court appeal and subsequent revocation order the Civil courts refuse to let me sue them for damages and to have their criminally false statements they insist are fact removed from their records. They persist today claiming all their (criminal) actions were 100% legal and that there was no revocation order.

That's one segment of history I can prove was blatantly criminally falsified by Government public officers then obviously that's irrefutable proof falsifying facts are their custom of practice for all history recordings. Its not restricted to significant matters or a few persons in one department. Its a global pandemic of false records committed by all government officials globally to make their political party appear to be performing duties within the parameters of State law when clearly they're not.

In my own life since I witnessed murder of and by Freemason police officer (offender & victim) I can prove I've been targeted for attacks by hundreds of Australia officials in separate matters who've also criminally falsified documents and records falsifying my identity and actions.

These are the sorts of immigrant who SHOULD be deported. but that jurisdiction was directly prohibited to the They have illegal orders made by a tribunal that not only had no jurisdiction but that the Act they claim to give them jurisdiction expressly and directly prohibits orders under those sections the tribunal claimed authority to make the orders. This is not a 'poor me' story its proof Australia's political parties are terrorist organizations, I'm an intelligent person, got perfect score in my 2018 defamation law assignment for my Bachelor of Laws university degree at UniSA --- yet since I witnessed FREEMASON police murder in 1988 I've been blocked in my right to secure employment. When I go to court or tribunal they claim they can't see my evidence. That's BLIND JUSTICE. For budding lawyers who may wish to pursue this crime as misfeasance in public office or trespass & invasion of privacy this is the LINK to SACAT illegal orders to political criminals at housing SA public officers since 2008. No point asking local Christies Beach or Aldinga police officers to investigate as they promote and foster Freemason crimes like this one. The ETSA for STATE illegally cancelled my gas for stove & hot water for 12 months (2008-2009) after I moved in BECAUSE I refused to sign up with ORIGIN ENERGY (a NSW Government retail energy company) I'd been illegally rendered homeless for two years by another tribunal in 2006 when I was n private rental. Main reason came to South Australia in September 2004 was to get evidence against NSW Freemason medical crimes not realizing they're all the same across Australia in SA they wasted no tome to start defaming me proving its not me its them. I was born in Cooma NSW. Something the SA State government refute, they believe I'm "Leanne Walters, shot dead" as per 2012 Government funded TV mini-series. https://icedrive.net/s/D7kFhZuu4SiSNGxiuThyF4C9afji ETSA Electricity Trust of South Australia (ETSA) was the South Australian Government-owned monopoly vertically integrated electricity provider from 1946 until its privatization in 1999. Using mass immigration into public office, every Labor or Liberal party member in every parliament across Australia participate in homeland terrorism by illegally stripping Australian citizens of their legal rights to cover up political crimes of the Party faithful which includes the secret political party named FREEMASONS --- every last one of them. --- I have legal claims against these departments since 1989. Its not a matter of the more the merrier, so many proves the terrorist element thrives in Australian public office:

1) *Electricity Trust of South Australia.*

2) *Housing Trust of South Australia, Housing.*

3) *Health SA.*

4) *Education SA.*

5) *Transport SA.*

6) *SA Attorney-General's tribunals & court.*

7) *Police SA.*

8) FED Centrelink - Dept Social Security (since 1990).

9) FED Australia Post.

10) FED health's Therapeutic Goods Administration (ILLEGAL IMPLANTS).

11) FED family law court refused me right of property settlement).

12) FED Insolvency and Trustee Service Australia (ITSA) stole my real estate.

13) Police FED. 14) Police NSW.

15) Health NSW.

16) Wollondilly Shire Council.

Then there are the criminal activities by public officers in New South Wales and the Federal Government blatantly mirrored global news industry who falsified my identity and my alleged actions on those alleged by the Freemason centric global publishing family ALLEN UNWIN HYMAN.

Like who am I? I've not invented something that threatens **capitalist pigs** in big industry. I've not claimed to be someone I'm not or done something I've not. I'm simply an **obscure average person** trying to live my life peacefully and happily just like everyone else — who isn't part of the global fake news industry claiming those opposing them are the ones pumping out fake news, by telling the truth.

Its the mirror effect, smoke and mirrors and other ancient fake magic tricks. Tactics of blaming the innocent victims for the crimes of the blatantly guilty deemed as fact when many Party Faithful tell the same lie on social media or in the print news.

Criminal actions of Australia's genocidally inclined Government of public officers and what we see globally of the infighting amongst citizens of areas in Europe — this proves irrefutably that poor Jesus if he existed was no Christian "**son of God**" or Muslim "**prophet**". The evidence, all the evidence which is all of recorded history since, proves 100% Jesus of the bible was no different to you and I, just an average citizen or resident attempting to play the role of peacemaker and good Samaritan in his community.

All the evidence includes the fact that religions have been incorporated as integral to laws globally. Perfect example is the ten commandments allegedly from Moses after a night on some hallucinogenic — customary for all prophets or indigenous Shamans since people formed communities necessitating implementation of local fears or taboos to control undesirable actions. Elementary history.

The global recognition of indigenous and alternate gender persons by

Governments has evolved to get them onside for the glut of illegal and secret medical experiments since the 1980s using computerized electronics and nanotechnology on people as the new Government political weapons — without knowledge of target dissidents opposing Government crimes and without any lawful authority whatsoever.

They're infringing every human rights agreement formulated with their own government participation in United Nations conferences since the end of the second world war between Germany and England, the second (bullshit) **global war to end all wars,** marketed that way to con young people to give up their life for a greater good that has never existed in the real world of planet Earth.

I'm yet to realize my legal right to damages for any infringements against my legal rights as Australian in Australia. Only terrorists in these fake democracies[2]." ☿

THE BIG PICTURE

WWII core reason was turf war to decide which "world power" controlled a globally secret & illegal medical experiments market. We all lost that one. Since I had evidence to prove I've been illegally experimented on in 1990s & tortured perpetually along my spine through wirelessly controlled illegal devices, only response I've had is people in the street point me out to snigger or laugh at me, government public officers trespass on my property to illegally imprison me & illegally drug me, news industry & police tell me, "you've a history of mental illness" when that's the only insanely false part.

This is a collage of words from whet the health Minister's representatives wrote in their secret mental record:

> *"Janette's delusional content seems to involve wider government conspiracy* (towards) *premeditated crime in relation to her long*

---

[2] *See section 168 of the CRIMINAL LAW CONSOLIDATION ACT 1935 (s168 serious criminal trespass, section 15C(3) definition of home invasion, section 5AA aggravated offense because I'm over 60 years of age & the matter is intended as alleged retaliation for my websites and intent to sue the bastards) http://www8.austlii.edu.au/cgi-bin/viewdb/au/legis/sa/consol_act/clca1935262/*

See Residential Tenancies Act 1995 (SA) section 5(2). Tribunal made orders under prohibited sections 72 & 80. https://www.austlii.edu.au/cgi-bin/viewdb/au/legis/sa/consol_act/rta1995207/ https://www.legislation.sa.gov.au/__legislation/lz/c/a/residential%20tenancies%20act%201995/current/1995.63.auth.pdf"

standing belief regarding a government conspiracy involving medical professionals being involved (with) *multiple government agencies after an alledged* (sic) *sexual assault by a government minister in 1999. She has a complex belief system involving being the victim of 'implants'. As such, she is convinced of a conspiracy and has been vociferous in her allegations, to the point of naming and slandering doctors, politicians and medical services, online. Ms Francis is articulate and her delusional beliefs are encapsulated. I understand she expressed herself well, during her recent appearance at the District Court."*

So well in fact that with my solicitor's research and my testimony I won the appeal against Government Party Faithful's illegal orders — because they had no evidence of me having mental illness in the hundreds of pages of their hundreds of criminal defamations in words. That dear reader is what **Government public officer's criminal insanity by delusional detachment from reality** looks like in their own records.

I still don't know how "**Rebecca SCHEFE**" and Mr "**WEATHERILL**" came about this information in 2012, or who the "**1999 Minister**" is or which Government he represented as a **rapist** or who the health department's **victim** was and how this statement was justified being in any health record under **my personal identity**. Its another bit of fake news from terrorists in Australia's Government.

I do however know it was recorded by the health department public officers six (6) days after I had secured irrefutable evidence of an illegal implant in the "cochlear" (hearing) region inside my head — and do know Cochlear Ltd is multibillion company owned by State of New South Wales and in 1999 I was resident in New South Wales.

- Is this a veiled psychopathically sarcastic admission Labor Party Premier Jay Wilson WEATHERILL and health minister John David HILL (**alias Bandido Motorcycle club member Lance WELLINGTON**) were both directly involved in my surgically rape in 1990s New South Wales?

- Was Jay Wilson WEATHERILL prison hanged Anthony Mark SPENCER president of 1984 **Bandido Motorcycle club both given fake identity as Labor Party parliamentarians because they're also Freemasons?**

It would appear that the above dear reader is fact of it. Which gives rise to the question:

How the hell do you consider that mindset civilized?

This isn't a story about whose wrong and whose right. Its a true story about the disgusting pack-animal savagery inherent in vast majority of people who criminally infiltrate Government public office churning out decade after decade of repetition by enforced crimes from within and under the "flag" or "colors" of any government, inflicting on the less powerful by sadistic psychopaths in positions of any measure of control of the laws of a town, region or country. They're not just a little eccentric — they're completely insanely dangerous to the entire population believing they possess superior power to enforce whatever they choose on a whim, like they said of Nero. Delusions of grandeur. Nero had the lead waterpipe excuse causing his brain damage — perhaps they don't eat iodized[3] salt which contains enough iodine for good mental health, not enough is like too much lead and why unleaded petrol was made mandatory. Therefore those who grew up prior to unleaded petrol and were over also exposed to flaking lead paint are susceptible to brain damage from the lead[4] in the environment much the same as Nero had been. There's no lead in lead pencils its always been graphite. The paint on the outside last century was probably lead paint. I never chewed painted school pencils but knew many who did. Another 20th century poison harming mental health was amalgam in dental fillings. Being a target of Freemason crimes they blocked my access to dental health and fillings to cause me physical harm as primary school child whilst creating massive tooth decay resulting in my front lower adult teeth being removed c1968 (12 years old) and two more when I was in puberty I had half a top front tooth thanks to the irrational anger of my sibling who had lots of amalgam fillings. My Freemason male parent refused me access to any dental implants despite that he paid for my brother's dental plate after his front teeth were kicked out during football. Meaning I never smiled large due to no bottom teeth. However, I evaded mental harm of amalgam. Are you seeing a pattern? I see that our poor ancestors ate hard grains and vegetables, while the power hungry wealthy ate white flour products and fatty meats ensuing impoverished persons had better health.

The block of eight logos at start of each chapter represent organizations who at the material times act in the same manner as each other to outsiders, dictatorially oppressive. Its a relevant fact and obviously intentional that the New South Wales State Railways use the same angular "S" style symbol as the Gestapo Secret Service (police) used on their uniforms.

Being born 11 years after the war ended I don't profess to know what German societies were like before the second world war last century. I do know from experience what societies were like in the 15 to 20 years and beyond after the war ended. From that eye witness experience I can formulate the reasonably statement that there were no better side, merely one side that was the extroverted psychopath and the other who remain the

---

[3] *Reduced mental ability occurs in almost 300 million . Ncbi.nim.nih.gov*

[4] *Exposure to low level of lead & irreversible brain damage mayoclinic.org*

introverted psychopath. I can say this with 100% authority because I have many illegal implants inside me that would have made the Nazi Germans proud if they had that technology to use on the ideologies and religions that history tells us they detested so overtly. However, as history is written by the victors the fact Nazis Party supporters detested the Freemasons politics as much as Jewish influences has not been honestly recorded. Same as the Christian Bible that was translated from Hebrew by authority of a King James of England.

I suspect if Germany had won the war the only difference is that they would not only be less of the Jewish religion, they'd also be considerably less Freemasons globally. While I don't ever agree with the Germany holocaust I do agree that *less Freemasons can never be a bad thing considering that they function in the medical industry and Government with the same level of hate we see from terrorist organizations and the same ferocity as we're informed the Gestapo Secret Service inflicted on their targets.* I remind you dear reader I was pregnant in 1991 when Freemasons stormed my residence, drugged me and abducted me to surgically rape me cutting my spine open to insert illegal implants to inflict pain on me by remote controlled operated by persons living around my residence since 1991 to this very day in 2024. All I did was witness Freemason crimes. So tell me how it is you believe the *Freemason party, Labor Party, Liberal Party and supporters* are honorable persons and better than Germany's *Nazi Party Gestapo Secret Service.*

I'm all ears.

Many Australians being targeted unfairly or illegally by Government are under the misapprehension that they're alone in it or are in the line of fire because they belong to a specific minority.

Some Australians are spreading false rumors about why I'm publishing my book series. The inner sanctum believe they've fooled everyone with their schemes and scams.

I have the evidence that proves Australia's consecutive Governments have been operating as terrorists since at least from the passing through both houses in parliament the Bill that become *the Australia Act 1986.*

The *Australia Act* means Australia has no laws only guidelines that are ignored or followed when it suits a political cause for the Labor Party or Liberal Party.

The *Australia Act* undermines the Australian Constitution by indirectly defeating the "appeal from court to the King" part of the Australian Constitution.

The *Australia Act* illegally and indirectly altered the Australian

Constitution as a majority of Australia's Judges and Lawyers stood in cowardly silence waiting for their payment as co-conspirators in that terrorist plan for a political cause trashing hundreds of years of planning for a civilized society.

The ***Australia Act*** plunged us deeper in barbarism than we've ever been before. Now torture rape and pillaging of dissidents goes on in private away from the stare of the news industry and the reprisals of our now quite toothless court system as the Kings and Queens are too afraid to take a stand else their entire families are assassinated.

The ***Australia Act*** is the dawn of the second dark age where the truth is buried under virtual mountains of electronic propagandas.

The future of humanity verses the overlording of humans forced back into centuries of servitude by power hungry psychopathic overlords — ***society on slow boil, that is what and why*** I'm publishing this book series.

I'm also hoping to attract lawyers and barristers with enough foresight, courage, love of their own family and community to stand by me to sue the Government on what we agree is the best lawsuit. I say its misfeasance in public office and terrorism as a tort, with the Governments own documents that falsely defame me on 100% lies as 100% fact.

I'd imagine the same applies Britain, America and all other fake constitutional democracy countries. When the population of a specific group is deemed burdensome then genocide is practiced by stealth on birds, animals and people.

In densely human populated city areas when the noise and poop become discomfort in parklands Government bait hundreds of sulphur crested cockatoos to cull them.

In the outback farming regions and Government shoot hundreds of the kangaroos because they eat the natural fodder for introduced meat-eater food animals to cull them.

In city areas when Born-Australians register discontent with Party policy they too are culled from their community. They're silenced and negated by illegal arrest, rendered unemployed or homeless so they're too impoverished to naturally socialize to reproduce, and replaced by selective submissive immigrants from overcrowded or war-torn Europe happy with any Labor Party or Liberal Party Freemason style policy. The replacements get jobs and public housing before Born-Australia dissidents to sing the praises of the Government who took them in. Some like my neighbor are enrolled to vote at their public housing rental address in the name of a deceased Australian voter.

Everything in this and all my publications are facts, not based on facts

but facts I've discovered and or have irrefutable documented evidence of; the latter the evidence, its quite extensive.

Where a "marked dissident" in Australia is someone who remains in vocal opposition to child rape and murder even after failing to encourage police to investigate said crimes amongst their own police departments with irrefutable extensive evidence of said crimes harming themselves or their own family or police who support them in their quest to rid Australia of child rape and murder terrorists in Government, *the evidence says that marked dissidents* (like me) are selected for multiple levels of targeted crimes which include illegal implants to torture the marked dissident, along with further secret and illegal Government activity intended to frustrate their target to embark on desperate illegal conduct. When that fails they invent illegal conduct in secret records, as they did to me claiming, police found that I falsely accused an unidentified parliament Minister of rape in 1999; and falsely accused an unidentified psychiatrist of rape on unknown date. The latter bringing with it the belief I've been diagnosed long-term with mental illness.

Only place these false rape claims happened was between the ears of their original, obviously psychopathic, authors.

Even without me knowing about the double false rape allegations, I was able to prove them wrong and get their 'mental department' orders revoked. Still they insist their original criminally false documents are legal records despite my successful appeal and subsequent revocation order made because the half-witted Government Public Officer sycophant supporters of Labor-Liberal-Freemason terrorism in South Australia had no evidence whatsoever of mental illness on me — its all their own. You know what they say, people write about what they know best.

With over 100 names of people adding to baseless claims on my actions and my thoughts in South Australia mental department records Government refuse to apologize for and refuse to remove, what is there left for me to do?

These are some of those adding to or willingly participating in my false criminal defamation (for a political cause) without any evidence of me having done anything wrong in any way whatsoever. There names were extracted from Government records as of 2018. One is the parent of my daughter's boyfriend who didn't even bother to let me know what was going on.

From a female perspective its considerably more treacherous when females betray females to cover up the almost exclusively male cause of pederasty and pedophilia.

'Defamation' is a 'no fault' common law tort but under criminal law it means you need intent or reckless as to harm your defamation causes.

Both defamations require only that you identity the person and publish the defamations, verbally or in documents of any kind – no actual harm needs to have occurred.

The effects of my defamations did & still do cause me serious harm that is physical. Which makes these defamations terrorism with political or ideology cause generally, to render me an unreliable witness against Freemasons who committed child rape and murder of many.

The many include my MtDNA grandmother 1907—1989 Olive Agnes Harriet Hussey Strachan BUNDOCH murdered in Ashfield New South Wales nursing home by a physician. Murdered because she recognized my face as the Freemason fake 1989 person LEANNE WALTERS, SHOT DEAD.

It would also appear on the evidence that's also why my husband died 1953—2008 another murder by stealth being challenging o determine due to fact he became alcoholic. Addictions — that's what these Freemasons aim for. Generating enough Government originating harm causing extreme stress in their target's life anticipating they'll turn to some form of addiction to be able to cope.

My husband was police charged and sentenced to imprisonment in a 21st century Sydney region New South Wales court because prison officers at the low security Silverwater Detention Centre had allegedly (according to police) released him something like 15 minutes early in 1979 from his less than one year sentence. The entire process was abuse of process and abuse of public office involving obvious Freemasons because my husband identified me as *Freemason fake 1989 person LEANNE WALTERS, SHOT DEAD.*

Evidently all these murderous South Australia Health Department associated public officer sycophants possess the all too common psychopathic mindset in Australia that deems it OK to falsely and maliciously defame someone in South Australia or New South Wales or Federal Government records if that maliciously illegal activity is sanctioned by a majority in their terrorist group.

1. WRIGHT, Denise
2. WILLCOCKS, Marg
3. WILKINS, David
4. WEATHERILL, Anonymous, Christies Beach police station
5. WEATHERILL, Jay, Labor Party SA State Premier
6. UNKNOWN, Housing SA, Toby
7. UNKNOWN, Housing SA, Rachael
8. TINGAY, Dr Helen Regina
9. TILDESLEY, Dr Celia Emmeline
10. THOMSON, Dr Kieron Joseph
11. THOMAS, Ben

12. THOMAS, Dr Ian
13. THOMAS, Katherine
14. THOMAS, Kerry-Lee
15. TELFER, Dr Richard Thomas
16. TAYLOR, Renee
17. TAVKOFF, Yasmin
18. SWAN, David, CEO Health SA
19. STRAUSS, Leonie
20. STRACHAN, John
21. SNELLING, John James
22. SHILLDARIEN-HENLEY, Paul alias as public housing tenant; alias Alexander PAUL [deceased person] on Federal voters roll where PAUL is the family name; and alias Paul HENLEY when falsely & criminally defaming me in mental department's secret Freemason terrorist record.
23. SHERBON, Tony, CEO Health SA
24. SETAYESH, Dr Saman
25. SCHEFE, Rebecca, compulsive luiar & hardened terrorist
26. SAUNDERSON, Dr Ernest Wilfred
27. SAGE, Dr Michael Radford
28. RODNEY, Vic
29. ROBERTSON, Greg
30. RAWLIUK, Tanya
31. RANKINE, Heidi
32. PRIOR, Alex
33. PETRUCCO, Dr Michael
34. PETRIE, Janece
35. NIELSEN, Dr Kate
36. NELSON, Dr Allan
37. NARANIA, Umesh
38. NANCE, Dr Michael John
39. MOYES, Belinda, CEO Health SA
40. MORPHETT, Dr Antony Andrew
41. MOIR, Janette Anne, hardened terrorist
42. MINNIS, Dr Neville Lister
43. MILLER, Sean
44. MCKINLAY, Heidi, insanely attacked me in Seaford SA Woolworths supermarket.
45. MCCARTHY, Sue
46. MASON, Jody
47. MAH, Dr Jee Ken
48. MAERSCHEL, R, Guardianship Board RE: G CHENG, A Nelson, RT Telfer (revoked criminally illegal mental health orders)

49. MACDONALD, Cathy
50. LOFTUS, Dr William Kingsley
51. LAY, Shannen
52. LAWRY, Christina Elizabeth
53. LANGFORD, Lesley
54. KENT, Sara Louise (immigrant from England wrote up English language music playing on my property as *"foreign language"*.)
55. KEEN, Alexandra
56. KAYES, Dulcey
57. JOSLIN, Priscilla
58. JONES, Annette, hardened terrorist
59. JAMES, Sian
60. HODGE, Don, Christies Beach or Aldinga police officer
61. HILL, John David, Labor Party 21st century SA State Health Minister & Brothers In Arms paperback, New South Wales 20th Century 1%er outlaw Bandido Motorcycle Club convicted murderer`` Lance Wellington
62. HIGGINS, Sue
63. HENDRICKX, Julie
64. GOODYEAR, Dr Shane Andrew
65. GIANNAKOUREAS, Dr Angelos
66. FURLER, Darien
67. FORWARD, Madeline
68. FORBES, Lynda
69. FONG, Dr Sonnie Wah Onn
70. DOWELL, Dr Barry Simon
71. DANG, Dr Diem Tran Quynh Dang
72. COX, Helen
73. COVENTRY, Dr Elizabeth Rachael Tavell
74. COULTER, Robyn
75. COSCIA, Dr Claudio
76. COLE, Dr Alison Barbara Jane
77. CHENG, Dr Georgina Ai-Chin (Asian ancestry psychiatrist wrote up English language music playing on my property as *"foreign language"*.)
78. CHAMPION, Dr Andrew Robert (evidently a long-term Freemason terrorist who conspired with surgeons who surgically mutilated me in New South Wales)
79. BYRNE, Shaun E
80. BROWN, Naomi
81. BOTHA, Dr Isobel Stephina
82. BISSONAUTH, Dr Luveen
83. BISHOP, Susan
84. BIENEWITZ, Daniel

85. BEE, Police detective Alison
86. BARKER, Judith
87. BALLESTRIN, Matt
88. BAIRD, Alan
89. BACKHOUSE, Julia
90. ANDERSON, Ann
91. ALTMAN, Emma
92. AHMED, Dr Mohamed Riyazuddin, surgical rapist & pathological liar.

Reality is there's nothing, literally nothing to stop Government public officers in Australia from acting criminally as a willing part of a terrorist organization. Nothing. Police refuse to stop them. Self-representing litigants are refused their legal right to sue them under civil law in all of Australian courts. I've tried.

Lets look at a summery of the last time I attempted to block State Housing from enforcing a non-existent contract and unenforceable policy to defeat statute — specifically the **Residential Tenancies Act**. In response to my legally correct arguments in writing the State Civil & Administrative Tribunal ordered **(without jurisdiction)** that the State Housing staff can take an hour **(to home invade by serious criminal trespass)** at my residence to poke around in my house and shed snapping as many photos of anything they choose to send them wherever they choose or any purpose they choose.

Don't believe me? Lets look at the documents. But first let me inform you I have the equal of just over half a law degree. What I haven't passed a test for isn't worth my time or logistically necessary to have a law degree. Its just so the Government can charge well over Au$1k per three months course; and I got a perfect score in my defamation law assignment so I'm allowed to boast.

Let me remind you that living in a community of any kind requires reciprocal trust. The unwritten agreement that you won't be subjected to crime when you're vulnerable. The guarantee in Parliament's legislation that if you are targeted with crime in participating in any community then the police department and the courts will make sure you are compensated by a claim of damages in civil law or prosecution by police under criminal law.

When neither of those two things happen as is the truth of the facts in y life and the lives of my children and older relatives, then that in itself is irrefutable proof, not evidence but **proof** that you don't live in a democracy but that **you live under terrorist rule**. Every country on this wretched planet live under terrorist rule not just Australia.

I don't just have evidence of criminal activity between the Housing department and the Civil & Administrative Tribunal who are controlled by none other than the State Attorney-General and the State Govenor for the King in England.

My evidence also proves a ***three way terrorist conspiracies*** between State Housing, State Health , and State police departments.

Not only do I have the two sets of terrorist conspiracies in my evidence I have another between State police and State transport.

That's three sets of terrorist conspiracies designed to pervert the course of justice and due administration of law and undermine Government public services for a political cause not just to defame me as an unreliable witness but to block my access to medical services to have illegal implants removed from my person — implants that cause me serious physical harm.

That dear reader be a Celtic Trilogy.

My **Celtic Trilogy** evidence of criminal activity from the five State department activities establishes clear proof of criminal custom of practice in all Government departments across Australia, none of whom fear reprisals from the news industry or the Attorney-General's civil courts, the police department or the Attorney-General's public prosecutor because they are all members of the one   national terrorist organization secretly under the banner of Freemasons the political party you support when you don't want it known you're a member of a terrorist organization. ♉

POLICE THREAT PHONE CALL

On Thursday 22 September 2016, at about 6:01 pm a voice message was left on my message bank for my mobile phone number 0481100043.

The female caller said, **"Hi Jenny, Janette, this is Bree from Christies Beach police, could you please call me back on 83929000, 8392900, thank you, bye-bye."**

I tried to call back at 6:11pm, 6:18pm, 6:34pm every time the phone rang out. I rang again at 7:09pm, a male answered the phone with, "Christies Beach police."

I asked, "Is Bree there?"

He said, "Who?"

I replied, "Bree."

He said, "What's your name?"

I replied, "Janette Francis."

He asked, "What's it about?"

I replied, "I don't know, she rang me and left a message asking me to call her back."

He said, "She's tied up with another matter can you hold on?"

Me, "Yes"

A female came to the phone, greeted me calling herself Bree, then launched with this, **"I've had a visit from a resident in your street today, complaining that you've been putting letters in letterboxes."**

I responded, "That was some time ago"

Bree, "What's the letters about?"

Me, "That's self-explanatory."

Bree, "I want you to tell me."

I started to explain, "Well a neighbour erected a camera the angle of the camera indicates its pointing down my driveway, his landlord told him I was going to take civil action, I haven't even started, and he's been retaliating severely, a few times."

Then realised the situation did not feel quite right, I asked "Which letter?"

Bree, "That's what I want you to tell me; they said you were saying he was recording everyone in the street."

Me, "Who's complaining?"

Bree, aggressively raising her voice, "Your neighbour, there is no law saying he can't put video cameras on your house[5]."

Me, "Pardon, It's a civil matter not a police matter."

Bree, "There is no law saying he can't put video cameras on your house."

Me, "Excuse me this is not a police matter, you can't tell me how to run a civil matter."

Bree, "Don't mouth off at me, yes I can."

Me, "I'm not mouthing off at you, are you uniformed police or clerical?"

Bree, "I'm a you com."

Me, "A what?"

Bree, "A you com."

Me, "What's your police number?"

Bree replied, "79053." I had a pen in my hand and wrote the number as she spoke it.

Me, "I'd like to end this conversation now." Waited for Bree to acknowledge me. She hung up.

---

[5] *Yes there was and still is, Surveillance Devices Act 2016, South Australia.*

I made this record of the conversation. Then I looked up the phone number on the internet which told me "08 8392 9000 is phone number of Christies Beach Police Station located at 94 Dyson Rd Christies Beach, SA 5165" I felt as if the female identifying herself as police officer 79053, intended her actions to be a malicious threat of violence to scare me off pursuing civil action against Paul SHILLDARIEN-HENLEY and his 2nd wife.

SURVEILLANCE DEVICES ACT 2016

"section 5—Optical surveillance devices

(1) Subject to this section and section 6, a person must not knowingly install, use or maintain an optical surveillance device on or in premises, a vehicle or any other thing, (whether or not the person has lawful possession or lawful control of the premises, vehicle or thing) to record visually or observe the carrying on of a private activity without the express or implied consent of each party to the activity.

Maximum penalty:

(a) in the case of a body corporate—$75 000;

(b) in the case of a natural person—$15 000 or imprisonment for 3 years ...section 5(4) Subsections (1) to (3) (inclusive) do not apply ...

(b) to the installation, use or maintenance of an optical surveillance device on premises by a person if the use of the device is reasonably necessary for the protection of the lawful interests of that person ..."

Its a classic case of police officers facilitating organized crime. I've not charged and convicted of any crime or been subject of any lawful police investigation, he cannot establish any *reasonable necessity* to have several cameras pointing at the entry points to my residence **therefore,** he's acting illegally and liable to penalty of *"$15 000 or imprisonment for 3 years imprisonment"*

My youtube.com video records that on 3 March 2023 two male police detectives came to my residence with two more mental department females with obvious intent to entrap me into saying something that might give them excuse to imprison me under Mental Health Act they did this as this neighbour was erecting his illegal front spiked fence to (illegally) fortify his residence. They attended on his request because I'd asked him to remove his spot light from my driveway, as you can see he didn't but he has erected another flood light pointing at the other side of the front of my property. He's criminally harassing me and Christies Beach - Aldinga police and mental department are his Government public officer accomplices. In my local area what police do in South Australia after they retire is join the Liberal Party and run for Local Council, State or Federal Parliament, evidently they seek affiliation with the criminal elements in our community.

This BREE transcript, https://youtu.be/-VnhxAw9Yk0 that video and most of my other youtube.com videos prove in their own right that Australian government public officers are seriously organized terrorists whose sole purpose is to facilitate crime for a political ideological or religious cause associated with the Freemason secret political party, and the registered political parties Labor and Liberal who take turns controlling Government in generally stacked elections, depending on which one has the most evidence of crimes committed by the other. ♔ **That's what my evidence screams.** ♉

LANCELOT'S EVIL TWIN

Freemason Lance Wellington killed in cold blood unarmed young Ivan Romcek in the car park of the Viking Tavern in Beaconsfield near suburb of Milperra Sydney, Australia on Fathers' Day 1984. Freemason police criminally fabricated evidence of the death & life of seven people including a fake 'innocent bystander' they Christened, Leanne Gaye Walters. Thant's my opinion based on material evidence. Hundreds if not thousands of ACT, NSW, NT, QLD, SA, TAS, VIC, WA, NZ, UK, USA Freemasons & their Tripartizans bribed for their silence. All Freemason globally, global news industry & Australia's police departments are guilty of harboring those conspiring to murder or torture witnesses to Freemason infant or child rape & murder crimes. Parliaments willfully change the Constitution without referendum. Australian Labor Party slot Ivan's murderer into parliament as Minister for Health to help Freemasons cover up their 300 plus years globally of child rape, murder, surgical rape & other medical research crimes. Freemason's Tripartizans only want you to see that: 1%er outlaw bikers murdered an innocent bystander — a child that never existed. These are all "*substantially true facts*". That's what all relevant evidence proves. That's terrorism.

Paperback quote:

"Lance Wellington 36 (imprisoned circa 1987) manslaughter 12 years, affray 6 years, non-parole period 7 years."

If he did kill Ivan should have been murder & life. Being in BIA penny-dreadful proves little, for HILL it indicates terrorism.

There's nothing honorable about being a convicted killer or lying about it to pervert the course of justice by covering up the truth of Ivan ROMCEK's cold blooded murder and the fake identity of a fake dead child sold globally as an innocent bystander. All evidence says Ivan ROMCEK and 5 others were assassinated in Viking Tavern's scheduled Fathers' Day ambush by Freemasons and their police.

There can be no doubt that *"Lance like a boil"* WELLINGTON in the SIMPSON & HARVEY paperback John David HILL are the same person.

Two photos as "Lance WELLINGTON" are mirror reversed to the UniSA deputy Chancellor photo, in that photo you can see his nose is bent dramatically to his right ear is slightly smaller than his left ear — the Lance WELLINGTON photos show the same physical differences in mirror reverse and same features when accounting for age difference.

2005 I'd moved into a rental property around the corner form this John David HILL's 99 Dyson Road Christies Beach SA electorate office. Ergo, he was my representative in State parliament with that legal obligation. I'd made appointment to ask for his parliamentary representation on matter of Freemason police terrorism and my stolen biometric identity advertised as 'dead' in same SIMPSON & HARVEY 'Brothers In Arms' paperback since 1989. Which appeared to be inhabiting my access to medical services. This was *before* I made any allegations of illegal implants.

I was aware that this John David HILL was a member of Labor Party and had been elected on their political platform. I was there to give him the benefit of doubt, to prove whether of not he was a willing terrorist for this Freemason & Labor Party[6] common cause. Seconds in I placed my 1989 copy of SIMPSON & HARVEY's 'Brothers In Arms' on his desk between us and begun speaking, calmly, in measured tones. John David HILL stared at the paperback and started mumbling asked me rhetorically why I was there, before he ran from the room saying

"I can't do this I have a conflict of interest with that."

John David HILL unjustly cancelled any other appointment I made to see him the rest of the years he was my 'voice in parliament'.

His replacement as the member for Kaurna, Christopher PICTON was also allocated as Minister for Health who treats me with the same level of contempt without provocation as John David HILL did. They do little — full of words but no action. For instance in his possible first speech after his 2014 election Christopher PICTON said:

"I come to this parliament as an advocate for health service ..."

Which means he was trained by Labor Party to replace John David HILL as he's also the Minister of health same as HILL. Not a coincidence one would believe based on a;ll the evidence. I'm stuck in public housing in Kaurna having been blocked in my access to gainful employment and my right to sue those involved with this crime so I can leave this Freemason dominated prison-camp called Adelaide. What's PICTON's qualifications in Health? None. He was office boy for Amanda RISHWORTH in her federal electorate office when I contacted her, where he was taught how to evade making the

---

[6] *2 September 1984 Australian Labor Party held the balance of power in parliament in both NSW & Canberra, when all NSW police were Freemason.*

government responsible for their medical industry crime. He sent me a letter in response to my Medicare Australia complaint giving me attachments from Internet on how to complain to Medicare in United States of America about Medical Australia matters. That's how both Liberal & Labor goons are trained to respond.

Only the best psychopathic liars are nominated by 'the Party' for election. This is proved on the documents they sent me in response to my valid complaints, or the 100% lack of any response or lawful response. Proved in the existence of the illegal and unconstitutional block on my driver's license to this day in 2024. Proved in the fact no person's been arrested for the many crimes against my person. Proved by fact I can't get legal representation despite the virtual mountain of evidence that proves the SIMPSON & HARVEY's 'Brothers In Arms' matter was written and published with premeditated intent to pervert the course of justice and due administration of law.

John David HILL may or may not be outlaw Bandido motorcycle club member Lance WELLINGTON but he is the person in SIMPSON & HARVEY's 'Brothers In Arms' holding himself up to all and sundry as a convicted killer.

As such he has illegally taken office in State parliament infringing Australian Constitution at section 44 which is applicable in both Federal and State parliaments as it outlines how Stare government is structured therefore it applies equally to matters of section 44 in State parliament which stipulates thus:

> *Any person who: (ii) is attainted of treason, or* **has been convicted** *and is under sentence, or subject to be sentenced,* **for any offence punishable under the law** *of the Commonwealth or* **of a State by imprisonment for one year or longer;** *or ... shall be incapable of being chosen or of sitting as a senator or a member of the House of Representatives.*

However he wasn't elected to Canberra's parliament, he was elected to South Australia's State parliament whose Constitution is much the same, thus:

"17—Vacation of seat in Council[7]

(1) If any member of the Legislative Council—

(a) without permission of the Council fails for twelve sitting days consecutively of any session of the Council to attend therein; or

(ab) is not or ceases to be an Australian citizen; or

(b) takes any oath or makes any declaration or act of acknowledgment or

---

[7] *section 17 of the Constitution Act 1934 South Australia*

allegiance to any foreign prince or power; or

(c) does, concurs in, or adopts any act whereby the member may become a subject or citizen of any foreign state or power; or

(d) becomes bankrupt; or

(e) takes the benefit of any law relating to insolvent debtors; or

(f) becomes a public defaulter; or

(g) is attainted of treason; or

(h) is convicted of an indictable offence; *or*

(i) becomes of insane mind,

the member's seat in the Council shall thereby become vacant.

31—Vacation of seat in Assembly[8]

(1) If any member of the House of Assembly—

(a) for twelve sitting days consecutively of any session of the House of Assembly without the permission of the House entered upon its journals fails to attend in the House; or

(ab) is not or ceases to be an Australian citizen; or

(b) takes any oath or makes any declaration or acknowledgment of allegiance, obedience, or adherence to any foreign prince or power; or

(c) does, concurs in, or adopts any act whereby the member may become a subject or citizen of any foreign state or power; or

(e) becomes bankrupt or an insolvent debtor within the meaning of the laws in force in the State relating to bankrupts or insolvent debtors; or

(f) becomes a public defaulter; or

(g) is attainted of treason; or

(h) is convicted of an indictable offence; *or*

(i) becomes of unsound mind,

the member's seat in the House of Assembly shall thereby become vacant."

The above extract from Constitution Act 1934 South Australia means John David HILL was illegally allowed to take office in State parliament. He illegally accepted payment from State treasury, is illegally in receipt of a parliamentary pension, illegally uses the "Honourable" title. That is if he was once known as outlaw Bandido motorcycle club member Lance

---

[8] *section 31 of the Constitution Act 1934 South Australia*

WELLINGTON, regardless of whether or not he's been given an alternate identity under witness protection that doesn't erase the effect of the Federal Constitution which imposes the same obligation on the States and Territories.

If John David HILL isn't outlaw Bandido motorcycle club member Lance WELLINGTON as he holds himself up as being that person that makes him mortally unfit to be a "voice in parliament" moreover he's proved and established his lack of fitness by his refusals to be my voice in parliament because he declared his "conflict of interest" not by his words — by his actions or deeds by lack of reasonable action in response to me that contradicted his legal obligation to me as a resident in his State electorate to be my voice in parliament on this issue of my criminal defamation and my many criminal assaults on my person.

John David HILL and the Australian Labor Party need to be outed for the terrorist they are. Discredited and declared a terrorist organization in response to their own repeat actions in response to me and this situation decade after decade in New South Wales and South Australia. Had they been then the Freemasons would have already fallen on their own sword, also would have been declared a terrorist organization at same time various alleged outlaw motorcycle clubs were. The Federal parliament were able to fix their member's 'dual citizenship' errors then the States can and must fix their 'terrorists in parliament' errors. There is no question that the people who elect their parliaments expect their voice in parliament to be capable of impartially representing the interests of every person in their electorate, regardless of Party police. If they can only represent the interests of their political party who nominated them under the party ticket — then they're not fit to be a voice in parliament because that dear reader is the very short slippery slope to full blown terrorism. Every parliamentarian must be equally capable of complete impartiality as every Judge or Magistrate must be, else they're not fit to sit in judgment in any Court of law and parliamentarians are not fit to make laws for *'the peace, order and good government* [9] *"* in Australia. Parliament is no different to the maximum for data entry into a computer — *"rubbish in rubbish out".*

Its undeniable that the SIMPSON & HARVEY's 'Brothers In Arms' paperback which infringes Australian Consumer Law by being advertised as "true". John David HILL has had his biometric identity in SIMPSON & HARVEY's 'Brothers In Arms' same amount of time as I have. According to an internet website that's since April Fools Day 1989. He's managed to progress into parliament while everything I owned has been stolen and my excellent charter besmirched by people I've never met. That alone indicates his

---

[9] *ss 51 and 52 of the Commonwealth of Australia Constitution Act.*

criminal involvement in the creation of the SIMPSON & HARVEY's 'Brothers In Arms' printed story and television miniseries. That the book has him in a confrontation with young Ivan ROMCEK in the moments before Ivan was murdered leaves John David HILL as the prime suspect in that individual one on one murder of unarmed young Ivan.

The Fake death of the fake Leanne Gaye WALTERS is described in SIMPSON & HARVEY's 'Brothers In Arms' thus:

> *"The force sent her backwards through the air, lifting her up and throwing her to the ground like a battered mannequin. The bullet lodged itself in her right collarbone. Blood and pieces of her flesh splattered Shifty's shirt before he hit the ground beside her. He saw her body twitch. He grabbed her arm and felt for a pulse. It was faint, and then it was gone."*

Its wrong on so many levels. Starters why would a parent want their child's brutal killing be described in graphic detail? Its in the same box of responses with the answer to the question — why would a parent want their child described as a *"cheap little slut"* They wouldn't. Yet SIMPSON & HARVEY's did in their gutter-trash 'true crime' they called 'Brothers In Arms'.

Many people have suffered firearm damage to their jaw and lived to tell the story.

The subsequent outcomes in John David HILL life prove he's a Freemason terrorist enemy of Australia. Its irrefutable on the documents held true by State of New South Wales and Commonwealth of Australia since the decided to fund the TV miniseries on this book in 2011 or 2012 through their Arts departments. Because I'd published the images of the falsified evidence to the New South Wales police Commissioner in 2003 (next page) to be told the police department planned to do nothing to investigate that Freemason crime (all police were Freemason) and in same letter I was illegally outlawed by effect of the decision not to respond to anything else I could prove (see French Letters)

Its just as undeniable the propose of John David HILL's face being in that paperback is to criminally defame me specifically to discredit me as a witness against Freemason child rape and the cold blooded shooting murder of police officer Jack BASSET on 24 April 1988, before my eyes inside the Camden New South Wales police station by police detective Peter Robert (Bob) BRADBURY.

For that reason John David HILL should spend the rest of his life in an Australian prison as a terrorist for the Freemason cause. Every cent he and his family have derived from his association with the Australian Labor Party should be subject to forfeit as *"proceeds of crime"*.

These are, but are not merely my moral beliefs, this is the effect of what's written in Australian law if it was lawfully applied to the willful actions of this John David HILL who was or is impersonating the belief that he once was outlaw Bandido motorcycle club member Lance WELLINGTON.

Australia's parliaments claim and advertise they're a Constitutional democracy, they need to start acting the part as right now and since Federation they're been a terrorist organization with the best interests of the global fraternity of Freemason's lore held over and above the imposition of Australian law. That's unconstitutional.

The **Australia Act 1986** is not a law for *"peace, order and good government"* its intent and action has been unconstitutional from the moment it was a proposed Bill before parliament. Its a terrorist's Act that should never succeeded. In 2024 Australia is still being governed in a manner that is no different to having Muslim's sharia lore. cancelling out Australia's constitutional laws. The legal maxim — *"What can't be done directly can't be done indirectly"* isn't a reference to physicality — its a reference to legality. That the **Australia Act 1986** passed through both houses of parliament successfully in Australia then was accepted by the Queen and her parliament indicates what? The presence of Freemason influence in both parliaments.

The reason Freemasons had (at material times) photo of Queen Elizabeth inside their Freemason (lodge) meeting room was because the head of the British Royal family is seen as the Patron of Australian Freemasonry — according to the murdering pederast pedophile who is my male parent and who was **grand poo-bar of his Freemason cult** since I was a teenager.

They don't need to be a 'member' they're the Parton, the figure head who approves of Freemason terrorist activity, the Royal who allows that terrorist organization to control the parliaments in secret fear they and their entire family will be murdered as their cousins in Russia had been. ☿

INTRINSIC INSANITIES

NSW police charged **43** persons with 2 September **84** shooting deaths.

I've been fighting to expose Freemason crimes virtually all my life, after being brutally raped by State employed Freemason on Federal Government property as a toddler on 3 March 1959. **Silence only protects perpetrators**.

Freemasons have been secretly plotting to kill me "by accident" since I was a child. When I'd inexplicably walked away unscathed in first week of 1977, after my 1967 HR Holden was shunted from standing at a temporary DMR[10]

---

[10] *DMR means Department of Main Roads in New South Wales.*

stop sign by a fast moving extra-long semitrailer travelling down hill reportedly with smoke billowing from all of its brakes because it had been travelling 100kph before cresting the maybe 100 meres long very steep descent being fully laden with high rise construction steel bound for Sydney, staff at Camden Hospital New South Wales called police to arrest me as mentally ill — because I was uninjured.

Australia's HR Holden sedans only ever had a front bench seat, the back of it stops below shoulder height. Because my neck didn't snap and kill me I was called everything from an extraterrestrial alien to a Russian spy. I was lucky. Some may believe I'm "blessed" I say thank you but, there's no God to bless us we need to have those thoughts for each other. There were two entities in my HR who protected me neither were a God, I don't believe in 'ghosts' or 'spirits' either. The were entities with a tangible yet elusive presence. There but not there. Seen but not seen I could certainly feel their presence. There have been more than them around me at various times. They are not a God or many Gods or angles I can't understand why its so problematic to understand we are not the most intelligent species on this planet. Evidently such a problem exists because some people are afraid of what they can't immediately understand others are so full of their own self worth they refuse to admit there may be others better than them. Whatever the reason. I'm not one who cares to attempt to convince anyone of anything I can't prove with documents.

However, I can prove I walked away from that crash when no other person could understand how I managed not to die. There is no blind faith to believe anything its obvious fact. I walked away from a crash in a car with a bench seat and without any headrest. I was still sitting upright when I stopped. I can't add anything more to that apart from fact the staff at Camden hospital fond it impossible to poke a needle into my skin to stitch up the cut on my elbow from a cup hook. So lets think of other things we really can't explain. We can't see ultraviolet light. What else can't we see around us you should be asking yourself. I couldn't see them. I could feel the air pressure changes from their movement around me as they rapidly passed between me and the front windscreen and me and the closed driver's side window all the while yelling instructions at me in their voice. Yelling because I was ignoring them when they first started talking calmly. Yelling at me to put my seat belt on — this was before it was mandatory. My car radio was long broken. I had no fillings in my teeth to pick up radio transmissions if that is a thing.

All my windows were closed. I was only person in my car I had no one in my boot, actually I've never had anyone in my boot. There was no traffic around me, no houses nearby. I was effectively alone as we understand alone. Who do "I" think they are? I suspect they're the ones people errantly refer to as God. I suspect they're just as native to planet Earth as people and other animals are. I suspect they're not dead people risen but they are a species who have lived amongst us on this planet as long or longer than people have. I suspect they are the superior entities on this planet not people. They are where our technology comes from. We are their virtual puppets because they have no physical presence, however they have physical powers. They stopped me from being killed inside that car and the only reason I can imagine is that I'm not afraid of cowards bullies and terrorists like Freemasons and their Tripartizans. I was born 'not afraid' but by the same token I'm no fool, I never take risks. I suspect they like me because ethically and intellectually, I'm like them.

January 1977 police officers came to my house. I asked them if they planned to arrest me for surviving a car accident? They looked at my slight figure, looked long at my car, they stared at each other for some moments speechless, then they left without further discussion never to return.

Two weeks later 18 January 1977 Granville train tragedy crushing to death 84 people, scarring 100s more. I became old news. In 1977 all New South Wales police were Freemasons a few of them have been trying to kill me, on and off since, 1967 when I witnessed ritualistic child rape & murder at Freemason meeting in Campbelltown, NSW. Don't for one moment believe propagandas inferring Freemasons protect the 'holy grail' it if it existed, they'd be more likely trying to destroy it.

Just to reiterate, I have no religion, and I'm just as much a person as anyone else only I'm "humane" I'm humane to almost every living thing. People who aren't respectful and humane are "psychopaths" they're mutants of humans.

How do I think they 'saved' my life inside my HR? Those seconds are lost to my conscious memory. I can say that I remember cutting my arm when it broke off the hard plastic cup-hook I'd glued the the pillar to hold up my seatbelt and that the back of my bench seat where I sat was bent back at a 45 degree angle during the accident. I can say that when the car was stationary and my memory returned I was sitting upright, both my hands on the steering wheel, my proper feet were still depressing the clutch and brake as they were when the semi-trailer first made contact before shunting me three or four spaces forward, the car's engine was still running as I recall switching it off in fear of a fuel leak after I'd looked in he rear vision mirror and saw the truck's bull bar, it was after that I realized where my feet were.

Evidently more relevant perhaps I can say that when I was at Camden public hospital's emergency department to have the deep cut near my elbow stitched the nursing sister and the male nurse there were both pushing on the suture needle their knuckles were white as they were unable to get it to pierce my skin. That's when she started calling me names and had a bit of a nervous breakdown I suspect. Took about an hour after impact before they could stitch my skin.

We in 1977 weren't as 'in love' with ourselves as present narcissistic generations are. I don't have many 1977 photos of myself, none with my white 1977 HR Holden after this. With very few pictures left on film in my camera, no money for more, my husband William Robert PETERS 1953—2008 snapped these photos, he said didn't think to get bent seat before film ended. Good thing considering how locals treated me, calling me "witch" then off to church they went praising their God. I'm not going into great detail here as this isn't about my family or my 1977 incident, I'm merely establishing that I was well known for being born in 1956 and known to police because they knew my Freemason parent, known generally as I'd lived long-term in the Campbelltown region.

You can search the Internet for independent photos evidence of the 1967 manufactured HR Holden Special vehicles they had bench seats and three speed column change manual gearbox. I personally loved the column change as opposed to the floor gearstick on my 1981 Holden Gemini. I feel the column change is safer as the stick in in your line of sight. With the floor change sometimes you have to take your eyes off the wheel to look for it and the seconds between your hands on the wheel and floor stick might be a life or death time delay. That's my opinion. With the growing popularity of the Bathurst 500 annual event as Holden and Ford battled it out for popularity with blokes the floor change was considered more 'manly' so that's why the safer column change was not supported in later models. Or ask Holden directly. Any old timer with their memory intact will tell you that it wasn't until about 1971 when Holden released the Premier models that automatic transmissions and seats started with headrests or individual bucket seats were manufactured. I remember as mum was reluctant to drive the automatic that male parent had bought was a silver green c1970-71 Premier with bucket seats.

On the evidence of the SIMPSON & HARVEY's 'Brothers In Arms' 'young Ivan' photos, there is no evidence that John David HILL could have given police to lawfully qualify for witness protection, change of identity and advancement into South Australia's State Parliament as Labor Party's (*Freemason terrorist*) Health Minister, who by absence of community expected actions and various High Court rulings involving the political defense for defamation, John David HILL did unconstitutionally block my right to medical services to have the NSW illegal implants removed from my person. That establishes *prima facie motive* to harm me as he has 'seriously physically harmed me, because of his political or Freemason affiliation with the terrorists who surgically raped me.

Other evidence indicates I was brainwashed to believe it was "my idea" to relocate to Adelaide, in South Australia from New South Wales.

John David HILL wasn't lawfully able to justly his verbal claim of "conflict of interest" as my voice in parliamentary in the matter of the SIMPSON & HARVEY 'Brothers In Arms' paperback, his actions or lack of indicate he did verbally claim 'conflict of interest' in the cold blooded murder cover up of young Ivan ROMCEK.

A 'conflict of interest in government' refers to a present or future 'financial' benefit.

Many government public officers treat their employment like the Catholic church confessional. There is no legal right to redact defamatory statements or actions entered into government records to secretly harm the person the record describes. We're not in America, we have no 5th amendment. Self incrimination protection only works on the court room when you're being tried for a crime.

No Australian resident can claim a 'conflict of interest' to protect themselves from liability for their willing and active participating in ongoing terrorist organization cover up crimes that undermine to services of a Government or the health and safety of any section of the community or serious harm that is physical to even one person. Yet they do with the full support of Australia's police departments. What's the deal? What benefits are senior police department executives getting from harboring TERRORISM from within the State and Federal governments themselves? Must be top-shelf benefits.

The documents herein establish the very high probability that **John David HILL is a terrorist *enemy of Australia***. Every person who provides him, terrorists, any support to evade criminal accountability for terrorist crimes specifically against me since 2007 are also terrorists enemies of Australia. This is my first letter I wrote to my elected voice in State parliament after he, John David HILL, ran from the appointment room mumbling his right to declare a 'conflict of interest' in Ivan ROMCEK's Sydney 1984 murder.

My ***7 Sep 2007*** letter to John David HILL as South Australia parliamentarian was treated exactly as my 2001 information to NSW police as evidenced by ***7 May 2003* NSW** police response to me, with contempt.

It was a copy-cat crime to pervert the course of justice and due administration of law. The prima facir evidence of crime I'd provided to State officials in New South Wales and South Australia were *filed away and not answered* in conflict with Australian law on 'law enforcement' and natural justice.

Federal and State government's built and contracted private physicians to operate ***GP Plus Super Clinics*** across Australia. Ergo the contracted 'private' physicians became Government Public Officers who *illegally* used the same ABN[11] for their private & Government income streams.

If you've already read it, you may recall in his letter of **20 March 2012** Health Minister John David HILL advised me to file a complaint to AHPRA, because its a national organization. In another letter **28 August 2011** same John David HILL Health Minister directed me to file a complaint with H&CSCC alleged 'independent' health industry watchdog.

The Health Minister is last port of call in complaints arena before court action to sue the State for misfeasance. Health Minister is legally responsible for all actions allegedly performed by virtue of (health matter) enactments of parliament (statute law) from State health services. All Minister are *the Clayton's High Court* the court you have before stepping into a proper court of law.

AHPRA registers all physicians and nurses. H&CSCC investigates only State government controlled health service providers and sends their recommendations to Health Minister whose been 'indentured apprentice' trained by other Ministers and elected zombies (evidently) to give you run-around, fobbing off to AHPRA and H&CSCC.

The High Court was created (unconstitutionally) after the Federales illegally (altered the constitution without a referendum) cancelled our Constitutional right to appeal to the British sovereign from a terrorist's Star Chamber Court decision in Australia — which means the Australia High Court impersonates the British Monarchy in the Privy Council. Others would call that treason[12]. Australia's parliaments since 1986 call it legal.

Lets start with AHPRA who for a long time had their business name (ABN[13]) registered under a different spelling to the one they were allocated. Dodgy from day one.

John David HILL bio at UniSA says he graduated from Sydney University. All his stated 'years' are presumed false based on the hard evidence of his face in SIMPSON & HARVEY's 'Brothers In Arms'. in 2010 I had already submitted various lawful complaints about physicians refusing to acknowledge my separated shoulder joint and my dislocated thumbs and the illegal electronic implants in my ear region of my skull — instead attempting to slot me into the mental health services as a complaining crackpot.

Richenda WEBB now at AHPRA in Adelaide, answered my complaints

---

[11] *ABN means Australian Business Number.*

[12] *Australia Act 1986 (Commonwealth of Australia).*

[13] *ABN means Australian Business Number registered with Taxation office.*

about physicians by dismissing them all as baseless. She graduated from same University of Sydney 1977 same era that John David HILL would have *if he did* as claimed. Not saying they knew each other, 'tis same neck of the woods, same State as Macquarie University's Cochlear Limited. I'll not bother with the dozens of AHPRA and Medical Board letters in this paperback, they're mentioned often enough in other State records but this paperback really isn't about the medical crimes in Adelaide its about the SIMPSON & HARVEY's 'Brothers In Arms' I've referenced some because of the intricate and interwoven connection between the SIMPSON & HARVEY's 'Brothers In Arms' and the State's illegal secret records "diagnosing" me schizophrenic delusional because of my letters of complaint to the police in New South Wales and South Australia, Health Ministers in South Australia and my evidence of medical crimes published on he internet they describe with words like "troubling" to infer the problems are between 'my' ears not theirs. Or as lawyers might call it "cause and effect".

> *Australian officials 'best practice' is to apply terrorist tactics in teams, to attack 'informants' in response to informant's lawful reports to officials of terrorist attacks on innocent law abiding Australians.*

Now lets have a little peak at H&CSCC, which stands for Health and Community Services Complaints Commission and their legal relationship to Christies Beach Medical Centre who you'll read about a little later. Briefly they were contracted to supply general health services under contract to either the State of South Australia or federal government, Commonwealth of Australia. The feds nationwide jointly funded 'GP Plus Super Clinics' with state or Territory Governments. Its unclear which contracts physicians, however the contracts turn private physicians into Government public officers. ♉

DISHONEST DEALINGS WITH DOCUMENTS

Evidently accessing medical services in Australia is a secret 'popularity' contest, based on political affiliations.

I attended the Noarlunga **GP Plus Super Clinic** located about 1 minute's drive from South Australia Minister for Health's electorate office in Christies Beach. I refer to the same John David HILL. It wasn't until during the Medicare Australia consultation that I discovered this Government business was contracted to private physicians at **Christies Beach Medical Centre.** Then I discovered Christies Beach Medical Centre had illegally transferred my medical records into the Government medical practice without my informed consent and were using the old Christies Beach Medical Centre ABN at GP Plus Super Clinic Noarlunga — because evidently, Australia's medical service centres are criminal organizations to cover up Government funded medical crimes. All this and more i've already proved by their documents published on my website for some years, because when the very same John David HILL MP was my voice in State Parliament and the only State Minister for Health, he and those party faithful who elected him were all active political terrorists for the Freemason's cause to cover up child rape.

Sure it too me many years to accept the glaring obvious of the Freemason child rape cover up. I had to go through the long and arduous task of eliminating all other probabilities. Including proving the alleged federal Privacy Act Principals and Australian Charter of Healthcare Rights are not recognized in the Adelaide region of South Australia where the Australian Labor Party hold balance of power in State and Federal parliaments in 2024.

Government executive being one third of Government agree to "policy" and Charters. They write the Charters same as they wrote the first Charter, the Great Charter also known as Magna Carter. Another third of Government (*parliament*) make and pass Enactments of parliament we're all supposed to comply with 'or else' the other third of Government (judiciary) will punich us. That's how is supposed to work in democracy.

In a totalitarian dictatorship that all of the falsely claimed democracies are, the Charters and Enactments are intended to lull the rest of us into a false sense of safety and security as they're never intended to be complied with when the political interests of the Celtic Trilogy of terrorist organizations in Australia are under threat of exposure for their crimes. This Celtic Trilogy is naturally Labor Party, Liberal Party and Freemason's secret unregistered political party that work in unison with Labor or Liberal depending who holds the balance of power in parliament. That dear reader is why its difficult to tell them apart.

The theory that capitalist corporate interests control Government is equally correct on account of the fact they are members or supporters of one, two or all of the Celtic Trilogy. The evidence tells all for thiose willing to see the truth of it.

Then we have their registered physicians who also support 1, 2, or all of the Celtic Trilogy to secure their financial future. This group of registered physicians believe they're some type of cowboy living in North Korea making up their own "business law" as they go along to negate Australian Consumer Law. They have no fear of accountability for their actions because they have politicians like John David HILL in their corner who willingly turn a blind eye to it to ensure they get reelected to parliament.

With this new mindset we must now reflect upon the obvious dear reader.

In the event John David HILL was once outlaw Bandido motorcycle club member Lance WELLINGTON — then he's a killer convicted to the shootings on 2 September 1984. In reflection of what is truthfully known about 20th century Australia Freemasons then the evidence indicates that John David

HILL murdered unarmed young Ivan ROMCEK in cold blood because he'd witnessed child rape crimes as a child. Or else some other did for the same reason and HILL agreed to be the "face" of that in exchange for his guarantee of future financial and social status.

In the event John David HILL never was Lance WELLINGTON, he just posed for or allowed those photo likenesses of him to be published in the SIMPSON & HARVEY's 'Brothers In Arms' paperback — then he's a political or ideological terrorist covering up Australia's long history of child rape crimes, some of which I witnessed as a child and adult by adding the the terrorist farce of the SIMPSON & HARVEY's 'Brothers In Arms' paperback. In the two scenarios he's either a cold blooded murderer or he's a Freemason terrorist. There is no 'get out of jail' card for John David HILL — that's what the global Freemason organization is for apparently. Ergo — John David HILL never qualified for his seat in State parliament he was evidently automatically disqualified since 1989 as a Freemason terrorist when SIMPSON & HARVEY's 'Brothers In Arms' paperback was first published. Yet, John David HILL therefore didn't qualify for his lifetime parliamentarian's pension he now enjoys as a Vice poo-bar and council member at the University of South Australia. All proceeds of crime.

Following photo on my foot had no edits whatsoever its a actual digital photo of my foot snapped when it was painfully electronically pulsing in 2007, I'd snapped many this was only one that proved the pulses. My research led me to suspect 'bionic neuron' or BION. They're all still in soles of my feet & arms. **Cochlear Limited is owned by the State of New South Wales, *Macquarie University*** the evidence says its they who provided the illegal implants to the Wollondilly Shire terrorist physicians to criminally experimented on me in 1990s for their Freemason and Labor-Liberal terrorist causes and that Freemasons are the "sponsors" of the illegal implants because covering up their child sex crimes is a "*mens health issue*". Naturally those variables of who what when where why how, they're fluid as I'm not part of their **"*inside story of two*" government "*gangs*"**.

It wasn't until 2012 I had 'their own' documented evidence to prove physicians at the Christies Beach Medical Centre, had criminally defamed me in both their private medical practice and the Government contracted medical service provision to illegally block my right to access services to have illegal implants removed from my physical person. Which is an act of terrorism and a crime against Australia.

Still despite all my evidence against these Government funded terrorists in Adelaide region of South Australia, the State and Federal police departments refuse to take any action to protect me from these political terrorists. This is why I've been forced to write this book to search nationally and internationally for lawyers to sue these terrorists on defamation and terrorism torts, that include the elements of misfeasance in public office and of a terrorist act pursuant to the federal **Criminal Code Act 1995, Schedule, The Criminal Code.**

An unidentified person **deleted** a September 2006 (dated) radiologist's report from Perret radiology (since absorbed by Jones Radiology who provide radiology services in State hospitals) which stated evidence of my prior surgery (I'd not authorized) and evidence of the illegal (vibrating) implant (still) in my jaw which appears to be a tracking device, from my research anyway.

"Barry DOWELL" on CBMC stationary he was at GP Plus Super Clinic Noarlunga as their 'physician team leader' when I had my first ever appointment with **Malaysian physician** Mr Jee Ken MAR who **racially defamed me as "entitled"** in State record because I wanted to control my medical service, my right under the Utopian Australian Charter of Healthcare Rights. The government forgot to inform physicians we have legal rights and protections from racial discrimination and criminal (intentionally willful or reckless) defamation innuendo of mental illness.

Which is very relevant as they had already signed the contract supply medical services at GP Plus Super Clinic[14]. Which means all directors are **contracted government public officers** and all Christies Beach Medical Centre staff are also **contracted government public officers** when working at GP Plus. Relevant as contracted government public officers are just as liable for investigation by ICAC as any other government public officer. Their actions must be impeccably lawful, honest and transparent, that's not what has happened in my records.

Following images from Christies Beach Medical Centre represent part of a criminally falsified Government medical record made buy registered physicians, very young Tasmania trained Ms Celia Emmeline TILDESLEY at private practice, Christies Beach Medical Centre near John David HILL's electorate office at the material times, and Malaysia trained mature aged Mr Jee Ken MAH at the Government's contracted medical centre where this dufuss can't possibly be clueless to the reality that he's a *State Government Public Officer* bound to hear me and medically investigate when I inform him I feel vibrations around my tailbone. Physician Jee Ken MAH didn't bother the hear me on the fact that I had illegal secret surgery there when I was mid term pregnant in 1991, leaving me with several dissolving black surgical stitches. No he was more interested in reaffirming the criminally false allegation made by his fellow Christies Beach Medical Centre physician, Cecilia Emmeline TILDESLEY who secretly wrote to psychiatrist Helen TINGAY in her diagnosis that I must be mentally ill because I speak of being

[14] *GP P,us Super Clinics are a* joint project for State & Federal Government.

victim of the crime associated with the Government funded propagandas in SIMPSON & HARVEY's 'Brothers In Arms'.

Government agree to Charters, enactments of parliament but their registered physicians still believe they're cowboys living in North Korea making up their own "business law" they believe negates Australian Consumer Law politicians like John David HILL turn a blind eye to it to ensure they get reelected.

In the event John David HILL was once outlaw Bandido motorcycle club member Lance WELLINGTON — then he's a killer convicted to the shootings on 2 September 1984 and as the evidence indicates he murdered unarmed young Ivan ROMCEK in cold blood because he'd witnessed child rape crimes as a child.

In the event John David HILL never was Lance WELLINGTON, he just posed for or allowed those photo likenesses of him to be published in the SIMPSON & HARVEY's 'Brothers In Arms' paperback — then he's a political or ideological terrorist covering up Australia's long history of child rape crimes, some of which I witnessed as a child and adult by adding the the terrorist farce of the SIMPSON & HARVEY's 'Brothers In Arms' paperback.

In the two scenarios he's either a cold blooded murderer or he's a Freemason terrorist. There is no 'get out of jail' card for John David HILL that's what the global Freemason organization is for apparently. Ergo — John David HILL never qualified for his seat in State parliament he was evidently automatically disqualified since 1989 as a Freemason terrorist when SIMPSON & HARVEY's 'Brothers In Arms' paperback was first published. John David HILL therefore didn't qualify for his lifetime parliamentarian's pension he now enjoys as a Vice poo-bar and council member at the University of South Australia. All proceeds of crime.

Be in no doubt dear reader, physicians, politicians, police and Freemasons globally are using, *gullible us, as their secret medical experiment targets* to feather their own nest for retirement and family fortunes. ☿

Copyright Act theft Micro Focus v NSW Police

Just in case you're not convinced New South Wales Government's police department and police officers aren't seasoned criminals, then take a look at this surely it will change your mind. The State of New South Wales **Crown Solicitor wasted taxpayer resources to unjustly defended this 'no win' lawsuit** which at the onset established that Australia's oldest parliament are indeed, unrepentant on their own federal government's **Copyright Act** thefts, which is what this same police department did to my own **Copyright Act** protected biometric identity (photo) since 1989. **This lawsuit proves 100%** that our Liberal Labor Australia parliaments in NSW actively ensure 'their' police are allies in just about any despicable political terrorist plan including the ongoing medical crimes they've inflicted upon me since at least 1991.

This is a perfect example of how CRIMINAL our public prosecutors our parliaments and our police really are. This criminal-police conduct is the real Australia. See litigation by *Micro Focus [US] Inc v State of New South Wales [New South Wales Police Force] [2011] FCA 787 [15 July 2011]*

This 2010 decade Government who will misappropriate public resources, *because its not their personal money*, to embark on a court battle that has no legal merit after they refused repeatedly to investigate and prosecute the evidence based crimes against State public officers in this matter since 1984. Direct quote by Brett Winterford Jan 29, 2013[15] with some "*the*" deletions.

The NSW Attorney General will this week sign an out of court settlement with software vendor Micro Focus, putting an end to a protracted and expensive dispute between the State's law enforcement services and the software vendor over licenses.

Micro Focus had accused the NSW Police, the NSW Ombudsman, the Police Integrity Commission, Corrective Services NSW and countless other NSW Government agencies of illegally distributing its software for the better part of a decade in a law suit filed in May 2011.

---

[15] *https://www.crn.com.au/news/nsw-police-settles-micro-focus-battle-330451*

These agencies have progressively signed small settlements with the British software vendor, but the main protagonist NSW Police continued to fight the matter in the Federal Court until late into 2012.

NSW Police and the NSW Department of Attorney General and Justice have finally settled out of court with Micro Focus.

Bruce Craig, general manager for Micro Focus Australia, told iTnews he could confirm that both parties have settled – NSW Police coming to the table shortly before a hearing scheduled for November, 2012 and the state's Attorney General last week.

The details of those settlements were attached to non-disclosure agreements that prevent software vendor from revealing how much case cost taxpayers.

Micro Focus had originally sued NSW Police for $10 million, but upped the damages sought to $12 million in June 2012 after viewing the results of a court-ordered audit of NSW Police systems.

A relieved Craig said he could not name a figure, saying only that the outcome was "more than satisfying" and had "achieved the desired result." — "It's done and dusted," he said. "All agencies are now fundamentally settled, but for some final paperwork."

TIMELINE: Policing the Police

1988: The NSW Police and Micro Focus sign a licensing deal for use of the NS mainframe terminal software suite.

2003: The NSW Police begins to use Micro Focus' ViewNow software – the next version on from NS - for terminals to connect to NSW Police's Computerised Operations Policing System (COPS), a centralised database containing all day-to-day operating information for police investigations.

May 2011: Micro Focus accuses NSW Police of using 16,000 copies of the ViewNow software, after only paying licenses for 6500. It further alleges NSW Police distributed the software to 27 Government agencies, including fellow law enforcement agencies, RailCorp and the Office of Fair Trading. The NSW Police alleges that its 1998 agreement entitled it to a "site-wide" license for an undisclosed number of terminals. This agreement had been updated in 1999 and 2000.

August 2011: The NSW Police Commission settles with Micro Focus for an undisclosed sum over 47 unlicensed copies of the ViewNow software.

September 2011: Federal Court Justice Jayne Jagot appoints KPMG associate director Stan Gallo to audit NSW Police systems at a cost of $120,000.

February 2012: Micro Focus adds the NSW Attorney General and Corrective Services NSW to its lawsuit over the alleged use of "at least" 60 copies of the ViewNow software.

April 2012: ABC's 7:30 Report airs an investigation into software piracy.

May 2012: The Attorney General's Department settles out of court over the ViewNow licenses, but is further sued over its use of another Micro Focus software program, SNA Server.

June 2012: Micro Focus increases its claim to $12 million after viewing the results of KPMG's audit of NSW Police.

Late October 2012: NSW Police settles with Micro Focus for an undisclosed sum, subject to a non-disclosure agreement.

*January 2013: The NSW Attorney General settles out of court with Micro Focus for **unlicensed use** of NS Server.* ♉

ALICE'S PEASANT TOES

Some government crimes are so huge they're impossible to see without stepping back. What's also true is that I'm long winded in my explanations of the facts, which is necessary to paint the full picture of this very elaborate confidence trick that's had taxpayer resources pumped into it to perpetuate these crimes for Freemason and party-faithful terrorist's causes.

Elaine SLOWMAN moved into her Kadar Street Bargo NSW residence to be near my only brother Alan, specifically to undermine the structure of my family and cause my brother distress. She made the mistake of believing my brother's neighbor was my brother, David AUCHTERLONIE. Elaine SLOWMAN is a self-proved psychopath. Psychopathy is often DNA inherited so too are your toe shape, mine are Egyptian[16] same as my mum's with very small little toe but my siblings are Greek same as our dad, I share his blood group with my brother. Eventually multiple Freemason terrorist members succeeded infiltrating my brother life through the Bargo Pony Club where my brothers wife took her children. I suspect that person was physician and hypnotist Mohmmed R AHMED the person who surgically raped me during the 1990s after the physicians in the Argyle Street PICTON NSW has surgically raped me with illegal implants requiring surgical stitches to close the wound over my tailbone when I was pregnant in 1991 — obvious that was the insertion of the pulse generator. Other puncture wounds were on my sternum (chest) and on my spine both on either side of my heart. The chest one was closed with super glue (crystalized) the spine closed with stitches. AHMED joined in some time later after I'd changed physicians from the Picton surgically him.

AHMED added his first illegal implants inserted behind my left shoulder and center of my spine at the base of my neck. Then circa 1998 when I was abducted from a Camden council MACROC meeting he added ones in my brain or at least on top of my skull that punctured my brain preventing me from speaking. I suspect that was intended to vegetate me. He'd also added one set of cables that punctured the skin inside my nose and upper pallet (mouth) that led into my stomach or abdomen generally. They vibrate these intermittently causing me to almost choke on food or liquid cough sneeze or

---

[16] *See toe chart on ninth page of this chapter.*

gag.

At same time they were all infiltrating my closest age sister's life Sharon. Sharon was living near me in Enderslie (Camden NSW) in 1984. They manipulated her relocation from Elderslie The persons my sister knew who claimed they "knew me" were "Peter and Rose" the same Peter and Rose who relocated themselves in direct live of sight about 100 meters from my front door, I was 30 William Street they were 39 Mary Street. I only got a look of them once she was the same person who Jennifer SHEEHAN from Visyboard called her aunt Rose. She looks identical enough to be Jennifer SHEEHAN's sister.

Elaine SLOWMAN also personally infiltrated the life of my sister through the Camden historical society. Camden Freemasons are the group who had intended to murder me on 24 April 1988 but murdered my families long-term family friend the only other man I'd known since my birth, retired police officer Jack BASSET who was stationed in Cooma NSW when at least when I was born. His family lived opposite our old style tiny country residence on a little off street from Monaro Highway we were other side of the highway in Government's residence at Bunyan siding proper. Mum ran the tiny country post office and switch telephone exchange. She also operated the railway gate for the State of New South Wales. Our house was owned by the Post Master General the old Attorney-General's domain that became telecom and Australia Post. Despite her contribution to early Cooma-Bunyan she's not been mentioned as pioneer resident despite that she clearly was. That's because Federal and State Freemason centric governments decided to cover up my rape as a toddler and the rapes of my siblings as small children by my Freemason male parent who was employed as a fettler for what is now known as NSW State Rail the day I was born. I was raped when 2 years 10 months old on 3 March 1959. Despite that the Cooma local court sentenced my male parent to prison for my rape the State's records on that criminal record don't exist, according the the State in 2023.

Elaine SLOWMAN was known to my brother and sister as Lynette STYLES. So who else apart from Peter, Rose and Mohammed R Ahmed infiltrated their lives? That's be some Irish Catholic family who'd approached my sister Sharon through the Camden heritage group claiming to be DNA related to our male parent. They claimed this on the basis of the fact someone in NSW State Parliament did to my male parent's grandfather exactly what the Freemasons in Government are doing to me in my lifetime — erased his life after his death. His marriage certificate was recalled to Sydney by an anonymous person. My own detective work in 2017 after Sharon was conned into believing we were associated with a Freemason Irish Catholic police family in Sydney with the family name of COFFEY based on old newspaper of a run-away Sydney boy Francis COFFEY made by his male parent a 1800s Sydney police officer and a DNA comparison test result which like my DNA tests was probably swapped in Australia Post mail by Granville post worker. My theory is they swapped the swab my male parent gave for one of their own family members when in transit with Australia Post.

Circa 1998 I had a 300 page registered mail of papers disappear from the Post Office I mailed it at, twice. Once in Bowral once in Mittagong. My application for compensation also disappeared. The mystery person I saw out the back in the Bowral Post Office I'd also seen out back in Branxtom Post office where my mail was held to ensure my illegal eviction of false documents in February 2002. They are a Freemason police family who use their status as police to intercept every facet of out lives illegally — as terrorist enemies of Australia by undermining Government services and communications systems.

My family detective work since 2017 says the alleged runaway Francis COFFEY died in Melbourne and was well connected to Melbourne community life.

The glaring obvious logic my dear sister is unable to grasp because she's not INTJ or even close to my logic mindedness, she had no overt ability to perceive utter stupidity when its before her as she used to. She's been effectively brainwashed to believe illogic garbage.

My darling sister's (Freemason brainwashed) entry in Camden history magazine entry she stated with words to the effect that:

'because our male parent "never tanned" and ate peas, potato and carrots and was an alcoholic therefore he was Irish.'

Here's the logic:

1. Our 'dad' tanned like a black-man. I didn't know any other white skinned person my age who could tan that dark.

2. If he was a Sydney police family child run-away in 1800 why didn't police find him in 1800s.?

3. If this Irish COFFEY police family knew 'Francis COFFEY' was a 'lost child' then why didn't they use GEDmatch to locate his descendants or police DNA tests available to police since 1980s long before they approached my sister through Elaine SLOWMAN as Lynette STYLES in 29017?

4. Obvious conclusion — the DNA was falsified by Freemason police families. My sister's been conned by another criminally minded Freemason Irish family or whomever else they claim to be. Probably changes from day to day.

My brother's wife was attacked in the same manner when she was tracing our FRANCIS family tree in the 1990s. She came to different conclusions she believed were correct but my research says was just another Freemason family confidence trick They even had 'sleep-overs' at residents of these alleged 'newly discovered' family members. (My hand slapped my forehead" How can my siblings be so daft? They're all older than me.

I won the DNA lottery. As I've written before my siblings and I we don't look like siblings. Don't even look similar enough to be cousins. We have the same parents but Mum has a huge gene pool this I know through her mtDNA and my family tree results before FamilySearch.org was tampered with — I downloaded my family tree a few times, over several days it took.

Mum has Irish DNA but my DNA shows almost no Irishness. I suspect my male parent's origins are similar to mums, Scandinavian Germanic mostly west Europe. However, mum has some Asian DNA she had thick dead strait black hair like the Asians. Male parent had ringlet curly black hair. I have brown hair born blonde same as my oldest sister Lynette, our very curly hair goes fuzzy in humidity demonstrating our African DNA. My hair falls into ringlets when shoulder length.

I have my male parent's A+ blood group like my brother who also gas curly fuzzy hair but his is black. My two sisters have O blood group same as Mum. My Sharon has a stumpy neck and (normal) big head like mum. Mine is head is very small and my neck is long. My oldest sister is similar to me but her jaw is thin mine is square. My sisters and brother have the same type os toes as male parent (from memory) second toe same length or longer than bif toe. They all have slight Roman nose bump except mum and I we don't have the Roman bump. My brother and sisters are all tall like male parent. I'm same height as mum we both have wide square hands perhaps from my Neanderthal DNA and same size feet with Egyptian type tapered toes. Put a flag on the toes concept.

From my research my paternal links include the poor side of the GROSVENOR family of London — I suspect I'm distant cousin to London's Hugh GROSVENOR who has Royal title of some such.

We're GROSVENOR related through Ruth GROSVENOR who married Henry FRANCIS 2 April 1801 Westminster, Middlesex, England, United Kingdom. No idea whether or not that was at Westminster Abby or not. Ruth's parents were William GROSVENOR & Anne LOWE. Henry died in Sydney before having my ancestor son who had a son who was my male parent's grandfather. His parents appear to have immigrated to San Francisco before the great earthquake but they survived it.

Since I've started researching my family in the church website FamilySearch.org the Freemasons infiltrated that by organizing manipulation of that family research internet website (free to everyone) through all State public Libraries. Whether it was ta a Library or at a home computer someone has been erasing my family associations in America. Since about February 2023 when I first published my happy findings on my Facebook page.

Its obvious that Freemasons have infiltrated Australia's governments to change history by erasing evidence of Freemason crimes specifically Freemason child rape. Illegally manipulating my family history and associations internationally.

If you've not noticed, Wikipedia is manipulated by State or Federal political interests in Australia — when I added my 2014 Federal Court of Australia Order and associated material to "Brothers In Arms Wikipedia.org page it was erased, again and again.

Australia is a terrorist nation I've proved that over and over on my documents. I'm one of several million Australians. Its more likely than not history is being erased globally by Freemasons in allied nations to cover up the huge prevalence of Freemason organized crime which includes altering any and all history records.

Best way to describe how they got away with this for so long without many more coming forward is by the fact so many Freemasons and their politically aligned Tripartizans are in Government and the News Industries, positioned to pull out and quash and evidence record that might split this story wide open — is this — put an open book to your face rest is against your nose then read the words you can see. You can't read any words because now they're so huge they're impossible to see, impossible to focus on they're all a blur and how they get away with so many crimes — the criminal infiltration in our false democratic Governments and news industry is so huge we the people on the outside of that crime syndicate see nothing of it in the news or the court system.

My toe's shape have altered slightly since the 1990s silicone fillers injected in my feet. The result is quite painful long-term as now when I walk I'm walking on skin that's under the toes next to the toe the skin belongs to. I suspect the intent was to make my tapered Egyption toes look like the square peasant toes of SLOWMAN WALTERS UNWIN or COFFEY family or pull a Freemason family name out of the hat for this lot who probably have forgotten their own names having, as it appears, altered it to deceive that many times. ☿

TOE FLAG

The 2014 Leanne toe lengths almost identical peasant toes. As noted before my family have "Egyptian & Greek toes" on this chart. When I've written I have 'head to toe' secret illegal silicone injections accomplished by first secretly drugging me, probably with traditional 'date rape' amnesia type drugs, I meant that literally.

The toe photos were first published on the Internet circa 2014. Believe me I've periodically scoured the internet for "Leanne Walters" photos.

These first appeared in 2014 after I started my Federal Court of Australia Copyright challenge against the Allen Unwin and their authors etcetera The article is about New South Wales Freemason Police superintendent Clive SMALL.

However as it was published in Queensland its just as likely it came from author Lindsay SIMPSON family who lives on Magnetic Island according to numerous sources. The article has several new images of the fake Leanne[17] Walters. The author or source of the article has addressed all the main points I've brought up in proving Freemason police falsified evidence at the murder scene of these shootings. They blacked out Ivan ROMCEK's feet in the photos previously published on the covers of the paperback SIMPSON & HARVEY Brothers In Arms as well as adding what I say are morphed photos or photos of now allegedly dead author Sandra HARVEY whose real name is Leanne SLOWMAN or one of the other SLOMAN or UNWIN sisters involved on the 1984 crime to fabricate the identity of fake Leanne Walters. These are photos that I accessed the feet from note how clear the images are. I have year 2000 photos that are nowhere near as excellent quality. Which leads to the accusation these are morphed brand new and digital in 2014 — not 1984 photos . They also have "JFIF" extensions which I'm informed:

> *"JFIF is pretty well obsolete, having been mostly replaced by the EXIF format. Both are primarily used for digital camera storage, and are not general purpose formats* [18]

Almost everything is different looking at the 1984 image compared to the 2014 image. No background, hair wider & darker, face distorted & wider, eyes larger, eyebrows larger & darker, teeth bigger, lips larger, chin longer, towel stripe missing, elbow shorter. Why is this coming from Queensland where author Lindsay SIMPSON lives when the alleged parents live in Sydney NSW? Why wasn't it in the 1989 book? Answer: Because its fake as fake gets you three: Tamara, Sharon and Camilla UNWIN.

The article is titled "Milperra Massacre: 30 years on, Father's Day will

---

[17]   https://www.couriermail.com.au/news/milperra-massacre-30-years-on-fathers-day-will-forever-be-a-symbol-of-death-and-terror/news-story/6e071eab762d414faefc27fe5718053e

[18] Author of "OOXML Hacking - Unlocking Microsoft Office's Secrets", ebook   now   out   John   Korchok,   Production   Manager production@brandwares.com   answers.microsoft.com/en-us/msoffice/forum/all/why-does-power   point-allow-jpg-and-jpeg-buft-not/6a8043a5-a810-465e-8b5b-27b48dc80028

forever be a symbol of death and terror[19]" this is how the Freemasons sensationalize their own crimes transforming their crimes into the crimes of others. That's three obvious actions to attempt to counteract my litigation in Federal Court of Australia:

- Network Nine Television documentary from State of NSW

- Author SIMPSON's Courier Mail story from State of Queensland.

- Author Lynette STYLES paperback Kangaroo Court to criminally defame me also from New South Wales.

These youtube.com photos behind the "DAD" glass, they're from Network Nine's documentary. As you may see this is supposed to be the same female wearing the same clothes. Look closer.

The outer two may be twins but they're not the same person. The biggest tell for my eyes is the proportions of their upper and lower arm length compared to the length of their torso. Righty is fatter in the face with no neck. Lefty is thinner with a long neck. Lefty appears to have longer arms proportionally to Righty. They're different clothes lines. One's against a brick wall the other a dark fence. These three females behind this glass thing which reads DAD may very well be the three look-alike daughters of Carol and Raynor UNWIN — Camilla, Sharon and Tamara. Or even the three author daughter of author Elaine SLOWMAN — Jennifer, Leanne and Lorraine. Maybe the UNWIN sisters and SLOWMAN sisters are same people and all the same fake Leanne Gaye WALTERS shot dead 1984.

Network Nine propaganda machine — 60 Minutes Australia image above https://youtu.be/h6G38Lbrn9Q "The Fathers Day Massacre: The worst bikie violence in the world" ☿

HOW MANY LIFE INSURANCE CLAIMS?

This is what the NSW Tripartizan Party Faithful GOVERNMENT of public officers do by custom of practice to my children and myself. We're food for their pleasure. My family Christmas tree photo was in my wallet when as elected Councillor HALL was stolen from my wallet at Council meeting, they (**Freemason & Labor Party faithful**) stole my entire bag with my wallet, and keys which obviously made it easy for them to deposit me back into my residence after they abducted me and surgically raped me in 1997 at the back of the Council office in the car park soon after I'd separated from my defacto Owen HALL and rented the house at 1 Swaine Drive Wilton, NSW.

---

[19]   *https://www.couriermail.com.au/news/milperra-massacre-30-years-on-fathers-day-will-forever-be-a-symbol-of-death-and-terror/news-story/6e071eab762d414faefc27fe5718053e*

I suspect that is the time I woken paralyzed in unimaginable agony during the illegal surgery on my face. These are people with no morals and no taboos. No limit to their criminal activities because they're psychopathic criminals for any cause that comes their way. Obviously they also stole my second photo to falsify yet another fake Leanne WALTERS face, this time using one of my (minor) under teenage children, my third son Lee. I refer to my son furthest right with no background behind him. Obviously they morphed his biometric data (face and head) with their first two Sydney 1984 newspaper photos of their face dead, fake Leanne. Their standard **modus operandi**, creating chaos from nothing to cover up their crimes.

Australia's Freemason police raped and pillaged their way through the lives of my children, my husband, my siblings, my mum, and myself leaving my children and I homeless and impoverished specifically necessary to to unjustly enrich themselves on our blood and tears — so I couldn't afford to hire lawyers to sue them.

They're so expert in their parasitic adventures their victims rarely understand what's happened. Its a Freemason trademark, anothert *modus operandi* possibly started with London England's unsolved *Jack The Ripper* misogynistic crimes community attributed to Freemasons. Logically that he-they murdered so many women in the street (not all prostitutes) indicates Jack-the-Ripper was probably one or two police officers, women turned their back on thinking they were safe before their throat was slit from behind.

Turning the facts to accuse victims of being prostitutes, gay or sex offenders as perpetrators, is what the Australia's Freemason police community do well. They continued in this manner to criminally harass me on 3 March 2023 as seen in my youtube.com videos.

I made the mistake of thinking there's only small number of terrorists in Government who'll be bribed or intimidated by or secret Tripartizans Government in Australia. I've proved on the documents they're almost all the same, deceitful, lawless, and psychopathic sycophants.

From here its obvious who have the most to gain from ensuring my side of these crimes never make it in mainstream news. Those persons who presently enjoy notoriety in the public arena however they don't deserve anyone's respect. They should be languishing in prison, should have been in prison for past 20 or 30 years for that what they've done to me. They've all done to me by participating in the crimes I've already covered to this poinbt in the book. They're just as criminally responsible for my assaults and torture and criminal defamations as those they funded to illegally and secretly impregnate me with illegal implants and those who fund the monitoring of their illegal vibrating implants inside me for past 30 something years. These implants aren't painless they cause me constant pain and constant discomfort because they're inside me and I'm refused medical treatment involving the illegal implants they threaten my early death from infection which appears to be part of their grand plan.

Apart from being the aforenoted and apart from being Freemason families who are they?

They and the Camden New South Wales police who murdered my friend of family, retired ex-Cooma police officer Jack BASSET. They are Camden police officer, my neighbor from 39 Mary Street The Oaks New South Wales, Peter Robert BRADBURY. They are are Camden Centrelink worker, my neighbor from 39 Mary Street The Oaks, Rose BRADBURY. They are the physicians from the Argyle Street Picton cottage medical practice who also work in the Bargo main road medical practice name sounds like Challender (he drove a VW van) and his other Freemason brothers from the Picton and Bargo medical practices. I don't remember their names as when I was consulting them I hadn't suspected the severity of what they were doing. They are 1968 India trained physician, Razorback Rd Picton NSW resident Mohamed Riyazuddin AHMED.

They stalk me to this day directly or through third parties. Many have groomed their own children to stalk me or harass me by finding fellow psychopaths in social or cultural groups, or simply knock on doors of my neighbors canvassing for candidates to stalk me at my residence, like my neighbor across the road with the same cultural background and psychopathic tenancies as Mohamed Riyazuddin AHMED.

Aye your hummin toes have it mingin blether muckle coos bairn of bigdog Rex — noo. **Or in Australian:** low-life mother-fuker drongo bottom-feeding scum. *Raucous sounds of female laughter fade into the distance broken by the crack of a steel prison door slamming shut.* ☿

SATAN'S CRUSADERS

This family of females are typical Freemason wenches they do the bidding of their -buddies with layer upon layer of blatant psychopathically malicious defamations. These parasites crawled into my life because I was an existing Freemason child rape witness targeted for suppression and secret murder. This publishing family invaded every facet of my life since 1988 with one goal, to cover up their specific involvement as the 1984 creators of the fake life and death of their fake person they call "Leanne Gaye Walters" officially in NSW Government records as aged 14 and 15 and 16 at time of her rather unlikely mode of violent death on Fathers' Day.

Because I was well aware I was different as child, understanding everyone else psychologically was my first thirst for knowledge.

Its fascinating that there are no female transvestites or female Kings. There is no word for a male *slut* or *whore*. These personality constructs or pretext were manufactured in the minds of the males of our species. The attention seeking males whose personalities are dominated by narcissistic feelings of superiority over women and the psychopath's lack of empathy.

Its true the males of our species are the ones who overwhelming possess this 'supremist' mindset. Its equally true that many of their female family members also possess these traits. Contrary to what most psychiatrists tell us the vast majority of people are narcissistic psychopaths — this is how our species has evolved since domestication.

Its the few who are still true humans, people like me.

Let me state clearly and loudly. Psychopaths are mutant humans they are not human, not human — because they're incapable of the natural trait of being human, being humane. They can only mimic what they've seen or heard same as a talking Galah (feathered bird) the favorite mascot of Allen & Unwin publishers.

As for my credentials as a psychologist. I've nothing formal. I didn't take a psychology exam I didn't study for circa 1990 as part of a tertiary course I never finished and secured a Distinction grade for that test. So I'd say I'm reasonably qualified as ma psychologist. Certainly more logically and factually qualified than the several State Health Government public officer psychologists who (criminally) falsified imprisonment orders infringing section 102 of South Australia's Mental Health Act — in concert with State Health Government public officers in New South Wales, 1,500 kilometers apart in January 2014. Making it quite evident that Freemasons and their Tripartizan political party faithful have falsified the grades of many like minded fellow child-rapist or possessing other criminal desires to give passing grades for parchment to be awarded to underserving students in many universities across Australia and probably beyond our shores.

Which is why I would never cast myself so low as to be counted in their numbers as a fellow degree holder. I have my morals and ethics limits that I adhere to vehemently. Moreover they'd most likely be certain to make sure my grades have been minimized as I've noted in the past where the university attended marked you down for your own personal assessment of how a joint assignment went. For Christ's sake how is that relevant to a law degree? I realized quite young that you can't make someone like you. You can't make someone do right by you if there's temptation that sways them to act abhorrently. Its in them to be honest or decent or humane or it isn't. That's why we have laws in our communities to force psychopaths to behave like humans — or else suffer the consequences. The problems in our communities arise when the psychopaths control all avenues of law enforcement. Then there is anarchy such as this Freemason's Leanne Walters fiction .

Each Freemason family member that joins this terrorist conspiracy all have their own theories about me. Conjecture based on hearsay and innuendo. Its the street definition of total bull. They are precisely what they accuse me of being. Deluded only their delusions are false beliefs in the grandeur of their own self importance.

Author Lynette STYLES (Elaine SLOWMAN) decided to publish her first paperback after I'd filed my claim in Federal Court, also expressly to criminally defame me also published under the auspice of State of New South wales in their public library system by about June 2014. SLOWMAN-STYLES' child reference to a nursery rhyme, Humpty-Dumpty, is what they her fellow councillors in concert had collectively conspiracy to do to me. In fact I recollect the Humpty-Dumpty "shattered" reference is from one of my website she's obviously plagiarized.

SLOWMAN-STYLES' Kangaroo Court paperback was obviously intended to be 'business as usual' for Sydney region Freemason police families — same **modus operandi** as Brothers In Arms was intended to be, little more than the medium to criminally defame me.

Kangaroo Court paperback was published some 14 years after both of us had left council. Only catalyst to prompt Freemasons to publish it with

SLOWMAN-STYLES' as the author as her "first" paperback was my Federal Court of Australia Copyright infringement.

The reason I came to the conclusion to file the Copyright infringement was me being illegally imprisoned by criminal abuse of public office and South Australia's Mental Health Act after Adelaide region Freemason families in Adelaide region criminally defamed me after I started gathering evidence of my surgical rape in 1990s at the hands of Sydney New South Wales Freemason police families.

That SLOWMAN-STYLES stood for council election same time as I did established her intent to criminally defame me. When I knew Elaine SLOWMAN and her three daughters in 1884 they lived in the State housing high-crime estate of Green Valley, a long way from Wollondilly Shire where I purchased my house in 1985.

SLOWMAN-STYLES and her NSW Police husband or sex partner had spread many false rumors to the Council office staff and elected members claiming I was "really Leanne Walters", according to Christine TOWNDROW who confided in me that Rex WALTERS approached her at a council meeting to "confide in her" that I was his "wife Pamela Walters" and I'd had a nervous breakdown, reinventing myself as Jenny HALL.

As time went by Wollondillyites accused me of being:

LEANNE WALTERS; AND
PAMELA WALTERS; AND
LINDSAY SIMPSON.

No I have no evidence of that directly. I have a virtual mountain of hard documented evidence inferring balance of probability. I'll start in this chapter with photos of the females they should have printed in their 1989 paperback instead of my face. Indicating whose **ear and hair was altered** face before published front page Sydney's The Sun Monday 2 Sep 1984 as "Leanne Walters aged 16".

The next few pages about photos of this fake Leanne WALTERS proves this family willfully participated in this criminal deception and that there never was a "shot dead" Leanne WALTERS pr any other female child in the car park of the Viking Tavern on 2 September 1984. It was 'smoke and mirrors, a voluntary **FREEMASON** police deception from the first moment Insert image "cherished photo" proves ear and hair were altered before releasing to press.

When sourcing the DailyMirror 'cherished' image from Mitchell Library staff informed prior copies were stolen asking me why I had wanted to see this roll of microfilm. I explained briefly. They threw back their head with sudden realization informing me any further access to this specific microfilm was strictly monitored. As should all of them in my opinion. As you can see the 21st century color photo of person labeled "Sharon BARTRAM" has dimple in her neck in same region as the 1984 photo of dead Leanne where BIA paperback alleges "Leanne" had a tracheostomy. "Sharon BARTRAM" person in my best guess for subject of adjacent newspaper photo. The six red background color photos, Internet sourced, were 21st century published, that's what their dates or circumstance claimed.

Sydney Mitchell Library is close to Supreme Court and NSW State parliament house where unethical persons with genuine motive to alter history records often congregate with ill intent.

Previous page: red photos clockwise author Lindsay SIMPSON photo television circa 2005. Sharon Unwin BARTRAM Twitter account @Batram1960. Fake LeanneWalters Sun Mirror 1984. author Jennifer Slowman COOKE, DoneLikeADinner' marketing 2008. author Elaine Slowman STYLES election photo 2015, I knew her from Visyboard too. Camilla Unwin CORBIN looks very more like internet photos of Karen McCall wife of Merlin Unwin, DailyMailAustralia 2012. Corner two photo are myself in 1980s my sunken cheeks are obvious I have Scottish DNA ergo prominent chin. I used to include photo of Anita Manning from BBC BarginHunt program to demonstrate era upturned end curls were popular, her mum allegedly lived in Sydney during 1980s being a Glasgow girl she has family resemblance with the other fat cheeked Glasgow females on this sheet and initially appeared to me to be subject of 1984 Daily Mirror's fake LeanneWalters newspaper photo about her image. Its obvious the real Leanne SLOWMAN is author Sandra HARVEY seen with her DNA sister Jennifer SLOWMAN who I knew very well by sight in 1984 as I'd been her transport to the same office employment at Richard PRATT's Visyboard Scrivener Street Warwick Farm behind Liverpool public hospital where fake Leanne stayed with fake nurse Karen BRENNAN. I have considerable Scottish DNA which is why with fillers in the right place I look like many big-chin Scottish women and when I bleach my brown hair it becomes copper blonde not white as I have a red base like many Europeans do.

If this alleged Merlin Unwin was 25 in 2016 that means he was born around same time my youngest child was born, the one I was pregnant with then I was extensively surgically raped by Freemason physicians based in Argyle Street Picton NSW. This family group of publishers have financially benefited by my surgical rape when pregnant, when an elected member of local council and my criminal defamations by their 1989 theft of my biometric identity before he was allegedly born. My family's criminal assaults in Australia funded the rural role he relishes in Scotland.

I don't personally know who the names of the children of Raynor Unwin and his wife. Only know what I sourced on the internet.

Not happy with just stealing my biometric identity to profit from book sales for that Copyright infringement, they decided to physically alter me as well to make their theft complete by claiming 'she doesn't look like her' where the "she" is me after their face rape and "her" is me before they face raped me.

They claim Rex Walters should know what his daughter looks like. Apparently not. When I called in on them from their 2003 electors roll address in Ingleburn NSW, he pulled out a yellowed copy of Monday 2 September 1984 The Sun with its front page photo sporting the Freemason fashionable doctored hair and ear (sarcasm) expressly to show me he still had a copy of the article that criminally perverted the course of Australia history for the NSW Australia Freemason child-rape cover up cause.

All image sources not identified in 'witch hunted' page are later in this chapter for verification of my source in this attempt to attract lawyers not aligned with terrorist Freemasons so I can sue this family of terrorists who stole my biometric identify and mutilated my face and person generally with illegal implants and silicone fillers. ♉

FIXATED STALKERS

There's been dozens of years of this family criminally stalking me and my family to seemingly undermine everything we do as their lies about us is integral to their contim=nual ecasions of accountability for their crimes against us and others.

At no time as Councillor Lynette STYLES had sElaine SLOWMAN used the name I'd known her by in 1984. She even looked different. — she was always Lynette STYLES at council. I didn't consciously realize that's who she was until I saw her 2015 election photo in about 2020 there her hair was short as it always was at Visyboard in 1984.

SLOWMAN-STYLES has never factored as being important to me in any way whatsoever, either when we were allegedly both employed as office staff at Visyboard in 1984 or at Wollondilly Shire Council as fellow councillors 1995–1999.

SLOWMAN-STYLES wasn't even in my electorate — she was in the south electorate, there was a central electorate that divided north and south, I was in north electorate with Rob WILSON and Marina VONCINA. I got on well with both of them, I thought. I'm a laissez-faire INTJ[20] personality which in-a-nutshell means *'I really don't give a tinkers'* about what anyone thinks of me. Unlike SLOWMAN-STYLES I don't try to intimidate anyone to get my way. That didn't change when we were both elected Wollondilly Shire

---

[20] *Myers-Briggs personality test. INTJ are*

Councillor. When they started claiming I was "Leanne WALTERS" I brushed it of as the stupidity it is. I grew up in Campbelltown. Attended the State's Campbelltown East primary and the only State high school in Campbelltown at that time.

I got my drivers license at Campbelltown motor registry in 1973 using my 1956 Cooma NSW birth certificate. My male parent knew many Campbelltown police and because of that Freemason relationship with him, they knew me. I did attend the Leumeah Inn with the father of my first child and other older ex-Campbelltown high school students and despite that police often wandered the drinking establishment knowing I was under age I was never removed because I was always sober and extremely well behaved — we were all well behaved. I would never associate with any other type of person. That's why I refused to friendship 'offer' from Rhonda WARK the loudmouth psychopathic bitch who arranged my rape in revenge of my refusal to accept her 'friendship'.

Elaine SLOWMAN (Lynette STYLES) has the exact personality type as Rhonda WARK. Exact they're not the dame person they've been born a decade apart they are the same personality 100%. Irrational, self-serving psychopaths who'll stop art nothing to get their own way. They are both effectively criminally insane. They have no taboos to their psychopathic actions. None. Its only others around them that stop them committing murder, the others they rely on for emotional sustenance and feedback.

Rather pathetic really.

At Wollondilly Shire I was the only councillor who didn't have after hours friendships with other councillors. They tried to rope me in but I'm an INTJ — just not interested in associating with gossiping backstabbers. Someone's alleged status in a community has never impressed or offended me. I don't give a tinkers curse really.

When I knew SLOWMAN-STYLES at Wollondilly Shire Council, she looked different to her appearance at Visyboard, and acted differently. She usually left the room when I entered so I wouldn't gaze at her or recognize her I suspect. She barely spoke at council meetings. I do vaguely recollect that I'd recognized her at one point but they's secretly roofied me so often to make me forget they'd done to me so I can't be specific not would I bother with the she said he said scenario. I'm a document person. Documents are harder to refute than words. Words that were never spoken can be cohobated by 100 liars.

One thing I knew about Elaine SLOWMAN she couldn't alter is that her arms were disproportioned — the top and lower sections are not same length as most people's are. As Lynette STYLES she always wore long sleeves. Like I said I vagally recollect seeing her once with no sleeves and that'd be when I recognized her. But I can only remember recognizing her as Elaine SLOWMAN smiling at her in a friendly manner saying "I know who you are" then forgetting completely mixed in with a memory of throwing a chair out a window after they'd refused to let me leave the council building after hours.

They'd drugged me to interrogate me to discover what I knew about them or how they could screw me over more likely. It was a big upstairs window, next to where I sat at the council chamber table. Had to be a record of the repair or insurance claim. Mongrel bastards.

In her aptly named "Kangaroo Court' STYLES-SLOWMAN plays the hard done by elected member everyone picked on, when in reality was the typical wicked-witch who'd caucused with the Labor left majority faction to deliver non independent decisions despite claiming they were "independent" as in not Party aligned. Nutbags. That she mentioned me when I was an elected member claiming I was always angry at her is rubbish. I don't get angry because if I do let myself feel that emotion I flip into a 'disassociate fugue state' — I black out apparently once I'd inflicted near death injuries on the male person who drugged me then told me:

"you're a little girl, I'm your daddy, I'm going to rape you"

I wasn't born with this. Its not a mental illness. Its an emotional distress no different to post traumatic distress which I've also experienced when I was a Wollondilly Shire Councillor for the first time in my life — Post Traumatic Shock and the Disassociate Fugue State — they're both direct result of me being raped by people I trusted.

All the hurt I've suppressed to force myself to feel ok despite having had a, not ok life. I coped by not discussing my childhood or my parents. SLOWMAN-STYLES and her gang used that to their advantage claiming my silence was "proof" of me being their Leanne Walters.

This family of psychopaths they don't let up, they keep psychologically torturing me with physical rape, something had to give. I suspect they were hoping their illegal implants in my frontal (brain) lobe region would alter my personality and cause me to forget my true childhood interweaving the reality with their fiction they keep 'play acting' verbally in my sleep even in 2024 through the illegal bone-phone they drilled into my head circa 1997. The illegal implants whose footprints and electronically vibrating presence seen in MRI and CT scans that multiple Ministers of Police and Health claim don't exist.

When I was Councillor HALL they drugged me and made me relive being betrayed by my girlfriends. I was completely shattered for several days couldn't stop crying. STYLES and her gang thought it greatly amusing. They secretly drugged me circa 1997 to steal every aspect of my memories my personal copyright on my version of my memories and experiences. Why? To find people in my past to come back into my present attack me on their behalf —   probably under threat of arrest and incarceration for my childhood rape.

That's how the Freemason police family of terrorists operate as terrorists. In her KANGAROO COURT – STYLES-SLOWMAN falsely claimed I was spitting angry at her during a council meeting then claim's I was "schizophrenic" then starts on about the "Brothers In Arms paperback I didn't see until 2001, two years after council. That means she was internet stalking me to plagiarize my literary works in my website to criminally defame me by manipulating my words and taking the information on my investigative journalistic crime reporting, out of context, expressly to defame me — she infringed my literary works copyright by abuse of my moral rights. Being an alleged "working" lawyer SLOWMAN-STYLES knows that. Unless her alleged lawyer status is also a lie.

Even that on its own implicates her however, a copy of her self-published paperback made its way into the hands of the Allen and Unwin lawyer who put it on the desk in front of him during mediation pointing to it as his evidence He promised to put it in evidence but never did. I got extracts from Google Books and I suspect its still published on the Internet as I can't get any lawyers in Australia to represent my interests in the real truth of any Government funded lie that's physically harmed me and my Australian born 'white' family so what's there excuse, can't be that I'm indigenous aboriginal as I'm not as you can see in the next image despite the poor quality from the cheap disposable camera, next to Marina's head which is pretty normal among most adults you see I have a very small head. Jan Ross also in this photo has a similar proportion head to mine only she's much shorter. I have ancient pigmy DNA.

Measuring circumference with old plastic dressmakers tape, above my ears across my forehead its 22 inches. Then from forehead behind one ear under chin back to forehead its 25 inches. I've a long neck like Marina but tad longer, she holds her chin up (in photos) I hold my chin down like my 12th cousin Princess Diana 1961—1997.

This council photo (below) failed to keep true proportions of everyone's head. Here Marina's head looks smaller than mine. With exception of perhaps Daniel Relyea my neck is the longest. Someone had already started secretly illegally filling in my cheeks with fillers circa 1984. Not being a mirror- gazer I didn't realize. Below right small image: Elaine SLOWMAN as 2012 One Nation Candidate Lynette STYLES same chin, small mouth, nose, cheeks & half moon eyes as author Lindsay SIMPSON & "Fake Leanne 1984"

Next group of photos are the SLOWMAN sisters, daughters of Elaine

SLOWMAN who now used the alias Lynette STYLES, starting with Jennifer's wedding photo snapped with my old Kodak 126 instamatic camera new in 1972 as my 16th birth present from Mum.

I was working at Smorgon Fibre containers when Jennifer telephoned me to tell me she was getting married inviting me to attend the church ceremony. I didn't instead I waited outside for them to come out. I snapped the two photos before a short stocky male (a fashion victim in a truly horrid brown suit) came over to me and threatened me with a pistol tucked in his pocket telling me not to snap photos 'or else'. I asked him sarcastically if he intended to shoot me on the street in front of his family. He didn't respond. I informed him it was a public footpath and Australia is a free country and Jennifer invited me.

This attitude tuned me into wondering why he was so aggressive. Its understandable he was on edge considering the females had been part of a global conspiracy to pervert the course of justice and he was most probably at the center of that. Instantly I'd suspected this cock was a off duty police officer, they were all Freemason. I'd never met Jennifer;s male parent. I wondered if he was fathers of the bride or groom.

However, as I knew Elaine SLOWMAN was in fact the bride's mother and he bore a resemblance to Elaine perhaps he's her brother. He may be the illusive Peter Robert (Bob) BRADBURY written about in the SIMPSON & HARVEY paperback.

I'd called out to the one I knew as Leanne, the short one "shorty". Jennifer and bridesmaid next to her laughed, I knew she was Jennifer's sister but hadn't known her personally she didn't work at Visy, it was her the tall bridesmaid that called back at me yelling:

motioning to the short bridesmaid therefore that's how I know whose who. Because of the laugh I snapped the first photo with Darren and waited for anyone else I knew. There were quite a few Visyboard staff.

I knew they'd been involved in something nasty that involved me but didn't know what. I'd just presumed I was the butt of their psychopathic jokes. Quite clearly I was Jennifer's friend but she wasn't mine. It was December 1985, I'd been at a family gathering and went to the church to snap photos, then went back to my gathering.

I'd only gone with my camera because of what I'd remembered happening at Visyboard. Because I had fractured memories of things I couldn't explain. That was why I snapped so many photos inside Visy in 1983 and 1984. It was obvious in retrospect I was secretly drugged by this family back then. Just as obvious is the probability that they had planned for me to be at the Viking Tavern as I'd said I'd go but had no intention of being there. I'd stopped going to pubs as a social outing once I was old enough to drink at them.

I'd been dismissed from Visyboard in May and got a job at Smorgon Visy's competitor.

I had taken Jennifer and several other girls who worked at Visy to and from work in my car a few times. I'd met her husband, Peter CURTIS is who she told me he was. I've wondered in retrospect if he was a police officer. I'm fairly certain Jennifer told me her male parent was a police officer. I'm not Catholic but have noticed that when I called my male parent my father to the suited males who illegally drugged me and abducted me to illegally interrogate me over these crimes associated with falsification of Leanne Walters identity, they thought I was talking about a priest.

All my siblings were married in same church Jennifer SLOWMAN chose to get married in. St Peters in Cordeaux Street Campbelltown NSW. Its become overtly obvious to me that this SLOWMAN family be they also the UNWIN family I don't know nor does it matter to me only matters to police who need to lay criminal charges of fraud etc. this SLOWMAN family had attempted to confuse themselves with me any my family. Obviously a Freemason vendetta thing. Why I know this is hundreds of little things that started circa 1984 when Visy office staff had a social gathering at horrid place called "Dirty Dicks'. I have super hearing due to my poor eyesight. At one point in evening I heard Elaine scold daughter Lorraine, words to this effect:

"She smokes you have to smoke to be exactly like her"

In my peripherical vision I saw them both glaring at me. Its not rocket science. They are dangerous psychopaths. It was as much a lie as everything STYLES-SLOWMAN wrote in he insane rendition of my life and my "thoughts". Yes she claims to "know" my thoughts. Same as her daughter author Sandra HARVEY (Leanne SLOWMAN) wrote in Brothers In Arms with **"Leanne thought..."** That SLOWMAN was writing her own thoughts, Elaine SLOWMAN as author Lynette STYLES is evidently attempting to 'pull-offk' the same sort of success with her first paperback to defame me as her daughter did with her first paperback to defame me.

Unwin Hyman family were first publishers of the SIMPSON & HARVEY "Brothers In Arms" Douglas SLOWMAN was accountant, director, or secretary of a number of the ALLEN, UNWIN, HARPER, COLLINS publishing companies in Scotland UK according to their country's business name registrant. Following two sets of photos are 2 sets of SLOWMAN sisters, 3 women in total.

My character assassination by publishing family ALLEN UNWIN HYMAN by theft of my biometric identity is overtly intended to render me an unreliable witness against Freemasons in government and private business who conceal Australia's history of Freemason child rape.

That Allen & Unwin's Sydney lawyer Peter BANKI would use this published paperback to discredit me containing, no official legal documents, only words from unknown author — that indicates BANKI's ill-will and criminal intent. My litigation action isn't finalized due to inability to find Australian lawyers who aren't aligned with Freemasons or political parties in Government.

Method author STYLES describes me screams narcissistic desire for revenge. My children and husband love me. Only reason we were separated was because I love them. I knew if they weren't close to me the **Lynette STYLES-Elaine SLOWMAN**'s psychopathic family would stop criminally kidnapping drugging and brainwashing them against me, if we had no contact brainwashing them was pointless. Evidently the still did it anyway even after I relocated to Adelaide capitol city region of South Australia from to outer Sydney New South Wales and Canberra region of my birth in 1956.

Lynette STYLES baseless lies in her paperback proves she has a psychopathically unstable criminal mind. Perhaps not perhaps she's a mother protecting her two daughter from criminal accountability. I know her three daughters as Jennifer, Leanne and Lorraine. I know two of them are also known as authors Jennifer Cooke and author Sandra Harvey as established pictorially previously in this chapter with the "Done Like a Dinner' paperback advertisement and Jennifer's 1985 wedding photo. Its weird, to me anyway, that family members follow each other into business. When you have a family whose mother and two daughters are authors its more than likely that the other daughter and other family members are also associated with publishing paperbacks.

I'm a researcher. Its my thing. I was stumped initially when I came across the old video from 'A Current Affair' that showed the 'Brothers In Arms' authors together circa 1989 promoting their new book same as sisters Jenny & Leanne above are. That image had author Lindsay SIMPSON with a pointy chin. I forgot about it for a while until I started sorting through the archived images of the SLOWMAN sisters when I had a brand new action potential — a new electrical connection in my beautiful brain alerted me to the concept that Raynor UNWIN's three daughters and Elaine SLOWMAN's three daughters may be one in the same or even cousins.

Searching through the Internet researched images I realized every television video interview of Lindsay SIMPSON has her without that pointy chin. What's going on I pondered? It appears that in the recent interviews she been conscious of her pointy chin — never smiles broadly so her chin doesn't point as mine does when I smile; and literally keeps her chin up as lawyer Marina VONCINA does instead of chin down as Princess Diana had the tenancy to do. Psychologically speaking from personal experience, the chin down photo pose demonstrates shyness. So I suppose the chin up demonstrates the opposite of shyness.

This convincing (unaltered) photographic evidence that both of the "Brothers In Arms authors Lindsay SIMPSON and Sandra HARVEY are author Lynette STYLES daughter gives a better understanding to why she is literarily not literally spitting with anger as she writes about always factual and truthful, yours truly, when I was known as Wollondilly Shire Councillor Mrs Janette (Jenny) Gail HALL and Miss FRANCIS.

Point of fact I always wrote of myself as Jeni before I came to work at Visyboard in 1981, they all wrote of me as Jenny. So not to create a fuss I conceded. I could be just as psychopathic as others if I were to let myself be drunk or take drugs, the so called Norwegian Viking beserka trait is inherent in my DNA. I choose not to. **Psychopathic harm is a voluntary mental illness** same as assault and battery are voluntary torts.

The ancient Christian in me forgives you for being a lying scheming psychopath Elaine SLOWMAN (Lynette STYLES) however, the ancient Crusader in me never will.

I also have many Scottish ancestors adding to my DNA. I suspect all Scotland's descendants are cousins. Mine are royals on both sides of my ancestry tree. I'd wanted to immigrate back to United Kingdom in 1970s to study archaeology, but the extensively inbred criminal network of sycophants and psychopaths in Australia's Freemasons terrorist cults had other plans for my future. Its probably impossible to locate someone who **isn't** related to some royal family.

Following six pages of images are extract from the paperback lawyers representing respondent's in my 2014 Copyright Act infringement **Francis v Allen & Unwin Pty Lty ORS** plonked on the table in the Federal Court of Australia (Sydney) intending to personality-wise discredit me and have my application dismissed because of what author Lynette STYLES wrote in her self published paperback I'm yet to see its content otherwise in person. The Sydney lawyer, Peter BANKI obviously a Freemason like the 1994 police use paperbacks authored by this extended FAMILY with only words, no documented evidence, as their 'evidence in chief' to make serious allegations of others 'ill-will' or criminal intent. Its the Freemason **modus operandi.** For character assassination. Hit hard, hit often, and hit with the most outrageous lies all Freemasons will recognize it as their own mindset.
ᛣ

KANGAROO'S CAUGHT

The paperback '**Kangaroo Court by Lynette Styles**" is a double entendre

— the nouns and the verb of her intent, the author is the Kangaroo court where others are being tried, mostly me as I'm the one most mentioned evidently according to the Google Books online version. I've been known as Jenny to all my friends and family since I was 16 years old. I was in a common law marriage relationship, de-facto Owen HALL came to my residence to live before he agreed to join the Freemasons and steal everything from me. William PETERS is my only lawful husband. Owen HALL tricked me into divorcing Mr PETERS pretending he loved me and wanted to marry me. Owen was a party to the Allen Unwin Hyman publishing fraud.

My application on Copyright theft of 3rd fake Leanne Walters biometric identity resulted in the 2014 decision of Judge Katzmann and her reasons to refuse respondent's application to dismiss my application as vexatious or frivolous abuse of process.

In 2024, this Copyright Act infringement matter is yet to be finalized as I had to withdraw despite this decision because I was dramatically affected by being illegally drugged for several months during 2014 (by the Australian Labor Party and their Government public officer Freemasons).

I was being illegally drugged at the time I authored and filed this application early in 2014, the decision was delivered in late in 2014 after I'd been illegally drugged for the better part of 2014.

Despite this decision in my favor, or because of it, not sure which, I've been unable to secure any legal representation from any lawyer I've approached personally in Adelaide, or electronically in Australia and elsewhere.

Even my attempts to advertise for legal representation in national newspapers has been blocked and refused.

Australia's State police in Adelaide refuse to investigate the crimes blocking my legal rights but are keen to unconstitutionally, criminally harass me, because I exercised my right not to be subjected criminal defamation, illegal stalking and light pollution by private nuisance (Goon Squad 2023) and why I've been forced to write my book to address the intentional lies in this trash written by pen named authors Sandra HARVEY & Lindsay SIMPSON.

Also busying themselves in 2014 disgraced retirement evidently, as it would appear involves multiple police terrorists; 2002 assistant commissioner Clive SMALL; deputy commissioner David B(bastard) MADDERN (like CADDEN and CAMDEN see volume 2) who illegally outlawed me in his letter dated 7 May 2003; and someone who would like us to believe they live in Queensland — perhaps it was author Lindsay SIMPSON who is not really named Lindsay SIMPSON (below) on her birth certificate. Published by online *"The Courier Mail"* in a Freemason-fiction *true-crime* story *"Milperra Massacre: 30 years on, Father's (sic) Day will forever be s symbol of death and terror"* That's an example of government funded propaganda, psychological brain-washing linking a happy day to celebrate a parent with eternal fear. Appears they want us to fear the fathers of Freemasonry Terrorism in Australia — New South Wales police and parliament.

Clive SMALL is inferred as the informant for the illegally falsified image of Ivan ROMCEK's leg and foot. As you can see before it was printed in the Queensland Courier Mail the publisher criminally **redacted** Ivan's left leg and foot to pervert the course of justice and due administration of law. This photo without redaction is on back cover (one I'm holding) for 2001 SIMPSON & HARVEY's 'Brothers In Arms' copy and inside all three versions — Ivan's leg and foot without redaction prove New South Wales senior police ordered that the bodies of another or two others were moved to be near Ivan Romcek in the middle — to criminally falsify Ivan's death evidence and their claim "**three fell side by side**". Its not rocket science. It is terrorism.

Not close enough Clive SMALL, I'm sure a seat in hell is being kept warm for you Brother SMALL. & Brother ROSS.

One thing judgmental I'll lower myself to say about my fellow 1984 Visyboard office worker Elaine SLOWMAN, alias disguised Lynette STYLES the secret stalker at Wollondilly Shire Council, she's a compulsive liar with criminally psychopathic desires but I guess that's in your DNA so maybe the temptation is too strong to resist same as 99% of Australians in government public office, **res ipsa loquitur** us honest ones are the 1%ERS. Careful what you wish for, it might come true but not as you expect it.

Do you think the 1984 female in pink jumper hiding behind her glass (my photo) has the same droopy eyes as Lindsay Simpson's internet photo from her Facebook account I think it was, the one with the hat. Fat Pinky called herself Loraine, she worked in the factory at Visyboard and allegedly drove a car with personalized number plates. Next to her is Judy Stevens she was the telephone and reception person who married Barry Quon from upstairs in production they moved to Mimosa in a brand new house. They went waterskiing with my closest office worker Mary Azzopardi HILL and her husband, Dennis HILL.

More photos that are relevant to this chapter are the vehicle ones from my car's little CCTV camera on peak hour morning of 14 August 2017. I noticed the vehicle had been on old South Road when I entered the road near my house in Seaford Rise, presumably she came from Willunga or Aldinga south of me which means she's living near me. I followed the vehicle to the Flinders University hospital car park complex, because she had attempted to cause a high speed vehicle collision, threatening to kill me. Perhaps she's also Nurse Karen BRENAN or Bree for short. Its anyone's guess I suspect they all take turns being the same persons. Like those interchangeable cross cut paper flip books we used to have in the olden days before the Internet and TV for some of us. My security camera wasn't great but as I read the letters the footage establishes enough confirmation to confirm her **SIMPSON** number plate on a white Toyota Kluger. This is what she looked like, without the hat, when I peaked in her car as she was blocking my progress on the 100 kph expressway zone in a menacing manner. She was snarling and yelling at me from her car I couldn't hear her but could see her lips moving as she was attempting to make it look like she was going to ram the driver's side of my little Holden Barina.

Its a bit tough to keep up to date with their antics in perverting the course of justice in this matter. However it would appear at around the time I was suing those directly involved with the Copyright *theft of the first photo they all stole from me for profit,* to falsely claim as the biometric identity of their fake Leanne in the SIMPSON & HARVER Brothers In Arms penny dreadful.

Seemingly retired police officer Clive SMALL or Author (fake) Lindsay J SIMPSON had falsified an inferred original photo of young Ivan ROMCEK's deceased body by darkening his left leg and feet to obliterate the evidence I proved about the feet to the NSW police Commissioner back in 2003 - the evidence the Commissioner's office claimed was not relevent. It was so not relevant superintendent Clive SMALL or another falsified the evidence thirty YEARS later when the original photo was allegedly published for the first time in 2014. With senior police officers like Clive SMALL conducting crime investigations you start to suspect Ivan MILAT was probably innocent, Freemason police probably did it.

Seemingly, just after I'd filed my Copyright action in Federal Court of Australia, Sydney registry (April 2014) Freemasons in NSW State Government decided to release a paperback defaming me under the title "Kangaroo Court by Lynette Styles"they published it in the Wollondilly Shire Council Library at Picton and wrote about it in local newspaper, not sure if it was the print as well as the Internet. I stumbled on it several years later.

I've been fair whenever I've published something defamatory but true about someone I've been sending them emails to let them know. They on the Other Hand Do The Opposite When They Falsely Defame Me. Even When I contacted the Wollondilly Advertiser (below) about their story they refused to print my side of it. Refused outright and despite that I had by then a Federal Court ruling indicating I was in the right all along.

The following six pages if an extract of the rubbish they wrote about me 14 years after I left Council, and 10 years after I left NSW. They plagiarized my websites to get 1% of fact to fabricate their 99% of fiction to claim it all happened when I'm Wollondilly Shire s Councillor Jenny HALL, most didn't.

CRIMINAL defamation Elaine, means willfully maliciously *FALSE*. ♉

MY WORDS & FRENCH LETTERS

Terrorist politicians protect terrorist police who protect terrorist politicians who protect terrorist Freemasons who are terrorist police. That's the secret cycle of local serious terrorism harms that are physical in Australia.

Best way to catch a Freemason terrorist is to let them believe they're more intelligent than you because its true, I can't prove several New South Wales Freemason employed and active police officers brutally murdered Jack BASSET in front of me on 24 April 1988 in Camden.

I can't prove my 1988 residential neighbor in the village of The Oaks New South Wales, Freemason Peter Robert (Bob) BRADBURY is a police detective who illegally entered my house when I was alone with my youngest child and stole photographs from my residence at gunpoint.

I can't prove 1991 Camden Freemason physicians at Picton and Mount Annan New South Wales surgically raped me when I was pregnant during the totality of the 1990s.

I can't prove the same Camden Freemason police conspired with and financially bribed in my presence some staff and my fellow elected councillors to Wollondilly Shire Council, and Camden Council, and Campbelltown Council during the 1990s to pack rape and surgically rape me.

I can't prove Australia's Freemason police have illegally refused to take my statement and investigate all these crimes and subsequent crimes proved herewith.

I can't even prove the persons of the names affixed to these letters actually authored or approved these letters.

I can prove that these letters exist.

I can prove I was illegally arrested in 2004 by New South Wales police after these letters were written and sent to me, arrested and charged in 2007 without any lawful authority whatsoever, with something like a sex offence:

"*offensive in a public place or near a school*"

I was illegally (unconstitutionally) charged by police with offending police by reporting police crime to the police mates of the police criminal offenders.

Australia's police openly criminally abused their position in public office in 2024 but in 2004 they were more secretive about it. Me reporting a police 'family' member had illegally broken into my residence was "offensive conduct" to Goulburn police where the State police cadets are trained how to be policer officers.

when I lived in Goulburn NSW I published the name of a senior NSW police detective "Bob BRADBURY" on my private vehicle as being a suspect in the theft of my biometric identity circa 1989 and break and enter into me residence in 2004. Goulburn police refused to charge the public officers who freely admitted to 'ordering' the break and enter from within State housing (my landlord) they had no lawful authority to order the break and enter yret police stool back and did nothing to uphold Australian law. Instead of charging the offenders they trumped up charges against me making it look like I was a sex offender for reporting a break and enter. Goulburn claimed to me this "Bob BRADBURY" wasn't associated with their lover Leisa BRADBURY yet they issued an illegal court process to have me illegally controlled by an illegal "five year apprehended violence order" (unlawfully) protecting Leisa BRADBURY who I claim is the daughter of Bob BRADBURY.

The 2004 court order was not just misfeasance in public office, its a direct result of a terrorist conspiracy to illegally undermine the government for a political or ideological cause. Criminal conspiracy between 2004 Goulburn police station employees (uniformed and detectives) and magistrate "R. RABBIDGE" of Goulburn Local Court in 2004, probably also a Freemason. More on that 2004 matter later.

I can prove I'd republished the following letters on my websites since at least 2005 between NSW government officials (2001 to 2003) from terrorist Bob BRADBURY's police department before he caused my house to be criminally ransacked. Departmental whose response was to refuse police investigation of every crime inflicted on me because every crime was caused by the New South Wales police department's own 'police' terrorists.

__Australia's Tripartizan political parties are pleased Vladimir PUTIN's mentality of eradicating political opponents is alive and well in Australia's police departments and Freemason fraternities.__

Australia's news industry have refused to republish the matters of these letters and the subsequent 201e4 Federal Court ruling that supports my assertions that police faked the life and death of Rex John WALTERS' *"cheap little slut"* Leanne Gaye WALTERS as described in the SIMPSON & HARVEY's 'Brothers In Arms' paperback since 1989. I have to persist with the long description in case some parent decided to name their child "Leanne Gaye

WALTERS" before or since 1984, else I may be sued for defamation of that other real person.

Subsequently these letters have been a green light for other Australian police, Australian Freemasons and other politically organized terrorists in Australian government or community generally to criminally harass and intimidate me in solidarity with the Camden New South Wales police who murdered senior citizen, retired police officer and Freemason Jack BASSET's before my eyes on 24 April 1988.

Just because they don't know I witnessed Jack's murder is no reason they should be excused for their active part in criminally harassing or intimidating me by abuse of public office. Like Australia Post staff criminally intercepting all my mail to filter out what they don't want me to get destroying mail, manufacturing false mail and making forged address labels on my parcels from China to prevent delivery into my large letterbox; and illegally holding all my very small parcels at a Post Office without lawful authority even when the original address label from Ukraine had express instruction to leave it in my residential post box—which is outright theft of my postal article.

The evidence proves that someone has created a sophisticated process to illegally filter all my snail-mail and email correspondence. That's terrorism.

I can prove I've been subjected to ridicule for almost two years from 17 December 2005 in conspiracy to criminally defame me and provoke others to physically assault me in the internet forum www.whirlpool.net by persons who threatened others who complained about South Australia police, and another using the pen-name **SHOOTER**.

SHOOTER falsely claimed to know me when I lived at Goulburn, claiming to know me 'personally' in greater Adelaide region of South Australia.

I can prove I was *criminally* assaulted by seven medical personnel and two police on two separate days in March, April 2007, without any lawful authority whatsoever.

I can prove that from 2006 to 2014 State Government public officers in South Australia and New South Wales criminally conspired to pervert the course of justice and due administration of law on the matters in these letters and had 'falsified government records to claim *'police proved'* I'd *'falsely alleged being raped by New South Wales Minsker of Parliament in 1999'.*

I can also prove that the 2014 Sydney Federal Court of Australia ordered there was enough evidence to prove my case against the publishers and authors and WALTERS family in the *'Brothers In Arms' story*.

Likewise I can prove by these people named, if they exist at all, are a small number of the Government public officers who have failed to look at the evidence before participating in the secret conspiracy to criminally falsely defame me by inference, for the *'Brothers In Arms' story*. Considering the implications of their willing involvement in falsifying this story by inaction, these people as identified in the *'Brothers In Arms' story* are therefore *terrorist enemies of Australia*, because their decision of inaction as police to charge the persons responsible for theft of my biometric identity and the many medical crimes harming me is evidently done *with the intention of advancing a political, religious or ideological cause; and with the intention of coercing, or influencing by intimidation, the government of the Commonwealth or a State, Territory or of part of a State, Territory or intimidating the public or a section of the public, these actions or inactions as police officers have caused me and my family serious harm that is physical, and serious damage to my property, have caused a person's death, have endangered other's lives, have created serious risk to the health or safety of me and my family and others in the community generally, and have seriously interfered with electronic systems delivering my Internet and telephone services, and have seriously interfered with the retail gas system, the medical systems and driver licensing systems used for the delivery of essential government services*[21].

Morgue Senior Supervisor Jim
New South Wales Police Minister Peter **ANDERSON**
Detective Senior Constable Greg **BAMFORD**
Constable Peter **BLINMAN**
Crown Prosecutor Peter **BODOR**
Police CIB Superintendent Bob **BRADBURY**
Morgue Dr **BRIGHTON**
Detective Sergeant **BUDGE**
Ambulance person Colin **BURTON**
Parklea Prison Officer Peter **CARRUTHERS**
Detective Bruce **DEMMERY**
Parklea Prison Assist. Superintendent Clarence **DRIES**
Detective **DUFF**
Paramedic David **ELLIS**
Ambulance person Brian **EVERETT**
Detective **FARTHING**
Detective **FENNELL**
Ambulance person Fred **FRAZER**
Detective John **GARVEY**

---

[21] *Criminal Code Act 1995 (Cth) Schedule The Criminal Code, section 100.1 "terrorist act means".*

Detective Steve **GRANDIDGE**
Constable **KOHLOGAN**
Police officer Fluffy Geoff **McDOWELL**
Detective (Silver) Peter **McERLAINE**
Constable Lindsay **McGILLICUDDY**
Detective **McHUGH**
Detective Sergeant Paul **McKINNON**
Detective Chris **McMILLAN**
Detective Senior Constable Geoff **McNEVIN**
Ambulance person **MOSLEY**
Sergeant Des **MUSSING**
Detective Constable Mark Charles **NICHOLLS**
Detective Sergeant Greg **NOMCHONG**
Detective Senior Sergeant Wayne **POPPELWELL**
Constable **POWTER**
Senior Constable Brian **RASSMUSSEN**
Detective **REYNOLDS**
Detective **ROBERTS**
Deputy Police Commissioner Barney **ROSS**
NEW SOUTH WALES ATTORNEY-GENERAL Terry **SHEAHAN**
Detective Sergeant Paul **SHIELDS**
Detective Barry **SMITH**
Constable **SOUTHEY**
Police Superintendent Ron **STEPHENSON**
Detective **SWEENEY**
Detective Aarnie **TEES**
Ambulance person Paul **VASSALLO**
Institute of Criminology in Canberra Dr Paul **WILSON**
Detective David **WILSON**
Detective Darryl **WILSON**
Detective **WOODS**
NEW SOUTH WALES PREMIER Neville **WRAN** (1926–2014.

Neville WRAN evidently died 20 April 2014 within three weeks after I'd filed my lawsuit on 1st April 2014. He was about 88 so no spring chicken. Not claiming any cause and effect merely noting the coincidence and the fact he's

BROTHERS IN ARMS BIKIE WARS SIMPSON & HARVEY FREEMASON LIES — ISBN 9780645597578

listed as a Queens Council22, an expert in the field of law, he would have known what the lawsuit meant to his reputation if he had heard about it. He was member of the Australian Labor Party and Premier from 1976 to 198623 therefore, he was well and truly involved in the 1984 Fathers Day Freemason and Labor Party international terrorist scam.

Since 1988, like many women in third world communist countries such that Australia really is, I've been drugged and pack raped by Government officials more times than I could possibly remember to count. Their extended family members and Tripartizan 'Brotherhood' across Australia evidently believe it's their legal right to defend their 'family' honor by perpetuating their own brand of terrorism and false criminal defamations about me initiated by their **Freemason** terrorist grandfathers and grandmothers last century germinating this unchecked forty year taxpayer funded **Freemasons** crime spree now able to be proved by their own psychopathically crafted evidence and in their own narcissistically evil words, despite Australian law.

Prison Island means its harder to escape from Australia in 2024 than legendary Alcatraz was in its day, once Australia's government organized terrorists have systematically impoverished their target as they've done to me since 24 April 1988.

Back in winter of 1994 three Campbelltown New South Wales **Freemason** police staged a pretend arrest of me at gunpoint inside the Camden Toastmasters meeting held for the first time at Campbelltown's Catholic Club one of them, Paul SHIELDS was waving a paperback above his head as his evidence he claimed of me: ***"You faked your own death this is the proof."*** Paul SHIELDS was named in SIMPSON & HARVEY's 'Brothers In Arms' and was comically waving it over his head, overtly forcing himself not to smile as he faced me with his back to everyone else in the room except his two fellow uniformed **Freemason** police terrorists menacing their loaded New South Wales State Government issued police pistols at me.

Fast forward to June 2001 with the SIMPSON & HARVEY's 'Brothers In Arms' paperback having been out of print since 1994 I'd relocated away from Camden to prove or disprove to myself that the crimes targeting me and my children in Wollondilly and surrounds were localized there.

I was organizing my garage at 21 Cessnock Road in Branxton New South

---

[22] *QC (now KC) is a senior barrister or solicitor advocate that has been chosen to serve as counsel to the British Crown. A QC barrister is appointed by the Queen on the recommendation of the UK Lord Chancellor, and in recognition for their excellence in advocacy. https://www.thelawyerportal.com/*

[23] *www.Wikipedia.org*

Wales when I overheard my new neighbor at number 23 in discussion with his motorcycle (riding) friends and noticed their volume lowered every time I emerged from the garage and increased again once I was out of sight. I heard the words "brothers in arms" several times. I suspect that I didn't look at them that had lulled them into a false belief I couldn't hear them.

I was aware they were perched on their raised verandah its floor level at about the height of the top of my fence suspecting they were soaking up the vista over the nearby golf course when I looked up in their direction to see if they were all looking directly at me. Reasonable to presume that their reaction to my direct glare without words indicated they were indeed talking about me, else that was their opportunity to speak to me. I was 41, slender and moderately attractive wearing tight jeans and t-shirt. They were four or five jeans-clad males around my age, from my experience that was their golden opportunity for at least one to make some comment about what I was doing.

When I looked up I saw them all lined up facing the railing edge all looking directly at me, their heads turned at about a 45 degree angle to their left. As if joined by string they all turned their heads in unison to the other direction. The sight of it caused me to burst into laughter. They quickly dissipated without a word to me.

The neighbor soon vacated the residence permanently never taking the opportunity to strike up a conversation with me despite that I positioned myself near the fence and attempted once or twice to entice a response from him, expecting he was curious enough to ask me something about the paperback. Perhaps then I could learn a it more about it myself. Perhaps he was part of the 'team' who had criminally defamed me in the paperback in the first instance and that was behind his rumor mongering with men younger than himself without talking to me on the matter.

I suspect the new tenant was one of the fifty-one Government officials named in SIMPSON & HARVEY's 'Brothers In Arms'. He took every opportunity to snarl at me as he stood on the back patio. An elderly male neighbor across the road, presumably a Freemason, was seen a number of times crossing the road to poison my front flower bed. That's what they had done before I moved to Branxton, I saw a man jump my six-foot fence and start to poison about Au$500.00 of potted plants I'd not long purchased from the local Bunnings. They were in my locked backyard, we were living in a half-house, in the back of it. That was in Denison Street at Broadmeadow, Newcastle. We only stayed there for six months coming from another region so I had no local "enemies" just the Freemason stalkers who've criminally stalked my movements (with my very young children) across Australia. I hosed them off but he must have come back again they all died. That was the Summer of 2000-2001 long before I went to the police about the 2001 paperback. We left the Denison rental because the neighbor across the street started falsely accusing me of hitting his car and the neighbor in the front of the house falsely defamed us to the real estate agent claiming we were having sex orgies and the playing children were jumping from their nonexistent double decker bed. It was the washing machine he was hearing. The children used to have a double-decker but we didn't bring it to the new house. That he specifically mentioned it made me suspect the stalkers were talking to him spreading rumors — blokes love to bad-mouth women supporting children and without a male partner.

Single-mum defaming is the national Australian sport.

It was mid 2001 before I went to The Book Den store in Cessnock New South Wales where I'd purchased a copy of the new 2001 SIMPSON & HARVEY's 'Brothers In Arms' paperback opening it as the salesperson rank up my sale.

When I saw that my biometric photograph (my face) was still in it my first reaction was outrage that New South Wales police had failed to prevent the perpetuation of this identity theft crime. The young male at the bookstore stood waiting for my payment, I looked up pointing to my face in the book saying, "That's me but that's not my name." Then paid and left. I was going to wait until I was back home at Branxton to do anything. Being in shock I hadn't thought of what to do next. When I was about halfway home I felt compelled by outrage to telephone the office of Allen and Unwin publisher in Sydney. I asked quietly and politely to make an appointment to discuss the error in this publication.

A few days later I drove to their Sydney office where once again I asked quietly and politely to to speak to the most senior person present at the office. In response, I was treated like a complete fool. No person would come to the reception to talk to me. None. They left a very young female receptionist to face me. Evidently, when she went into the back office she was told not to give me anything. She was underhandedly remorseful when she refused to give me the contact details of the authors or anyone else responsible for my photograph being in the paperback.

I was left to do nothing other than drive back to Braxton none the wiser. I decided to read the paperback front to back which was not easy as I detest fiction, this was obvious fiction. Many alleged 'true' facts contradict each other and reality itself.

After I finished the content I realized this paperback story with my stolen biometric identity in it, is the root cause of all the criminal assaults myself and my children had been forced by police to endure since 1989.

I realized this paperback story is why I've been criminally stalked for forty years to cause me serious harm that is physical by blocking my access to medical and court services so that I can lawfully and safely have their illegal implants removed that are causing me significant pain, physical disability, and the threat of death by undiagnosed infection.

I realized this SIMPSON & HARVEY's 'Brothers In Arms' paperback story was obviously intentionally published with false information so that the ALLEN HYMAN UNWIN publishing family could assist their Freemason Brothers to globally *pervert the course of justice and due administration of law* in the matter of the alleged 1984 deaths of seven persons in Sydney Australia and cover up the long history of child rape by Freemasons in Australia, Scotland and their forty something allied countries falsely alleged as constitutional democracies.

But perhaps more damning in the next few months the evidence was stacking up that proved every other person *photographed or named* in the SIMPSON & HARVEY's 'Brothers In Arms' had seemingly accepted bribes or gratuities to perpetuate the lies — and they were either children of immigrants or themselves immigrants to Australia from the United Kingdom in the second wave of land grabs stealing from new indigenous residents like me to be protected by Australia's new world Governments.

This is the TRUE AUSTRALIA, stocked with a majority of narcissistic psychopaths in the news industry, the medical industry, the legal fraternity, all Government departments and all parliaments. Top-down terrorists. Not the rubbish spun in their fake-friendly tourism commercials. Australia is a secretly oppressive totalitarian dictatorship overlorded by Freemasons and their formal political party Tripartizan terrorists all seemingly genuinely believing this crap is perfectly normal under Australia's constitution.

These are the letters that started my journey of evidence gathering. If Australia is a constitutional democracy then my evidence will repeat what my many famous ancient ancestors have done many times over — sack an entire country. I'll do it without physical aggression on my part.

Following are not all letters sent or received in these matters — however, I'm sure you'll find not one but a few *smoking guns*[24] in the following letters to government officials on what they've often called the most expensive police investigation in the history of NSW policing.

I was never there before 2002 (Viking Tavern) and never knew anyone who had been. I've never been on a motorcycle with an engine. I've never socially associated with anyone who owned a motorcycle. I've never known any person who admitted to me they were a member of any motorcycle club. I've never gone to a pub without a partner. I've never 'hung around outside a pub or hung around Liverpool'. Never known anyone named Shifty, Melinda,

---

[24] *Smoking gun: an document of incontrovertible incriminating evidence.*

Cheryl or Karen Brennen. Never drank beer or been in habit of drinking Vodka. Never had a tattoo. Never wagged school. Never left my house from a window. Never been expelled from school. Never went to an all girls school. Never had a criminal record. ***Being perhaps the only 100% innocent party in this Tripartizan of Freemason and political party's series of crimes, it was almost 16 years after the event and 25 years ago*** that at my own expense I was driving from Newcastle to Sydney trying to sort this rubbish out not realizing it was a very extensive Government funded terrorist crime. I'm no closer to attaining my day in court for this extensive series of political terrorist harms inflicted upon me and my five children by Australia, the Government and her people.

Its because I wasn't part of this motorcycle culture that was placed at a significant disadvantage in not knowing this horrible crime had targeted me and my children. That is why the Government hand selected me and my children to be their scapegoat. They decided we are a calculated loss in their success at achieving their own individual financial security.

I was sending multiple letters to multiple government officials — not just Allen & Unwin publishers as they claimed in their 2014 affidavit material. I was sending expensive registered or person-to-person letters that the receivers chose not to answer or answer in contravention of Australian law. A 'nutter' wouldn't have had the patients for all that.

I had no irrefutable evidence in 2001 therefore I had to force it out of them through my intelligent psychological manipulation. An art I learned as a small child soon after I witnessed rape and murder at my male parent's Freemason meeting. I learned how to act quite convincingly clueless so I could gather evidence to prove what had happened. So I could live to prove what they did.

They decided we were to have no legal rights in order to pad out their bank balance. That is the true face of a predatory terrorist.

What can a reasonable person say in the knowledge of that? Its relatively easy, they say:

"Thanks you'll for your donations to my evidence stack."

Commission Peter Francis RYAN resigned his tenure quite suddenly 2 years early on 17 April 2002. That was eight months after I wrote my first letter. He then fled Australia back to England. I'm quietly confident this issue was the catalyst. Why I say that is obvious when you read SIMPSON & HARVEY's short authors biography in front of their 2001 'new' copy of 'Brothers In Arms' at very last line below which reads:

> ***"Sandra HARVEY … is currently senior media adviser to the NSW Minister for Police"***

It appears to have become a political war between the elected police minister with Australia's Freemasons, the Labor Party and Liberal Party, most of senior management in police department, with Australia news industry sucking up to the majority with power, on one side their heels dug in against one Englishman head-hunted from UK on promise he'd be supported by Australian law and parliament as police commissioner tasked to clean up a deeply entrenched department of radical 1%ERS with loaded guns issued to them by taxpayers, clueless to fact our police are armed terrorists for the Tripartizan organization of Labor Party, Liberal Party and Freemasons.

With his back against the proverbial wall straight-laces Commission Peter Francis RYAN was forced to resigned his tenure quite suddenly 2 years early on 17 April 2002. Following letters *res ipsa loquitur*[25] are significant evidence supporting that allegation that police commissioner Peter RYAN come to the conclusion that there was simply far too much extensively functioning terrorism in Australia's government for any police commissioner to address as the lone gladiator.

It was because of this "author Sandra HARVEY" advertised employment statement and thre Commissioner's shock resignation that I didn't waste time writing to terrorists in parliament — the office of the Minister for police in New South Wales, until 2003. I gave New South Wales police Commissioner's office and the Attorney-General's department both enough proverbial rope to hang themselves. They obliged me.

NSW police Commissioner's office employed many other senior police calling themselves "assistant commissioner" or "acting" whatever role they were pretending to play.

Was in about July I'd initially contacted the publishers to contact the authors to give them the benefit of doubt that they made a simple error. It wasn't likely in my mind however, its best to cover all vulnerable points before you launch your main attack. ☿

2ND WAVE BRITISH INVADERS

Dated the same day, 7 August 2001 — I dispatched several letters. One to the publishers of SIMPSON & HARVEY's 'Brothers In Arms'. One to State Attorney-General's coroner. One to State police department. One to New South Wales Ombudsman.

Publishers Allen & Unwin never bothered themselves with responding to any communication from me outside the court room I was forced to frag them into. Evidently not fearing Australian law because they were ion the proverbial bed with Brother Freemasons terrorists. Absence of fear from

---

[25] *res ipsa loquitur means inference is reasonably drawn from a set of facts.*

publishers and authors is understood as being a willing party to Government terrorism against Australians by 2003 when the **new** era for NSW police commissioner's office declared me as a victim of terrorism, an outlaw — refusing to recognize my legal rights as Australian citizen by birth in favor of protecting the ALLEN UNWIN HYMAN HARPER COLLINS publishing family conglomerate of UK immigrant terrorists.

They became the second wave of British overthrowing Australian by stealth stealing our own resources to defeat us by abuse of public office within the police departments.

You'll notice in letter to the Coroner (7 August 2001) that I was covering all bases. I didn't know how extensive this terrorism was. I thought maybe it was just a few staff who swapped bodies or paperwork around as had been done in a number of Sydney cemeteries as reported in the press.

With my 'couch' lawyer's hat on I was fishing for clues. Trust me I was looking everywhere not just writing letters. Been scouring the then, still new Internet, looking for traces of police records but only found disrespectful photos of the deceased males, obviously Government owned photos of the six deceased males faces. There was nothing else in 2001 Internet search engine responses about this 1984 crime. Nothing. Now its flooded with misinformation. No prizes for correctly guessing whose responsible for that propaganda outpour.

I'm a scribbler. As the notation says on my copy their professional response to criminal defamation and identity theft is **typically Freemason — maintain the status quo**.

As women synchronize menses, two parliamentarians arranged joint response, same day 30 August 2001, from Attorney-General and Police Minster departments.

You'll notice the sudden change in 'tone' of the letters from Attorney-General's Coroner after they'd synchronized their same-day anally-guarded response. They morphed from formally indifferent to outright contemptuous of Australian law. It was at this point it was far from 'just me' being harmed by this matter.

As you may recall it was o this gap period between letters 11 September 2001, that the twin towers at the World Trade Centre was attacked in America.

It had the same effect on the continuation of this matter as the 18 January 1977 Granville train disaster had on me being harassed by miracle seekers after my 3 January 1977 car accident.

Logically the twin tower incident in America couldn't possibly have effected domestic business within Australia. I admit I was on the side on=f conspiracy theorists. It is obvious in retrospect someone wanted to create subterfuge by blaming the Arabs for everything that perhaps the Freemasons do to cover their own crimes,

Its 7½ months before climax of the obvious political storm that hit Sydney causing police Commissioner RYAN to resign and moves back to England after 6 years here.

This dear reader is where it gets interesting. Its discrete but a 'smoking gun' none the less. You see I wrote the the Police Commissioner's office (above) as the Coroner gave police a direction.

I had to handwrite this next letter as I was illegally, secretly evicted by a false statement to residential tribunal by Harry and Cheryl OOSTERVEEN my landlords. I was notified of the hearing after it was over. The eviction was ordered for Valentines Day, 14 February 2002. My children and I were thrown out onto the street. I was under no delusion that the Freemasons and New South Wales police were not behind having me secretly evicted by illegal process. I wrote the letter to Police to let these them know they hadn't beaten me. Still fishing with string when eventually with patience, I caught a killer whale.

I wrote to the Police but the Coroner responded as if I'd written to them. The second smoking gun.

EIGHT WEEKS from RYAN's resignation. The next letter dated 13 February (resignation 17 April) apart from whatever else pressure he was under (I'm guessing he was inundated as I was evicted) the next three letters add to grounds that probably prompted the Commissioner to leave his tenure two years early then leave Australia after being here for six years. I recall the fuss the media made about the resignation and lack of information to public on this issue.

On 11th February 2002 I wrote my handwritten letter to **police** sent by snail mail from Cessnock NSW, the Attorney-General's **coroner** department in West Sydney supposedly received the letter to police, and got it in **one day**. Then respond by **instantly**. As if.

This 13 February 2002 Coroner letter is a forged document. A false document specifically intended to pervert the course of justice and due administration of law on the identification of a child Freemason police named "Leanne WALTERS". This letter is a smoking gun.

 ↝   With a road distance of 148 kilometers from where I posted it in Cessnock,and where it was replied from in Westmead. There's no way Australia Post had this letter delivered in less than one day.

 ↝   There's no way the Coroner could have had so little to do to answer it immediately.

☞   There's no way a Clerk of the Coroner's Court would not have noticed they were responding to a letter I'd addressed to:

"Terry O'Brien / NSW Police Service Sydney"

Who was actually responding? Police Commissioner's office or Coroner's office or author Sandra HARVEY at the Police Minister's office or someone working at the Australia Post sorting centre near Cessnock? My guess, is the (Tripartizan) postal workers they're still illegally intercepting and criminally forging documents to my address twenty five years later.

You notice the writer of the fraudulent *"Noel Drew WESTMEAD"* letter tells me to run off and chase the civil court angle and forget I have legal rights that police are statutorily obligated to address as crimes of the publishers and crimes of the fake named authors **Lindsay SIMPSON Sandra HARVEY** claim to have the ear of the Labor Party by alleging HARVEY is a 2001 political employee of the New South Wales Minister for police.

Everything in the falsified (Attorney-General Coroner) response indicates errors in identification of this 'child's' body anyway it was a poorly constructed response by persons with, below average, intelligence.

Recapping the facts: Six months ago the Senior Deputy State Coroner directed police to investigate but this letter declares by inference the 'clerk' decided police investigation isn't required after all.

> *Australian law dictates that when a child dies under violent circumstances police must identify the child with the parents — not some remote party who knew the early teen for "five years" as the writer describing coroner's record claimed in their 13 February 2002 forged New South Wales Attorney-General coroner's COURT document.*

Perhaps most telling to me is that the writer is giving me 'legal advice' as seen in the last paragraph. Also known on street as 'a bum steer' or 'leading me up the garden path'.

The tension in the (22 February 2002) letter writer's words indicates something is amiss in Commissioner RYAN's office. Sort of like pooping a watermelon, you can tell the writer is trying to say something they're incompetent as expressing. The *"the inside story"* biography was screaming Tripartizan cover-up on basis the SIMPSON & HARVEY's 'Brothers In Arms' paperback's extended title is also *"the inside story on two ... gangs"* The claims of "other issues" causing his resignation coupled with police Commissioner's department's O'BRIEN response effectively absent of content' told me what had happened. I was the only person outside the Government who knew I was stirring up this hornet's nest because the news industry refused all my attempts to make this public then when New South Wales police Commissioner Peter RYAN was battling his side of this national terrorist crime.

Blind Freddy can see that there can be no doubt this 1984 New South Wales Freemason police crime was behind New South Wales police Commissioner Peter RYAN being forcibly squeezed out of the New South Wales police department and Australia almost twenty years later in 2002. Within another ten years the federal and New South Wales government expended millions of their 2012 television mini series to further cement into history the lies of fake Leanne Gaye WALTERS murder Fathers Day 1984.

Despite the 2014 Federal Court ruling in Sydney that deemed the photo in the SIMPSON & HARVEY's 'Brothers In Arms' paperback was not the same person as published as the same person in 1984 Sydney newspapers. Sydney newspapers in 2014 remained conspicuously silent on that crime they are directly implicated in perpetrating by the innocent decision in Federal Court (see Fail of Two Cities.)

SIX WEEKS from RYAN's resignation on 17 April 2002 the below false document dated 7 March 2002 was also falsified to criminally misrepresent a lawful record in a COURT of the New South Wales attorney-general.

FOUR WEEKS from RYAN's resignation on 17 April 2002 the below false document dated 12 March 2002 was also falsified to criminally misrepresent a lawful record in the police department. One relevant thing to notice is that in 2002 the New South Wales police called themselves a "service" within ten years they start calling themselves a "force" no longer a service, they infer what they really are — terrorists forcing their ideologies on us despite Australian law, manipulating Australian law to suit their terrorist causes.

In the 12 March 2002 police commissioner's office letter signed off with "Terry O'BRIEN" the letter writer failed to note that in August 2001 the Senior deputy Coroner had *"directed police* (to) *investigate"* on identification of alleged female child and that they have refused 100% to address that Coroner's direction, in preference of persisting with the 'seven murders cover up' — their political or ideological cause.

Police to investigate was Senior deputy Coroner coroner's direction. Not for Noel DREW to search the archives at the coroner's court.

Police to investigate their records on the formal identification of this alleged dead child by police officers which had not been mentioned in any letter from police or the Attorney-General coroner's court. Instead the forged coroner's COURT document claims by inference that police don't need to establish the true identity of a child killed under violent circumstances to ensure the alleged parents didn't steal and murder someone else's child.

The point that indicates to my this matter was at the top of the list of reasons Peter RYAN left his role was that there was not a peep in the

press about Police Commissioner RYAN or New South Wales police refusal to follow a Coroner's direction.

Despite that I'd been bashing on doors with my letters in hand giving the breaking news tip of the century to an industry who remain silent to this day on the true facts of the '1984 seven murders'. Therefore RYAN's almost half-million payout was illegal 'hush money' a terrorist's bribe from Australian Labor Party laundered illegal donations from corporate sponsors like the Freemasons through 'another' New South Wales parliament scam.

I was refueling when driving between Goulburn and Adelaide in 2004 as a country cop was reading terrorist police Commissioner Kenny MORONEY's 7 May 2003 authorized letters sanctioning my outlawry for being target of police terrorism. The letter was openly published on the exterior of my Holden Calais. When they'd finished reading they pondered for a moment before turning to me with this before walking away shaking their head:

"They answered nothing just created more questions."

What would happen if junior police stormed the police commissioner's headquarters to arrest the Commissioner and all the assistant commissioners? Would the commissioner's "force" murder the law abiding junior staff claiming the youngers were "radicalized"?

FORTY years after the "Freemason police faked seven murders" on Fathers' Day in 1984 Australia's responsible parliaments are still refusing to a face the issue of this high level of terrorism in public office now deemed as 'best practice'. **No conscience no soul.** That's how State and Federal senior police and parliamentary ministers are selected on prison island Australia.

This is what Tripartizan terrorists have allowed Wikipedia to say about commissioner's shock resignation on 17 April 2002

In February 1999, Ryan was reappointed for a further 5 years. [4] Some aspects of the new contract were kept secret but the controversy over it caused it to be released in its entirety, and a parliamentary enquiry to investigate the circumstances surrounding its signing. The contract made Ryan the highest-paid public servant in Australia. [4] Prior to coming to Australia, Ryan had risen rapidly to very senior roles in British police ranks. His British career culminated as the Head of National Police Training. [5] He resigned from the New South Wales Police Service in 2002, two years early, and received a payout of A$455,000—12 months' salary. [6] Paul Whelan, the police minister who recommended Ryan as commissioner after approaching him in the United Kingdom, had recently retired from the ministry and it is believed that his successor Michael Costa did not want Ryan to remain as commissioner with the Opposition citing that Costa had made contradictory remarks about whether Ryan had resigned or was sacked and questioning whether Ryan was entitled to a *payout if he had resigned. [7] ... Ryan was covered widely by the Australian media and is the subject of the 2003 biography, Peter Ryan: The Inside Story, by Sydney author Sue Williams.[2]* **(my emphasis added)**

Bracketed references for above in Wikipedia below:

- *Ref [4] http://www.abc.net.au/4corners/stories/s614583.htm*

- *Ref [5] Baldwin, Paul (29 June 1999). "Australian police chief shortlisted for Met job" (https://www.theguardian.com/uk/1999/jun/29/paulbaldwin1).The Guardian. UK News. Retrieved 21 March 2014.*

- *Ref [6] John Lyons (14 April 2002). "Losing Peter Ryan" (https://web.archive.org/web/20140320041329/http://sgp1.paddington.ninemsn.com.au /sunday/feature_stories/article_1030.asp?s=1). Sgp1.paddington.ninemsn.com.au. Archived from the original (http://sgp1.paddington.ninemsn.com.au/sunday/ feature_stories/article_1030.asp?s=1) on 20 March 2014. Retrieved 21 March 2014.*

- *Ref [7] "Ryan not entitled to payout if he resigned, say Libs" (https://www.smh.com.au/national/ryan-not-entitled-to-payout-if-he-resigned-say-libs-20020413-gdf71t.html). 13 April 2002.[26]*

Note Commissioner RYAN's book has similar title to SIMPSON & HARVEY's ***"Brothers In Arms the inside story on two ... gangs"*** I get the feeling that Peter James RYAN had little or nothing to do with writing this book claiming to be his biography.

This evidence in Wikipedia with my evidence in my evidence in the preceding and following letters allegedly between me and the New South Wales Government's police Commissioner's Office and the Attorney-General's Coroner this together says RYAN is a **Freemason** and his resignation was because he didn't want to be a part of the 1984 (seven murders) cover up.

The evidence screams that NSW police Commissioner Peter James RYAN's payout is a ***Labor Party political cover up*** — and the subsequent "inside story" biography is a ***Freemason cover up*** whose author's name reminds me of the Johnny Cash song *'A boy named Sue'*. Note subtle satire "The Inside Story" are highlighted part of the title. Also take note that "Sandy" is a masculine name and ghost writers rarely ever come clean. I searched public records to find where the Rex WALTERS family from the SIMPSON & HARVEY's 'Brothers In Arms' paperback. Following 2 August 2002 letter was delivered by me in person to the publicly registered address of the alleged Leanne WALTERS and Rex WALTERS.

I wrote to this Rex John WALTERS family delivering that in person speaking to that pair of chronic liars face-to-face to be certain as anyone can of the intent of another. I realized by their initial actions when seeing me they'd known me by sight already and had been involved in my surgical rape but kept that to myself. I'm the sort of person who needs to be 100% certain of my facts (provable on documents or not) before I move onto the next step. After leaving the Ingleburn residence I was 100% certain they had willfully criminally defamed me with malice by their participation in the creation of the SIMPSON & HARVEY's 'Brothers In Arms' paperback. Next step was to prove that on the documents which I have.

Despite the catastrophic harm I've endured at that point in 2002, you can tell from the wording of my letter I'd intentionally left the door wide open for them to apologize to me. To admit including my photograph in the SIMPSON & HARVEY's 'Brothers In Arms' paperback was a horrible mistake, to contact publishing company to have paperback withdrawn from sale to replaced my photo before republishing. A photo like the superior digital quality color photo allegedly of an impoverished teenage factory worker in 1984 — the one they published in 2014 of their *"cheap little slut"* Leanne. See "Alice's Peasant Toes".

Instead Rex started fake crying, so fake I'm not certain I had hidden my facial disgust. Lorraine ducked into a back room and donned a long red wig. Rex phoned Elaine SLOWMAN pretending she was Pamela WALTERS. It felt like I was in an episode of the twilight zone. They chose not to take any action to relieve effects of the serious physical harm their actions had directly caused me and my equally innocent minor aged children all drugged and raped along with me for their 1984 Tripartizan Freemason cause. ♉

ET TU BRUTE!

Its true, there are a lot of absurd conspiracy theories floating about in cyber-space. Its true the flat earth pundits appear to be one slice short of a loaf. But that appears to be so and what is reality is often worlds apart.

What if most of the absurd conspiracy theories were created by those covering up genuine conspiracy theories to make all conspiracy theories appear to be absurd fictitious constructions of a troubled mind?

What if the original flat earth pundits begun their journey to poke fun of the absurd serious theories put forward by scientists researched in Government funded universities across the globe — the one that springs to mind is the outrageously ludicrous quantum theory.

What it if wasn't Julius Caesar who was the evil oppressor in ancient Rome?

What if most of our recorded history have been willfully distorted to suit a political power of that day or even hundreds of years after the actual events which I remind you is when the Christian Bible was authored from hearsay literally hundreds of years after every participant had long been rotting in the earth.

So lets contemplate for a moment on how much of what you think you know about history is true?

Because you do know there is no way to conclusively confirm anything written in modern texts. Indeed some of it stored in Australia's National library as true facts is criminal defamation — Like the SIMPSON & HARVEY's '**Brothers In Arms inside story of two ... gangs**' books and their mother's book "**Kangaroo Court by Lynette STYLES**" **specifically published in the National Library to criminally defame me as a witness to Freemason child rape during Freemason meeting in winter of circa 1967.**

We're supposed to that the word of the author on those claimed facts. Like the deaths of the seven persons on Fathers' Day 1974 as recorded by the New South Wales police and Attorney-General court system. The same pair controlled by the same Tripartizan terrorist political trilogy who used my (stolen) biometric identity to conceal the truth of their '**fake murdered female child**' invented on-the-fly to protect the Freemason who murdered unarmed Ivan ROMCEK who in all probability was same as some of the other motorcycle club members, a child victim of Freemason rape — as I was.

From 2002 to 2007 New South Wales police department's Tripartizan terrorist Kenny MORONEY was hand picked by his overlording terrorist political party to follow the fallen and failed crusader against political terrorism in the New South Wales deeply entrenched police department terrorist cell, England's Peter James RYAN.

Terrorist Kenny MORONEY was as crooked a police commissioner as there has ever been before retiring in Campbelltown NSW where I grew up. His contribution to terrorism in 'his' department was to have me illegally arrested, charged and sentenced on a fictitious police complaint of harassing a budding terrorist Leisa Maree BRADBURY who illegally order that my residence should have its locks drilled out and the content ransacked after someone failed to gain entry through the back door, before bending a corner of the back screen door to attempt entry then throwing a metal object through the small laundry window.

Terrorist Kenny MORONEY agreed to have me arrested because I complained about police refusing to enforce Australian law to protect me as a target of the BRADBURY crime — instead Goulburn police under the command of Terrorist Kenny MORONEY arrested and imprisoned me, the victim of the BRADBURY crime painting me the aggressor. Sound familiar. Its the same scenario as they used for the Fathers' Day 1984 Freemason organized murders.

In interesting mews item told that Kenny MORONEY put a curfew on the

Police Academy in Goulburn due to evidence of drug fueled sex-capades by police in training another slice of political propaganda from Government to make it appear terrorist MORONEY was doing a 'good' job.

Don't I have enough evidence, even before going further, to prove terrorist Kenny MORONEY's police department is "*just as relevant today*" as organized terrorism as it was 'back in the day'.

From 14 February 2002 my junior school aged children and I slept on the loungeroom floor of a neighbor's house, until New South Wales State government decided they'd give me a State rental in Goulburn, which was probably the Freemason's grand plan when they criminally conspired with Brother Freemason terrorist Harry OOSTERVEEN to illegally evict me. To get me closer to the more intensely corrupt terrorist police. The ones in Goulburn who expertly train their new police on how to be team-player terrorists.

Like I've said before, from 1996 after Wollondilly Shire Freemason police had me illegally secretly evicted from my own Torrens title residence by letting Mr Owen HALL my ex de-facto illegally squat on my real estate and illegally change the locks so I couldn't get back inside to get any of my possessions — they'd been illegally forcing the three of us from our rental house every two years, like clockwork.

First week of April 2002we moved into my first State housing rental property located at 53 Gibson Street Goulburn. Within days I noticed a middle-aged male stalking us from his small red Mitsubishi he'd parked out front of my next door neighbor's residence evidently so that he could see us leaving and entering our property and front door. Same as (presumably it was he) who lived in 39 Mary Street The Oaks positioned in direct libne of sight from my front door when I lived at 39 William Street The Oaks where when I sat outside on my front patio to have a cigarette and coffee after dark I'd occasionally see a small red dot dancing around my torso. That property was listed in the elector's roll as being the residence of police officer Peter Robert (Bob) BRADBURY.

He sat in his car watching our residence for hours at a time and for several days until two weeks after we moved in he moved into the house across the road — 80 Gibson Street Goulburn. It's my suspicion that he worked at Australia Post or at Goulburn police station and was illegally intercepting my mail in Branxton and in Goulburn. I say that because I'd seen him in the back room of the tiny Branxton Post Office. While I was resident in the 53 Gibson Street State rental in Goulburn from 2002 to 2004 I'd decided to confirm or refute my suspicions that it was police involved in intercepting my mail and all the associated assaults on my person since I'd witnessed the Camden New South Wales police murder of retired (honest) police officer and Freemason,

Jack BASSET.

I went to various local motorcycle clubs in the daylight hours with the SIMPSON & HARVEY's 'Brothers In Arms' book in hand to see how they responded to me in that circumstance. I confirmed what I thought. Most were clueless about this crime but weren't surprised about police involvement in it. I also sent faxes around to various typical 'biker' waterholes never expecting to get any reply but to spread the news that the news industry had been refusing to publish my evidence. To see if police were intercepting my outgoing calls and faxes I'd also sent a fax to every sitting member of New South Wales State and Federal parliament. Every single independent and political party member which appeared to number around 100 people. I only got a handful of replies from there persons whose legal responsibility was to represent the best interests of all Australia's residents and prevent terrorism.

I decided to search for legal representation anticipating that not every lawyer I contacted would be Freemasons or terrorist enemies of Australia. Freely admit I was wrong on that too.

AUSTRALIA IS A TRIPARTIZAN TERRORIST ORGANIZATION

Australia is a Tripartizan terrorist organization. Not a constitutional democracy that was proved when they enacted the Australia Act in federal parliament to undermine the Australian Constitution by unconstitutionally altering the Australian Constitution to unconstitutionally block the constitutional right of all Australians to appeal to the Queen/King on advise from their Privy Council, to overturn an illegally unjust Australian high court decisions.

If Australia was not a terrorist organization our Federal parliament would quash or rescind the **Australia Act 1986** and never allow any such travesty of justice to occur in future by decree of statute that such a move by any future parliament is terrorism, intended to undermine the **authority of Australia's Constitution** which is the highest authority on Australia. Not the High Court and not any parliament — the Australian Constitution is the highest power in Australia however, just because its on paper without physical form the public officers of parliament and departments with physical form have unconscionably abused their physical power over the Australian Constitution with the same mindset that an abled bodied person would taunt or starve to death, a paralyzed person.

Katrina HODGKINSON MP did her best however, because police Minister's staffer author Sandra HARVEY was one of the terrorists there was a similar block on this Member of Parliament ever reaching a non terrorist at the office of Minister for Police.

You'll notice these two August 2002 letters (5th and 21st) have exactly the same words in their body. Exactly. Terrorist Michael COSTA was police minister from 21 November 2001—2 April 2003. As police Minister He was well aware of the situation and the terrorism in the police department Terrorist Michael COSTA is the same police minister who forced police commissioner RYAN to vacate his tenure early. Terrorist Michael COSTA was elected into the State upper house in September 2001, just after I'd started writing to police commissioner RYAN.

Many federal parliamentarians stay in parliament long enough to get their six-figure retiring allowance, often called the parliamentary pension, which is eight years. Terrorist Michael COSTA stayed for 7 years 18 days. The evidence

2 May 2014 the Australian Broadcasting Corporation Internet news website published a list of thirteen parliamentarians from both Labor and Liberal ranks who were either sacked from the party or resigned from parliament after being found to have been liked to what ICAC call corrupt conduct. People intelligent people would reasonably label as **terrorists, who are people who undermine their government for a political, ideological or religious cause**[27]. Padding your own pocket may be classified as a self-fulfilling unjust enrichment ideology the individual considers is justified because its available for the taking. Like when **I overheard Ms Reiteke CHENOWETH verbally accept a bribe to throw out my application** for out of pocket damages in the New South Wales residential tribunal hearing 04-14258 from Mr R WEEKS for the NSW state government respondent — before they disappeared into a closed room together minutes before the hearing in Goulburn.

Wonder how many of the resigned terrorist parliamentarians have been given high paid private positions *because* they were self proved terrorists.

ABC chose to publish this but not the broader terrorism of identified by inference from the September 2014 Federal Court ruling in my Copyright Act matter that Michael LEE had the power to assist me with but declined due to his political affiliations with active terrorism in New South Wales government. It appears publishing the truth of terrorism outside of ICAC "**brings the party** (sic) **into disrepute**" therefore its frowned upon, essentially ignored as Michael COSTA ignored his fellow elected member representing all Australian's best interests in parliament. Something Michael

---

[27] *"Political Scalps of the NSW ICAC" https://www.abc.net.au/news/2014-05-02/political-scalps-of-nsw-icac/5427260*

COSTA and his gang has no intentions of doing when elected into parliament. They were there for their own personal enrichment and the perpetuation of terrorist power to their 'Party'.

Personally — I resigned from the **Labor** Party (1997) after fellow Labor Party members told me I had to vote a certain in the Council meeting to benefit a developer, or I'd be expelled. One of the Labor members was fellow elected councillor Michael BANASIK who went on to be Mayor of Wollondilly Shire several times. As far as I know is still an elected local councillor taking bribes from developers. I suspect **Labor** Party members are better at lying under oath, from my personal experience when my fellow councillor Helen KUIPER lied under oath in the Picton local court after seeing me being assaulted by author Lynette STYLES as they stood side-by-side then went on to be elected by her fellow councillors as Mayor of Wollondilly Shire Council. That's a bribe isn't it Helen? Was that in payment for voting to illegally expel me from my elected position on Council in 1999 or did you get a new Nissan Pajero like Michael BANASIK after you lot conspired to steal my Mazda 929 and then stole it with others? I never worked out what your friend (or daddy) Bob WALLER's problem was with me Helen. All I can think of is that he may be one of the MacArthur region Freemason pedophiles intent on defaming me as a witness to the 1967 Campbelltown New South Wales Royal Arch (blue lodge) Freemason (formal dinner) meeting of ritualistic child rape (the apprentice) that sometimes *"got out of hand"* ending in murder. Perhaps he was one of my male parent's Freemason cult, fellow members.

Internet says pajero in Spanish means someone who masturbates often. Bet the researcher at Nissan who let that one go was grass roots member of Australian Labor Party.

These New South Wales ICAC caused resignations in 2014[28] one decade after this terrorism physically harming me personally (my illegal implants) supported within the police department and State parliament by the terrorist police Minister Michael COSTA means and proves irrefutably by lawfully acceptable inference that, had NSW police Commissioner's office after Peter RYAN **not been criminally negligent** in investigating this 1984/1989 series of Sydney region Tripartizan Freemason government crimes, then (government undermining) terrorist politicians forced to resign in 2014 would never have been elected in the first instance, **which includes Labor Party's terrorist police Minister Michael COSTA** the self confessed Greek tragedy.

1. These resignations centre around Newcastle where COSTA was born and where I lived when I went to police with this terrorist crime in winter of

---

[28] *"Political Scalps of the NSW ICAC"* https://www.abc.net.au/news/2014-05-02/political-scalps-of-nsw-icac/5427260

2001 after leaving the Goulburn Canberra region where I moved from Sydney region.

2. NSW **Labor** minister Ian MacDONALD was expelled from the Party for his conspiratorial activity with Eddie OBEID to defraud the state.

3. NSW **Labor** Party's Eddie OBEID retired not resigned, he and others lobbied politicians to advance private company's interests.

4. NSW **Labor** Party's Eric ROOZENDAAL was expelled from the Party for his participation in a conspiracy with Eddie OBEID.

5. NSW **Labor** Party's upper house Tony KELLY resigned from parliament after being found to have backdated a letter to mislead investigators.

6. NSW **Liberal** Party leader Mr O'FARRELL resigned after it was proved he'd lied to ICAC when giving his evidence.

7. NSW **Liberal** Party's Andrew CORNWELL resigned from the Party after accepting a bribe from a developer disguised as payment for a painting.

8. NSW **Liberal** Party's backbencher Darren WEBBER resigned from the Party after accepting bribe funneled through a new company set up to pay bribes to MPs to favor property development.

9. NSW **Liberal** Party's backbencher Chris SPENCE resigned from the Party after accepting bribe funneled through a new company set up to pay bribes to MPs to favor property development.

10.   NSW **Liberal** Party's Craig BAUMANN resigned before admitting to ICAC he'd taken bribes from developers when he was on local council.

11.   NSW **Liberal** Party's Garry EDWARDS resigned from parliament or the Party over election bribe money conspiracy, he's also taken bribe (about Au$11,500.00) from developer Jeff McCLOY who went on to become Newcastle Mayor.

12.   NSW **Liberal** Party's Marie FICARRA resigned from the Party after being implicated in the same scheme as HARTCHER, WEBBER and SPENCE to solicit donations for the party.

13.   NSW **Liberal** Party's Minister Chris HARTCHER resigned from front bench after ICAC raided his office.

14.   NSW **Liberal** Party's police minister Mike GALLACHER resigned after the ICAC allegations of his conspiracy.

15.   NSW **Liberal** Party's Tim OWEN resigned from parliament over election bribe money conspiracy with a developer Jeff McCLOY who went on to become Newcastle Mayor.

16.   NSW **Liberal** Party's treasurer, Arthur SINODINOS, resigned as

Federal Government's assistant treasurer after ICAC about an inferred conspiracy with NSW Labor Party's Eddie OBEID.

I've not included the attached letter referenced in my letters below it was in my opinion created to cause discontent the Labor Liberal Freemason *modus operandi divide et imperia*[29]. Evidently as both of us appeared to be psychologically incorruptible (the State member and myself) not easily distracted from task neither of us took the bait. Again I suspect origins were a combination of Jack BASSET's murders and Mr Sandy HARVEY's mob.

The seemingly unassociated letter about Camden police department's Camden Local Area Command where Jack BASSET was murdered, is part of the paper trail that leads to more smoking guns at office of Minister *of* police. Title *"for police"* is an unconstitutional Freemason declaration.

Perhaps the Member of State Parliament recognized the issue as Party terrorism, which is it in deed. Still nothing come of the paper trail being pulled into the federal parliament arena by my State member via my Federal Member. I telephoned to make an appointment to talk to the Minister of police face to face. I was instructed to make the request in writing. Every Minister with a department portfolio responsibility in any parliament has a legal *"duty of care"* to persons effected by actions or lack of proper by Government public officers employed or contracted to facilitate statute or a Government service under the umbrella of their portfolio. Plain English: Labor Party member and Minister Michael COSTA MP willfully breached his duty of care to me as a consumer of State Government law enforcement services, under the circumstance its a matter of misfeasance in public office and an act of terrorism. Having children to consider first and foremost, I'd still not purchased a computer to write letters. When I did I forensically examined the SIMPSON & HARVEY's 'Brothers In Arms' photos to discover why this Tripartizan Government of terrorists had pulled up their iron curtain. I wrote to Minister the Commissioner answers. Whose signature do "I" see on the letter a **SLOWMAN**, Leanne SLOWMAN alias SIMPSON & HARVEY's 'Brothers In Arms' author **Sandra HARVEY** employed by the police Minister. Two months response for March 2003 letter. Still waiting for response from August 2002 letters about 1989 SIMPSON & HARVEY's 'Brothers In Arms' and linked 1984 'seven Freemason police falsified murders' matter. ☿

...THEN FALL CAESAR

I don't oppose Freemasons presa, I reasonably oppose terrorists and other criminals who seek and receive shelter for crime as Freemason cult member. You'd be right is saying its been my life's work. I've been at it snce I was

---

[29] *Tripartizan's common practice as terrorists is to divide to conquer.*

raped on 3 March 1959 aged 2 years 10 months 2 days. Jack BASSET was the first police officer I told. Despite that th rapist, my male parent was Mr BASSET's best friend he made sure my male parent was held accountable. His fellow police and Freemasons have made sure they burried all evidence of that crime along with me, my life and anyone who looked like they were standing by me at any time in my life right up to this day in 2024. Which is why my mum, my siblings, my domestic partners and my children were targeted with brainwashing to turn them against me. If I weren't a Taurus INTJ chances are I'd have imploded from despair. I'm the polar opposite. The tougher the challenge the more resilient I become. I may be closest genetic distance to the **Iron Age woman from Oxfordshire Yarnton England** (genetic distance 2.855) who lived c300 BCE (I21178) however, more significantly personality wise, I share the most number of DNA 'chunks' being tiny bits of 15 of 23 chromosomes, numbers 1, 3, 5, 6, 8, 10, 11, 13, 14, 16, 17, 19, 20, 21, 22 (segment matches) with the **Norwegian Viking male from Iceland** (genetic distance 7.035) who lived c1000 AD (STT-A2) most probably why my face naturally glows bright red in what most consider a nice hot summer, have pale blue eyes, like my own company better than any other person, have pretty good balance and reflexes, and other matters ensuring I'm a survivor under most conditions, physically and psychologically, without effort.

Peter RYAN was a good man squeezed out of his tenure early by the persistent undercurrent of Tripartizan terrorism in Australia. They anointed Freemason terrorist sympathizer Ken MORONEY as his replacement. With police commissioner Peter RYAN gone there's been no barrier to NSW police terrorism culture of police officer crime to cover up police officer crime for any cause that provided financial or social status incentives. The structure of freemasonry (*safe harbor for criminal activities of members*) its the one intrinsic component that makes organized crime work.

Freemasons begun 400 years ago with a group of biblical sodomists who'd give alibies to each other to cover up their homosexual activities in an era the act of sodomy was punished by hanging. That's the root of Freemasonry, the intrinsic "ancient tradition". Bible studiers know what is written about the Sodomites — they killed property owners to steal their land and wealth. Exactly as the NSW Freemasons did to me except failing many times to kill me. Each time they failed to kill me during the 1990s they physically injured me in other ways as retaliation for not being able to kill me. They always secretly drugged me so I'd have no solid memory of being physically assaulted but I do have many fractured memories. They dislocated my thumbs (still painfully dislocated) and they (males and females) treated me in a manner that any fiercely misogynistic person does to a female after they drug her to unconsciousness.

Misogyny is over-reactive jealously. Male misogynists are jealous of females who in their mind don't need to chase others for sex it comes to them. Female misogynists are jealous of other females they see as more attractive on the eye than themselves. Misogyny and narcissism walk arms entwined in the mind of so effected Homosapiens.

I'm not religious but I do admit that our Bible is just as much history as the ancient indigenous sagas passed down through the generations by recollections that contort the finer details.

Letter on CD (before USB storage) sent to my federal member of parliament included a very long set of facts in a single document. It was by basic understanding of facts **then** without all the relevent parts I've since discovered. *Like how the ancients thought volcano spew were angry Gods.* This was early days in my investigation of this 1984 crime. I was only made aware of this crime by the content of the criminally forged letter stating it was from the New South Wales police Commissioner's office.

I remind you dear reader that a document is forged if it attempts to convey misleading information about a fact. The misleading information is the inference that an Australian can be ignored by police when reporting a serious crime linked to political terrorism that has caused **serious harm that is physical**. Police would have been aware of all the facts if they bothered to take a statement from me — they **refused to hear** any crime I was reporting evidently because I was reporting crime committed by their police mates or Freemason Brotherhood. That's terrorism.

I followed my letter by making an appointment to speak to this Member however he was "too busy" to be present in the meeting. Always was too busy to hear my words, which was exactly same as John David HILL State MP in South Australia, a common response to these issues that was to be a conundrum before I realized how deeply Freemasons parliamentarians were entwined in this terrorist crime series with State police Freemasons.

To break up the word documents the picture documents are irrefutable evidence of **ongoing political terrorist attacks** inflicted on me by surgical rape since 1990s.

t is physical' which makes these assaults terrorism because they were committed for a 'political or ideological cause' — to cover up Freemason crimne the crime of the fake LEANNE WALTERS, which was perpetrated by police to cover up the murder committed that same day by a Freemason, see *"Lancelot's Evil Twin"* *"Satan's Crusaders"* and *"Alice in Peasant Toes"*.

The MRI evidence is evidence of my physical torture that would have been ceased soon after it started if NSW police Minister Michael COSTA wasn't a 'head hunted' bespoke terrorist, in love with being the star of theatrical performances and idea of being parliamentarian for "the Party" instead of representing Constitutional interest of all Australians against homeland political terrorists

My jaw's full of illegal silicone, injected after I was securely drugged when I was an elected town councillor (fake local GOVERNMENT.) The silicone has migrated from my face and painfully herniates into muscle under my tongue and around my jaw when I yawn. Silicone makes the skin cold to touch, **very painful** on my legs in winter. I've never been fat so shouldn't have double chin yet clearly I have a COLD silicone chin. Secretly injected silicone from my neck injected I was pregnant in 1987[30] has migrated to my upper chest that now makes by 'athletic chest' wobble like jelly, which attracts Oedipus complex pervert males to stare when I'm pushing a shopping trolley. Unattached silicone rolls away when I lay on my side. Its easy to see the cable inside my top lip, it vibrates with the one in my top gum and nose and wrapped around my left shoulder blade attached to the illegal implant in the centre of my spine behind my heart, evidently the vibrations are remotely controlled and used to 'punish' me. More secretly injected silicone in my nose has hardened, caused my nose tip and nostrils to collapse making it uncomfortable to nose breathe. There are no non political physicians in Australia who care to assist me to have this removed its like living in a third world country. Much worse than Russia or China.

Despite my gut feeling that I was being railroaded derived from STENBERG statement "ADVICE PUBLISHER" I'd decided to play the game to generate the associated evidence as this is precisely what had happened when I tried to find a lawyer to sue State Government for wrongful dismissal from my elected position from Wollondilly that was evidently funded by bribes from terrorists within the executive of the Australian Labor Party. I made and kept the appointment as STENBERG requested. Mr Michael LEE was automatically contrary, condescending and antagonistic. Hallmark **modus operandi** of Freemasons attempting to cause self-doubt and reduce self-esteem. Either he always wore a snarl on his face or he generated that special greeting just for my benefit. 'm a firm hand-shaker. His handshake was like he'd handed me what felt like a cold and clammy dead herring.

When presumed Labor Party-faithful Michael LEE realized he'd failed to enlist a change in my pleasant facial expression from a smile to horror or whatever, he flicked my hand out of his, flicked it away.

My grandmother taught us to play poker as a small child. This was when we lived in Bunyan before 1962, long before we owned a television. I was thankfully trained to selectively show no expression before I attained school age, five years old, in case you're a bit slow on that one. If I smile its natural if

---

[30] *Physician thought I'd goiter issue when silicone was injected into my throat*

I don't its my poker face.

Its reasonable to believe that any lawfully functioning lawyer / solicitor has more than one barrister they use for litigation. That Mark STENBERG expected me to believe Michael LEE was the God of defamation litigation indicated to me Mark STENBERG was not only a Freemason but also another in the long list of terrorist enemies of Australia. Any lawyer who refuses to sue any Government despite the evidence they'd win is a terrorist enemy of that country.

I achieved a perfect score in my defamation law assignment for my law degree in 2018 — I am therefore a proved expert in defamation law. An an expert in defamation law I can say with all confidence Michael LEE was looking to convince me I didn't have a case to dissuade me from pursuing what is my legal right to secure damages for malicious criminal defamation.

This defamation is no more difficult to prove than any other defamation lawsuit. It is also Copyright Act infringement of my photographic and moral rights. It is also infringement of the then Trade Practices Act and now Australian Consumer Law (Competition and Consumer Act 2010) in that it is still intentional false advertisement about the truth and quality of the content. It is also ACL misleading or deceptive conduct and not fit for purpose. Most of all it is ACL unconscionable conduct by gross abuse of power of the Government over my legal rights not to be defamed for a political or Freemason ideological cause.

It was not just the publisher[31] or authors who had infringed my legal rights the Government had by falsely claiming they'd provided the photo (of me) to police as the established biometric identification of a deceased person. When it gets to so many civil infringements the scale tips to the matter being defined as an intentional premeditated crime. Any lawyer or barrister of Queens/Kings Counsel knows that basic concept is established fact. Michael LEE and Mark STENBERG were obviously players on the side of politically organized terrorism that's the only reason they chose not to step up and honor Australian law and my legal right not to be a target of our Government's political terrorism for personal profit of the terrorist government public officers. Any legally trained monkey knows intent to 'pervert the course of justice and due administration of law' in criminal cases to prosecute alleged persons who allegedly contributed to the death, is a separate crime and every crime is an admission the offender is a tortfeasor.

---

[31] The publishers include **any person** involved with creating the story, which means the coroner, police, the criminal lawyers from the 1984 crime, the WALTERS family and the authors t name a few.

It's a Pandora's box of intercontinental[32] multiple political party and multiple Australia jurisdiction Government funded terrorism, clustered around the secret fraternity of Freemason sex offenders protected by Freemason police evidently since even before Federation as the *'Freemason membership within ranks of Government police'* problem wasn't addressed in the federal constitution for prevention.

Despite that Freemasonry was already deeply rooted in Britain before Australia was sacked and confiscated by the Brits since the First Fleet exactly as the Holy Roman Empire did to ancient Britain and the present Europeans still do to modern indigenous (United Kingdom descendant) Australians like myself. Psychopathy runs deep in their DNA while families like mine who came to Australia 200 years ago freely to escape the insanity in Europe are obviously in the main, less war like. Less psychopathic. We could do a survey to prove that only sycophantic Tripartizans would stack that to willfully falsify the outcome — like certified Sydney lawyer tag team Mark STENBERG and Michael LEE did in 2002.

There was no response from STENBERG to this 30 July 2002 request (below) to return the SIMPSON & HARVEY's 'Brothers In Arms' paperback STENBERG stole it, presumably out of petty childish spite.

Mark STENBERG's immediate personal response 31 July 2002 to my letter I'd faxed previous day contracts his "time constants" claim within the letter. Addressing terrorism in his own country is by far of more ethical value than any other matter he may have been asked to litigate.

Their low bar on their personal ethics scale is demonstrated in lying by inference on the issue of legal merit in the matter of the SIMPSON & HARVEY's 'Brothers In Arms' publication and willingness to join an existing terrorist conspiracy makes this pair of baton carriers doubly unfit persons to practice law.

RECAPPING: 2001 with new SIMPSON & HARVEY's 'Brothers In Arms' paperback I took this Freemason terrorist crime to police causing police commissioner RYAN to resign and flee Australia. Lawyers refused to represent me to sue. Next letter, my State Member sitting in Parliament. The official police ministerial response to a political terrorism crime they support is in perpetuity: *"The matters raised are currently being examined and a reply will be forwarded to you as soon as enquiries are completed."*

Typical official police commissioner 'Claytons' response is like this: *"The investigation is ongoing."*

Which means there is no intent for the minister to investigate the reason why the police are refusing to investigate because they all know they're 'paid'

---

[32] *Australia, New Zealand, United Kingdom, United States.*

participants in the terrorist plan that created the problem in the first instance.

When you ask terrorists to put a stop to terrorism perpetrated by their best mates and employer its not likely it'll ever stop under their 'watch'. ♉

HAVANA SYNDROME & COCHLEAR LTD

It would appear on casual obervation that that most of the photos in the SIMPSON & HARVEY fake "Brothers In Arms inside story of two ... gangs" had been someone else, or photoshopped, or mirror reversed before being published by the Rex John WALTERS Klan terrorist family consortium; not confined to Unwin Hyman Ltd (Scotland) and Allen & Unwin Pty Ltd (Au Uk, US, NZ) Perhaps it was with intent to make the images different therefore less likely to be recognized by the 'face owners' who don't stare at themselves in mirror all day as the Allen Hyman Unwin family evidentlydo.

Its not the Russians its Australia and her allies blaming falsely the Russians as they always have to generate support against Russia. Any reasonable adult will tell you that is you segregate and ridicule most children long enough they will retaliate with violence. In the scale of global misbehavior (lies) of adults in Australia, ISA and United Kingdom, Russia is no different to that theory child.

SECRET TORTURE & MEDICAL FRAUD

Because I witnessed their child rape and murder crimes, because they'd failed to murder me by accident, because they stole my biometric identity, they surgically raped me implanting devices in my cochlear ear region top of my head. The entwined connection cables around my face across both lips and my eyes and nose, and down my spine. Their criminally inserted implants include pulse generators and my own breathing as their power, they included aerial lengths extending to my hands and feet — as evidenced in my youtube video "8zdyTsq90Yw" on my channel @CallToArmsFromAustralia seeking lawyers to sue them and physicians to repair their damage.

Curiously despite that I've requested and paid Youtube to promote my video they failed to fulfil our contract. My channel is effectively invisible on the Internet. I'd imaging its the same hackers who unlocked my phone when I was calling the government's 'free legal advidce' hotline at the Attorney-General's Legal Services Commission in June 2024.

Greg ROBERTSON at Noarlunga Emergency Mental Health Service (photo from his online presence).

This inferred Freemason has criminally conspired with another and others to falsify the following document to begin a criminally secret mental health record on me because none existed.

In that Noarlunga file number 190329 (NHS) his associates criminally added hundreds of falsified documents. The pivotal moment that gave this opportunist his chance for promotion was that I'd added my name to the waiting list for public housing residential rentals. The murder He wrote about by his own hand was the murder of police officer Jack BASSET:

"Presented to SAHT (South Australia Housing Trust) today - is being

evicted from private rental has no electricity

Reported as behaving paranoidly

Talking of having to be relocated

to South Australia due to murders etc.

No (mental health record/diagnosis) under her name in

South Australia or New South Wales."

Other Freemasons falsified this document diagnosing me as "schizophrenic" because I filed a lawsuit against Health Minister John David HILL and his fellow conspirators the Police Minister, and Premier. The Christies Beach Star Chamber court refused to see or hear my evidence. ♉

CRIMINALLY FALSE SCHIZOPHRENIA DIAGNOSIS

Adelaide and Noarlunga mental department persisted with their federal crimes of "witness tampering" and using communications systems to create false documents (forgery) from c2006 to the present day. It wasn't until the end of 2018 that I was given these documents from their secret records they still insist is legal (to falsely defame a witness to a police officer murder by falsifying medical diagnosis of mental illness) Can't get much more ideologist TERRORIST than that.

Cochlear Ltd is a company owned by the same government who criminally assaulted me in the 1990s with an illegal cochlear region implant. The cochlear in the area around your inner ear. My implant includes a screw shape drilled into the bone of my skull through the roof skin of my left ear canal at the opening when the cochlear implant for deaf persons was developed in State of New South Wales at the Macquarie University in SYDNEY and I lived in Wollondilly Shire on the edge of greater Sydney. On the afternoon of 17 November 2005 I was struck with a huge mass of energy to back of my head and upper neck where I have suspected I had an illegal implant and have a very hard lump on left side of my neck and another in soft skin under my left ear and other matters proving foreign items inside my head. This energy was clearly wireless microwaves I heard double brick wall in front of me crack loud in milliseconds after this energy passed through me from a small window behind me. Ever since I've been experiencing vibration in my head (all vibration creates sound) and all over losing natural ability to hear from the ear due to at least three separate very loud sounds which appear to originate from behind the outer ear.

First high pitched sound is the unmistakable very high pitched sound too often termed tinnitus probably caused by the oversaturation of sound waves in our environment from radio, television, and mobile phones.

Second mid sound presents as my pulse as they injected silicone around the implants so I hear my pulse echo through the silicone.

The third is much deeper it n=beats at about 8 pulses per second and in time with the abnormal vibrations in my head, this is the illegal implant digital signal to and from the criminals in Sydney who illegally implanted me with this torture device designed to spy on my from the "inside".

THEY EMPLOY CRIME TO COVER UP CRIME. Government funded physicians surgically raped me because I'm only independent witnesses to Jack Basset's murder by the global freemason police brotherhood of assassins inside the Camden New South Wales police station on evening of Sunday 24 April 1988 as he was giving supporting evidence to my allegations of having witnessed long history of freemason child rape involving police & other government officials.

More about my 2013 right eye photo. That's yellow not green with (top) spot of brown but mainly blue. I'm guessing fat lines nose side (right) from chrysanthemum plant dry stick I fell on in 1960 age 4, waiting for the 'Puffer-Billy' train to pass by our house in Bunyan, stick punctured my eyelid & eyeball. I stayed at Canberra public hospital to have it surgically removed and eyelid stitched leaving permanent scar with slightly smaller eye opening, no change in vision.

My destiny to expose Freemason child rapists begun in my infancy my memories of then are strong and that's partially why 1990s Freemasons attempted to convert my brain to jello. I suspect they claim these lines are their efforts. They lie about everything that's their super-power.

Political philosophy in constitutional democratically ruled countries demands that its the "duty" of citizens to overthrow and abolish a government that turns on any number of its citizens by nullifying their inalienable rights as AUSTRALIA has done to me since 3 March 1959 — because it was a Freemason who rather brutally raped me on that day.

Day after ANZAC Day in 2014, one of Australia's Government funded political terrorists and illegally registered physician Mr Angelos GIANNAKOUREAS wrote a forged document as part of his terrorist conspiracy to seriously harm me physically. He's one of those 'like-minded' hundreds or thousands of terrorist enemies of Australia who've been planted by their terrorist organization in positions of authority in Australia's governments by Freemasons and other politically organized terrorists jostling to illegally control the purse strings of this country to secure unjust personal enrichment for their members through illegal power managed by perpetrating many crimes by falsely claiming the right in the name of Government.

No constitutional government has constitutional authority to commit any crime therefore such actions are automatically terrorism.

Australian based terrorist Angelos GIANNAKOUREAS forged his August 2014 letter by falsifying his right to do so in the capacity of his employment as senior consultant psychiatrist in the South Australia State government.

As I said government has no constitutional authority to perpetrate crime likewise nor do any of their employed, contracted, indentured, or elected public officers have any such authority to perpetrate crime. You've been brainwashed not to see this type of political terrorism as crime because it has been falsely labeled in enactments of parliament by '*democratic rule terrorists*' as "corruption" and that false label was affirmed by '*democratic rule terrorists*' in our news industries globally.

I have the duty as a citizen of Australia to stand firm against this tyranny. Because there is only one of me intellectually battling this enemy all I could do was gather evidence anticipating that, someday, I'd be able to break free of the censorship in Australia to find other like-minded non-terrorists anywhere globally to assist me in suing the terrorist Governments of Australia.

Terrorist Angelos GIANNAKOUREAS' letter is one of those noted elements of irrefutable evidence that established he and his State Government are controlled by terrorist enemies of Australia. He's been planted in the State health department within the Noarlunga "*emergency mental health service*" at Noarlunga, located within the outer metropolitan area of the capital city of South Australia. He wrote to the "*Guardianship Board*" of South Australia which is a group of Government public officer psychiatrists or general physicians tasked with determining whether or not a South Australian has a "*certifiable mental illness*" and is a danger to themselves or others because they're in need of psychiatric medication. This specific guardianship board have since been disbanded. They were a terrorist cell who politically imprisoned me and ordered my physical torture without any lawful authority under the Australian constitution and without any facts recognized under any democratic law allowing denial of any person's liberty and legal rights.

Those that followed in SACAT[33] are no different from my personal experience. (See Three Blind Mice.)

When terrorist Angelos GIANNAKOUREAS wrote his letter I was officially one of the aforenoted political prisoners in Australia whose liberty was taken away in an illegal tribunal (Star Chamber) without any lawful evidence whatsoever it was all on innuendo and hearsay and facts that are never a crime in a democracy. GIANNAKOUREAS was playing his part as a terrorist in order to silence me as a witness to terrorist crimes some 1500 kilometers away which precipitated my biometric identity being stolen by the Freemasons and politicians supporting the police who assassinated Jack BASSET inside the Camden police station on evening of Sunday 24 April 1988 for the Australian Freemason's political cause, being to perpetuate the cover-up of Freemason 'ritualistic' child rape in Australia during Freemason meetings involving a specific group of Freemasons - as I personally witnessed circa 1967.

My identity was stolen because the killers were unable to kill me as well due to their Freemason 'code' or frame me for Mr BASSET's '*shooting murder*' which I witnessed across the detective room.

Terrorist Angelos GIANNAKOUREAS evidently believes he's been appointed as a political arbitrator in South Australia tasked with controlling public opinion and my right to post true facts and evidence of political terrorism in Australia on the Internet. Terrorist Angelos GIANNAKOUREAS also believes he has the right to pass judicial '*judgment and sentence*' on what is defamation under Australian law. Some might refer to people like terrorist Angelos GIANNAKOUREAS as one of the government's "thought police".

Make no mistake, this mild-mannered softly spoken GIANNAKOUREAS is a psychopathic political terrorist whose sycophantic desire to please his superiors and maintain his political and social status, caused me serious physical harm, which automatically manifests into his willful intent to intimidate me. Makes no difference whether or not he knew me as an eye-witness to Freemason's sanctioned murder of a police officer — as a qualified senior psychiatrist he reasonably knew his actions were psychopathic, illegal and politically motivated. An expert on human psychology Angelos GIANNAKOUREAS knows he's a terrorist enemy of Australia. He's most probably in a brain fog of delusional denial of that fact.

I scored a Distinction (almost perfect) grade in my 1990 *Personnel*

---

[33] *South Australia* **Civil Administration Tribunal** *politically engineered specifically to politically* **undermine Federal Consumer Law** *when a political target is resident in public housing—nationally—CAT's are in every State.*

Management Certificate psychology exam. My 2018 *defamation law assignment for my Bachelor of Laws* degree resulted in a High Distinction (perfect score) despite being criminally assaulted with illegal and secret (from me) lobotomy by political terrorists in government, at the end of last century. I may be a seasoned target of Australian government terrorists, but that doesn't automatically make me unable to comprehend the world around me. It does however indicate terrorist Angelos GIANNAKOUREAS' conscience knowledge (through his terrorist organization) that I've been illegally lobotomized in New South Wales. Therefore due to his training as a physician, he believes my brain must have been turned to jello so he can say anything he likes about secure in the deluded thought I'll never understand even if I do stumble on his forged documents to criminally defame me as part of his part in the **underlying terrorist plan to murder me by illegal implant infection and medical neglect**, which is proved in the next image of my head.

Terrorist Angelos GIANNAKOUREAS' letter was intended to criminally defame me to the physicians at this "Guardianship Board".

Before we get to the terrorist's letter first let me point out that I was not a "patient" at the "Noarlinga Multidisciplinary Ambulatory Consulting Service" if that is what **MAC** means from my Google search. I was a political prisoner **deemed illegally detained by State District Court order in 2014** to have been forced there. That is still not recognized by the State Health Department in 2024 they still insist I was imprisoned legally contrary to the court ruling. They've ignored the Court completely because they're governed by a **Tripartizan1 political Party cult system**, not the Court system not Parliament's statute.

This is what terrorist Angelos GIANNAKOUREAS wrote when he defamed me one of many times in his malevolently focused political career:

> "Ms Francis is a patient of the Noarlunga MAC team. She came to the attention of mental health services, after a spate of uncharitable correspondence with prominent citizens. She was' detained and spent some time in a psychiatric ward at FMC, where she was diagnosed as suffering from Paranoid Schizophrenia. A CTO was applied for and Ms Francis is now obliged to receive Zuclopenthixol Decanoate 150mg, fortnightly.
>
> She has a complex belief system involving being the victim of 'implants'. As such, she is convinced of a conspiracy and has been vociferous in her allegations, to the point of naming and slandering doctors, politicians and medical services, online. Ms Francis is articulate and her delusional beliefs are encapsulated. I understand she expressed herself well, during her recent appearance at the District Court.
>
> I am not convinced she suffers from Schizophrenia. Her presentation

is more in keeping with a Delusional Disorder. This diagnosis is less amenable to treatment with medication, and I do not think there has been a shift in her beliefs. She attends reluctantly and is quite dismissive of advice. She has not demonstrated a predisposition for physical aggression and there has not been any ideation of self-harm disclosed. Despite this, her correspondence has attracted police contact.

Ms Francis is at risk of litigation, misadventure and harm to her reputation. Her online behaviour has been noted and she is vulnerable to being sued by defamed individuals.

I am yet to be convinced that the depot has helped. I am happy to discuss these matters with Ms Francis. She does however avoid me."

I've no conclusive knowledge of what "MAC team" is supposed to represent. Evidently nor does GIANNAKOUREAS as he's used an acronym instead of his words, an indicator of laziness of the mind usually demonstrated by Government officials who are customarily appointed due to their intellectual malleability rather than their intellectual capacity.

I'm yet to learn what's in his mentioned *"spate of uncharitable correspondence"* or indeed who the *"prominent citizens."* are I'm supposed to have contacted. Government officials like GIANNAKOUREAS get to write any shit they like about anyone to criminally defame their political or ideological target with complete impunity. Angelos GIANNAKOUREAS is public mates with Andrew Robert CHAMPION brother or father to South Australia Labor Party State president in 2006, 1972 born Nicholas David CHAMPION who was member of federal parliament from 2007—2022, has been South Australia State parliament member since 2022 presently the Minister for State Housing therefore effectively controls my right to have rental accommodation after Freemason Labor Party terrorists stole my real estate 1991—1999 Commonwealth conspiracy to make forged land title documents help by the MacArthur Credit Union Camden New South Wales where I saw Jack BASSET murdered by the Sydney police Freemason Brotherhood — shot in cold blood not six foot in front of me on evening of Sunday 24 April 1988 as he was giving evidence to the police who assassinated him to support my allegations of being eye-witness to Freemason child rape since 3 Match 1959 in Bunyan where we lived in the Post-Master-Generals (Attorney-General) post office residence. My mum was the postmistress and telephone exchange operate for Bunyan area. Police lie to this day claiming Mr Basset took his own life with his own gun — he was a police officer in Cooma and best friends with my male parent before I was born in Cooma on 1 May 1956.

Which leads to the 'why' of Angelos GIANNAKOUREAS reference to me 'avoiding him'. Like I've taught my children, if you come into contact with a crazy person don't make eye contact, because they're like any wild animal, eye contact is considered a 'threat' therefore likely to physically attack you falsely believing you are about to attack them. Sound familiar when reading about police shooting people dead?

I avoided all of these like-minded psychopaths in South Australia's (sick) health system. I've said it before, I blame this type of demonstrated mental illness seen in long-term Adelaide residents on genetic impact through recent ancestry and 'microscopic dust drift' from 1950s British atomic bomb tests in desert to northwest of Adelaide at Maralinga. They're amongst the craziest in government I've ever experienced. There is no isolated pocket — it's all of them. The 2006 MRI proves some locations of (illegal) implants and vibration mentioned by terrorist Angelos GIANNAKOUREAS in his authored Government records about me. The bright white parts are implant locations and vibration centers. I was illegally and secretly surgically opened on top of my head circa 2007. This simple MRI image irrefutable proves my brain is vibrating indicated by the lack of visual definition inside my brain and by what looks like vertical shock waves across the top of my head.

Terrorist Angelos GIANNAKOUREAS should be languishing in a prison for political terrorists. The only thing he and his comrades are entitled to is death in prison.

Terrorist Angelos GIANNAKOUREAS knows I've complained of 'vibrations' caused by illegal implants (three locations) down my spine — saw me vibrating, sitting across from his small office desk, 9 April 2014. — diagnosed those implant vibrations as *"mild dystonia"* with no follow-up medical investigation.

There's highly probable that terrorist Janette Anne MOIR the offsider of Terrorist Angelos GIANNAKOUREAS, had illegally and secretly injected another pulsing BION into my left gluteus muscle when they were illegally injecting me with drugs in 2014 under threat of criminal assault if I refused, in breach of Australian law, by dishonest dealings with documents, criminal defamation and criminal abuse of public office. Those documents can wait — except for the three main ones directly relating to the obvious terrorist conspiracy between **terrorist Angelos GIANNAKOUREAS** and **terrorist Janette Anne MOIR**.

The terrorist conspiracy between New South Wales police and parliament, proved in my documents from 2001, have harmed and continue to harm more (numbers of) innocent people so they're first on my list, see chapter *"French Letters Letters"*. It was **1 April 2014** I filed my winning Federal Court **Copyright Act** claim on the same (Brothers In Arms) matter. Which would be why Labor Party terrorist Michael COATA spilled the beans on the property development bribes precipitating the **2 May 2014** ICAC resignations story, presumably calculating that example of politician's greed were the least harmful to Labor Party in Government, as opposed to admitting I was surgically raped to cover up the Bob HAWKE and Paul KEATING nod of approval to the falsification of (Brothers In Arms) seven murders on Fathers Day 1984. Followed by Paul KEATING and subsequent treasurers funding my criminal surgical rape from circa 1987 and the television miniseries to cover that up in 2012 illegally funded by both the Federal and New South Wales governments.

The inalienable right to pen or speak the truth of crime perpetrated in the name of democratic Government isn't lawfully banned or censured in a Constitutional democracy by parliaments or Court such censorship is a terrorist's crime only perpetrated by terrorists who've illegally infiltrated government public office through partnership with a political party controlling Government specifically to criminally abuse statute with impunity from their terrorist partners in parliament. Every treacherous dog will have its day of reckoning *like Terrorists Angelos GIANNAKOUREAS*, Janette Anne MOIR, Andrew Robert CHAMPION and their Tripartizan cult 'family of allies' in State and Federal police departments and parliaments.

Logically: if this type of surgical rape can and obviously has been violently enforced on my by terrorists like *Angelos GIANNAKOUREAS and his partners in Government funded medical terrorism Janette Anne MOIR, Andrew Robert CHAMPION of Noarlunga - Christies Beach (Adelaide) Australia — along with all of their supporting government public officers in Adelaide's police, health and Attorney-General's court departments*.

If this can happen to someone as level headed and logical minded as myself then others less articulate must also be criminally targeted this way with devastating consequences.

As can be seen from my MRI of my head photographs, my head vibrates severely every night as I attempt to sleep, early morning around 4-5 am is the most violent even if I don't sleep. It appears the illegal implants inside me are monitored and varied by medical terrorists in possession of the remote control for this illegal implant. I'm forced to bind my head reducing blood circulation to lesson vibration bruising. To any reasonable person the illegal implants seen in part in 2006 and 2012 MRI[34] radiology of my head are obvious caused of this vibration bruise to my eyeball. These illegal implants are reason my eyebrows and eyelashes have stopped growing properly.

---

[34] *MRI **magnetic resonance imagery**, not to be confused with Adelaide's new AU$3 BILLION SAMRI as South Australia Medical Research Institute.. No prizes for accurately guessing they'd be secretly researching illegal medical implants and other political Government funded medical torture applications.*

Illegal implants terrorist claim since 2007 are in my imagination.

My District Court appeal win 16 June 2014 and Tribunal Revocation Order 2 October 2014 doesn't represent that I no longer had mental illness or it was being successfully treated — they represent fact that there **was no evidence whatsoever for South Australia State Government to diagnose me with any mental illness in first instance**, none whatsoever.

The entire South Australia experience tends to prove that Australia's Freemason (mens health) culture conceal illegal **anti-human-rights** medical research and other medical implant crimes to continue to keep the secret of their very long history of **Freemason family predators desiring to indecently sexually groom and exploit children in their own family**.

Rock Spiders. ♉

Myers-Briggs INTJ

Suspect that INTJ type make the best lawyers, judges & investigative journalists however, as I know of no other person like me I can't close off on that comment.

If you're old enough to remember or Google search that circa 1962 song *'Liberty Valance'* sung so well by Gene Pitney, I'm like the easterner with the law book. My (older) brother got the single for his birthday circa 1966. I played it more than he did, over and over driving everyone crazy with it. I related to it even then — I was only ten years old.

I was born with poor eyesight and didn't often wear my glasses. When it comes to recognizing someone I recognize them by sight yes, but more so by personality which is why I don't need to stare at people when they talk to me. I'd noticed people who move in on you when they're talking to you and stare into your eyes. They're looking to see if your pupil size changes. Avoid these types like the black plague. They're habitual compulsive liars. Poison with legs. When I was little my personality difference hurt me insomuch as it made me feel sad and a little lonely to be different. But I got over that soon enough. I'm able to entertain myself psychologically in any environment. Even when you have nothing you still have your own mind to entertain and occupy your thoughts. So long as you have core values no one can brainwash them out of you. On the inside in my mind, I was born to be the (metaphoric) man who shot Liberty Valance. I'm the virtual freight train that can't be derailed. I only think in terms of what can be logically proved. However, I'm still bemused and in awe that without reasonable logic I lived through my January 1977 car accident has no logical structure presently known to the people of my time on planet Earth. It's a total mystery, not to them but is to us. A mystery not a miracle there are no miracles, just events not yet explained to your brain.

This is how Isobel (Briggs) Myers and her husband describe my Myers-Briggs INTJ personality from the 16 personality 1940s model created with her mum Katherine [35]:

> *"INTJs are the most independent of all the sixteen personality types and take more or less conscious pride in that independence. Whatever their field, they are likely*

---

[35] *'Gifts Differing' Briggs Myers, I, Myers, P, 1995, ISBN: 0-89106-074-X.*

to be innovators. In business they are born reorganizers. Intuition gives the an iconoclastic imagination and an unhampered view of the possibilities; extroverted thinking supplies a keenly critical organizing facility. "Whatever is, could doubtless be improved!" They are likely however to organize themselves out of a job. They cannot continually reorganize the same thing, and a finished product has no more interest. Thus they need successive new assignments, with bigger and better problems, to stretch their powers. With technical interests they tend to be research scientist, inventors, and design engineers ... they can get things done, but they will be interested only when the problems involved are complicated enough to be challenging ... have the tendency to ignore the views and feelings of others."

My INTJ personality is why I found it so easy to overcome everything this Freemason family of criminally fixated parasitic psychopaths threw at me. My personality type is why I found it so easily unravel their tightly woven matrix of them secretly drugging me to surgically rape me and mutilate my face and entire structure with illegal silicone fillers — to recognize their many attempts to murder me using brainwashing of others — to recognize that Australia's parliament had indeed bankrolled the many terrorist styled physical attacks on my person carefully interwoven with the Freemason ideological cause of covering up a long history in Australia and probably globally of Freemason child rape and murder. All that while keeping my nerve, maintaining focus, constantly reassessing the evidence to make sure I was heading in the right direction, searching relevant leads, ignoring irrelevant distractions thrown in my path — there were more of those than anything else.

When I knew SLOWMAN-STYLES at Wollondilly Shire Council, she looked different from her appearance at Visyboard and she acted differently. At Visyboard she was openly a total bitch to everyone. At Wollondilly she was secretly the bitch to specific persons none of whom were me, I did overhear her being so to another. She usually left the room when I entered I suspect so that I wouldn't gaze at her or recognize her as Elaine SLOWMAN. She barely spoke at council meetings. I do vaguely recollect that I'd recognized her at one point but they'd secretly roofied me at Council meetings so often to make me forget they'd drugged me so I can't be specific. Nor would I bother with **the 'she said he said'** scenario. I'm a document person. Documents are harder to refute than words.

Words that were never spoken can be cohobated by 100 liars. Documents can be proved to be forged, words can't.

One thing I knew about Elaine SLOWMAN she couldn't alter is that her arms were disproportioned — the top and lower sections are not same length as most people's are. As Lynette STYLES she always wore long sleeves.

Like I said I vaguely recollect seeing her once with no sleeves and that'd be when I recognized her. But I can only remember recognizing her as Elaine SLOWMAN smiling at her in a friendly manner saying "I know who you are" then forgetting completely mixed in with a memory of throwing a chair out a window after they'd refused to let me leave the council building after hours.

They'd secretly drugged me to (illegally) interrogate me to discover what I knew about them or how they could screw me over more likely. It was a big upstairs window, next to where I sat at the council chamber table. Had to be a record of the repair or insurance claim. Mongrel bastards.

In her aptly named "Kangaroo Court' STYLES-SLOWMAN plays the, hard done by elected member everyone picked on, when in reality was the typical wicked-witch who'd caucused with the Labor left majority faction to deliver non-independent decisions despite claiming they were "independent" as in, not Party aligned. Nutbags. That she mentioned me when I was an elected member claiming I was always angry at her is rubbish. I don't get angry because if I do let myself feel that emotion I'm likely to flip into a 'disassociate fugue state' — I black out and inflict near-death injuries on my target completely unaware of my actions. It's happened three times, twice because I was illegally secretly drugged after psychopaths secretly drugged me to "know" all my "secrets" at the Wollondilly Shire Council office (1995-1999.) As Elaine SLOWMAN alias Lynette STYLES has never experienced such battery from me then I've never been angry towards her. I make a point of not being angry. I laugh a lot to keep the endorphins flowing. My often laughter renders predators to errantly believe me an air-head, the opposite of my intellect. They're clueless. I like it that way as when predators know what happens and how to trigger that response they tend to enjoy secretly drugging me for entertainment. My own male parent did it with beer, which makes my stomach automatically reject it on contact. Psychopaths enjoy seeing others react embarrassingly without control, humans would never do that. Elaine and her new friends at Wollondilly were her like-minded psychopaths. That sort of predator flocks to the government (employment or election) like the proverbial moth to a flame.

The first time it happened was (1972) when I was 16 years old was mild however, it meant I made sure I was never drunk or took drugs voluntarily. It may have been brought on by being raped the year before as during that I felt almost catatonic because of the conscious betrayal of my (3rd form) year 9 girlfriends Elizabeth SELSBY and Sharon LOVE who'd participated in arranging my rape with Elizabeth's old primary school friend Rhonda WARK who didn't understand the word "no" when she asked me to be her friend. That's the danger of lesbianism in schools. WARK is the psycho-daughter of a NSW police officer and she's never been charged for my statutory rape therefore she's a candidate for one of the many who have stalked me since

1970s to defame me so they're never held accountable for their crimes against me — that's what police officers do best. Elizabeth went on to be appointed to a Sydney region Local Council Management position. Rhonda's been criminally stalking me fever since to this very day (evidently) with the assistance of her police family.

Other two times I was secretly and illegally drugged 1995-2002 from the small newspaper notice, I almost killed him cracking his skull on the ground. The Newcastle Times (NSW) claimed he'd been gang-bashed and left for dead. I have partial before and after memories.

You can hear me on my youtube.com channel, I'm perfectly mentally balanced. Even when faced with the goon squad wanting to imprison me to protect their terrorist informant from accountability for his criminal defamation crimes against me, the one they housed directly opposite my driveway allowing him to illegally keep me under surveillance with video cameras pointed at my front door and driveway and floodlights at night illuminating my driveway so we only see the flood light when we walk out our front door at night or entering or leaving my property.

If I'd be inclined to be provoked to anger he'd be first on my list. He knows it which is why he lies about me, he knows I've tried to sue him but his political mates have illegally refused to let me file my lawsuit titled "Francis v Australian Labor Party and others".

So that STYLES-SLOWMAN falsely claimed I was spitting angrily at her during a council meeting then accused me of being "schizophrenic" and then started on about the SIMPSON & HARVEY Brothers In Arms paperback I didn't see until 2001 - which was two years after I left the council and Wollondilly Shire region to living in Branxton near Newcastle quite a long drive apart. So how did SLOWMAN aka STYLES know that I wrote anything about the SIMPSON & HARVEY Brothers In Arms paperback? That'd be because she too is criminally stalking my presence on the Internet, she plagiarized my literary works on my website claiming it as her work then criminally defamed me with that information she discovered on my website. It's a common modus operandi for Labor Party and their allied Freemason political terrorist family.

That means she was internet stalking me to plagiarize my literary works in my website to criminally defame me by manipulating my words and taking the information on my investigative journalistic crime reporting, out of context, expressly to defame me — she infringed my literary works copyright by abuse of my moral rights. Being an alleged "working" lawyer she knows that, unless that's also an exaggeration of her talents. Interestingly, a copy of her self-published paperback (she titled Kangaroo Court) made its way into the hands of the Allen and Unwin lawyer who put it on the desk in front of him during mediation pointing to it as his evidence I was a looney-tune. Their lawyer promised to put it in evidence but never did. Incidentally, on my website, I wrote that if I were to write about my time on council I'd call the book Kangaroo Court.

I got extracts of her malicious book (totally absent of evidence) from Google Books and I suspect it's still published on the Internet only because I can't get any lawyers in Australia to represent my interests in the real truth of any Government funded lie that's physically harmed me for the past thirty four (34) years. That's terrorism.

ANCESTORS, DNA LINKS AND A FAMILY TREE

Ultimately you are who you become in life partly by what your DNA dictates and partly by willful choice or partly by necessity. I'm artistically inclined like Louis Marc François GAUVIN, same as my mum, he's is one of my 3rd Great Grandfathers (mum's side) he's listed in my family tree record as being born in old Paris France circa 3 January 1827. This is interesting as 3 January 1975 was when I was married in Geelong Victoria.

Somewhere on the horns is a Freemason symbol however it may have been carved by someone else, even well after his death. The reformation of Freemasonry from a homosexual club for men into a secretly organized political group was relatively new in the 50 years before he was born. In my mind the 'modern' Freemason symbol wasn't carved by this Louis GAUVIN. His son from whom I'm descendant is named Louis Henry GAUVIN.

They had their own Stock Exchange there was that much gold in Charters Towers when my great grandparents were there towards the end of the Charters Towers gold rush period in Queensland,

(My great great grandfather) Louis Henry's daughter, *Jane GAUVIN[36] (1890-1920) was very young when she married an older English immigrant (Oliver George HUSSEY) who is the Freemason rapist male parent of my beloved maternal grandmother, Olive Harriett Hussey STRACHAN (Jane's oldest daughter) and murderer of his 30 years young wife Jane presumably because she stood between him and his sisters selling off his prepuberty girls into prostitution (presumably) through a local pub registered to Ester Fanny

---

[36] *Jane is the 5th great-granddaughter of Scotland's folk hero Rob Roy MacGREGOR (1671-1734) through her maternal grandmother Queensland born Jane MacGREGOR (Mrs) MacLACHLAN (1842-1932).*

GAUVIN [37].

One of this Charters Towers born family My maternal grandmother's younger sister Ann HUSSEY[38] married **William SIMPSON**, they had no children. Their mum's was *"Jane"* her birth name Jane GAUVIN[39], I'm suspecting that's where the SLOWMAN-UNWIN family derived the 'pen name' for author **Lindsay Jane SIMPSON**. The fullness of time will undoubtedly reveal all.

Thanks to my maternal grandmother's statements to me just before she was murdered by Freemason physician in 1989, I'm not only aware Australia's Freemasons have been ruining, injuring or murdering females lives in my family for past 100 years at the very least, I can prove it 100%. She was murdered by willful medical negligence because she recognized me from a television photo of me aired in the TV or newspaper when she lived in a Sydney nursing home. The photo they'd stolen for their SIMPSON & HARVEY's BIA 1989, falsely labeled as *"Leanne Walters murdered Fathers Day 1984"* She told me this days before she died. Despite being drugged up first thing she said to me was:

"I told them you're not dead., they didn't believe me."

I know it was murder because she contracted gangrene in her foot, as a diabetic. She told me she never cuts her own toenails because of the gangrene threat, she only had a physician cut them for her. No one else she said not even a nurse, only a physician. She was very particular about that. They murdered her just same as they tried to murder me many times –murder by accident. Its the Freemason coward's way.

Nana died in about November 1989. I harassed Ashfield police until they ordered an autopsy. They told me they found it was medical negligence that caused her death. I didn't get any more information as this was after I'd been estranged from my parents , since Jack BASSET's murder on 24 April 1988 which was the catalyst for New South Wales police stealing my biometric

---

[37] *Ester Fanny GAUVIN (unknown relationship to me however, she may be related to the terrorist descendant family of Raynor UNWIN from Scotland or author Lindsay SIMPSON herself who likes to live near where this family of mine had lived and died. Whether she does to perpetuate the belief we are the same person is not clear based on the evidence I have. Ester is listed as "Licensed Victualler" (pub owner) Cairns Queensland AUSTRALIA, in the Queensland Police Gazette, Volume XLV, No. 47, page 330, Saturday 1 August 1908.*

[38] *My Great Aunt Ann, I knew her up to my teenage years.*

[39] *My Great Grandmother, she was murdered by Queensland Freemasons.*

identity for the 1984 Freemason faked murder. The Freemasons had the SIMPSON & HARVEY's BIA published in about mid 1989.

They also killed my old dog Samson the night before my birthday in 1988, 30 April. He was defending me from assault inside my residence invoicing Owen HALL and Peter Robert BRADBURY, the Freemason who murdered Jack BASSET. I only have fractured memories of them attacking me the dog defending me then they killed the dog. Probably fractured as they'd hit me to knock me out then forced amnesia drugs into when semi conscious or totally out of it. I have distinct before and then nothing next morning. No idea how I got to bed. Its rubbish what they say about small towns in Australia — they don't give a damn about each other unless they're Freemason then they'll help the Freemasons kill you if that's what Freemasons want. I was being pack raped in my own bed in the middle of the day — neighbors heard me but decided they didn't want to get involved in our small village of The Oaks New South Wales, 39 William Street was my house — arseholes.

Around my residence were Julie & Graham OSWALD[40] north side my side, Lindy & Bob MAHER[41] south side my side, across the road were Bev & Tony , Caroline & John DURRINGTON, Nicola and Peter NICOLLS she's a nurse he's a teacher.

Owen HALL (1964–2010) my de-facto (from 1986–1996) is also in that double photo with Graham, Graham is 2nd from centre on left behind bloke with his hands on his hips and Owen 1st from centre on right with headband. Owen's slightly edited face-photo is also next to my stolen photo-biometric identity, he's listed as *"Snodgrass (Anthony Mark) Spencer, suicided in jail"* the BIA story goes that he got a Valentine's Day card from the dead Leanne Walters so he hung himself — as bloody if a bloke who allegedly carried firearms and other weapons on his motorcycle would cave in like that. Dream on Freemasons dream on.

Bob MAHER had twin daughters from a previous relationship he told me. I saw them visit him in his front yard few days before Bob & Lindy left to move to Tasmania c1990. I thought it was odd they weren't allowed to go inside his house they stood there on the boarder talking to him as if he was a stranger. Poor little things. They both had a bright white dress on as if they'd been to Holy Communion or such. I just happened to be mysteriously beaconed to look out the front window and see them there. Beckoned I suspect by the esoterics in my car 3 January 1977. The universe looks after me like that,

---

[40] *Graham OSWALD was photographed in SIMPSON & HARVEY's 'Brothers In Arms' as one of group in the only double page photograph,*

[41] *Bob MAHER was also photographed in BIA as "Foghorn (Robert) Lane Comanchero, shot dead.*

putting me in the right place to gather relevant evidence. You could say I was tailor made for the job. **You** could say it but I'll never believe it.

Bob & Lindy had a little boy about two years old when they left, his first name is the second name of one of my children. Its not the children's fault their parents made critically poor life choices. Bob MAHER made a point of apologizing to me before he left. When I asked what for? He said only this:

"We trusted the wrong people."

Bob MAHER also used to dye his lightish brown hair black.

Graham & Julie had a little girl a bit older they also moved house at the same time but to a different location, Mittagong. I saw Julie working in hospitality in Mittagong c1997. Right place right time. I randomly decided to take my children out for dinner, rarely did, Julie served me.

Seriously they couldn't have had better names for me to remember, long-term despite the brainwashing. Another Graham is name of the father of my first born. Another Bob (William Robert) name of father of my second born. Oswald is last name of Lee Harvey (JFK's alleged killer) and MAHER last name of General Manager of Woolworths MacArthur Square when I worked there c1980.

Therefore with John David HILL being named as BANDIDO, and from the COMANCHEROS we've Graham OSWALD and Bob MAHER, then logically John David HILL was the "undercover cop" noted on front page of newspaper (front of book) and as William George ROSS (1984 Comanchero Jock) was obviously also Freemason the police and the bikers had themselves a secret deal — fuk me over for impunity.

So the question is — exactly how many did they say were killed on Fathers Day 1984? There's at least three less than the six they claim being:

• **Anthony Lane not dead - BUSTED.**

• **Anthony Spencer not dead - BUSTED.**

• **Leanne Walters not dead - BUSTED.**

The neighborhood local 'mood' when I moved into my house at The Oaks was that there was something 'stewing' around me. I'd had a lifetime (even then) to understand how Freemasons worked. They virtually sent up red flares whenever they're up to dirty tricks. There's not one think I could point to there are dozens. The entertaining part is that Freemason police are no different to uneducated petty criminals, they believe they're too clever for everyone else. Hello, hello, hello!

MY TRUE ANCESTRY DOT COM & GEDMATCH

I'm aware that my written family tree has been very well matched by my DNA archaeogenetic comparisons from the good people at MyTrueAncestry.com which tells me I'm DNA related to Ludwig van BEETHOVEN and may explain why I was certain I could play the piano before I begged mum for one as small child — I couldn't. It was obviously in my DNA memory not necessarily from that BEETHOVEN.

Only recently discovered probability that I'm also DNA related to Rodrigo DÍAZ DE VIVAR "El Cid" of SPAIN through my male parent's mother. Which appears to be potentially associated with DNA either from his side or the Muslims he was fighting. Explains quite a lot about millions of us freedom fighters who are on the side of freedom and equality for all equally, not life as we know it across this warring planet in every country where all lie about everyone being equal. Religious or political oppression of any kind is for the era of barbarians not civilized persons.

I'm more inclined to take up a law book than a weapon as fighting with the law in a court of country generally has a further reaching, peaceful and longer lasting effect with significant potential to put terrorists in parliaments and police departments in terrorist prisons for the rest of their psychopathically driven lives. Creating safer communities in reality not just in words as painted on the side of police vehicles here in Adelaide of South Australia—dominated generally by lawless sycophantic, sadistic psychopaths. If you're like me then there is never "**us and them**" there can only ever be "**us**" all of us living by one set of rules applied the same by all police departments on all people, including all police department personnel. Us — is the only way forward to move out of this million something years of barbarism.

Theoretically, if I was hanging about as my spirit self in some hypothetical 'other realm' when someone asked for volunteer to inhabit my infant self as I was being born knowing what I was up against, I'd be the one to volunteer. Chew that over. How cool it would be to be recycled every couple of centuries as that heroic person sent to Planet Earth to filter out fodder for the hypothetical devil furnace and written about in history books for thousands of years. hypothetical there's natural water filters, natural air filters, logically there's also natural soul filters, a method for the universes to dispense with bad seeds to ensure they're never recycled. Theoretically of course, if I could I'd be one of them — soul filter. That be my first fiction story, when I eventually get '*a round tuit*'. I was trying to write when I was early teen but had to let go as any Freemason child who did anything imaginative back then was deemed as being intellectually retarded.

In MyTrueAncestry.com DNA matches, I'm linked to 23 ancient persons who settled Iceland between about 935 to 1100 CE and one more in 1678 CE and 18 in Pict Graveyard and dozen more identified as Pictish. About 100 identified as Viking. Only about 35 identified a Irish. Marked as England were 319 persons these are a mixture of Celts Britons Angles Saxons Vikings Apart from Cheddar Man, the oldest DNA match in MTA is Neolithic 2950 BCE at Summerhill in the Tyne and Wear county in England. My next closest ancient in MTA after Cheddar Man is in Switzerland at 2542 BCE. That means I'm indigenous to Wales, England, Scotland and Ireland. Where's my handout then as a disenfranchised indigenous descendant? That's the current trend, complain you've been displaced because you're lucky enough to still live in your ancestor's lands.

As a point of interest according to the MTA computer system, Cheddar Man is DNA related to Estonian and other Scandinavian Vikings murdered by England's residents during the Viking era as Viking invaders.

Interestingly in GEDmatch.com I'm DNA linked to persons who lived:

- 12,500 years ago in Clovis Montana USA.
- 13,000 years ago in Bichon Switzerland.
- 13,300 years ago Satsurblia Georgia.
- 24,000 years ago in Malta Siberia.
- 37,000 years ago in Pokrovsky Valley Russia.
- 40,000 years ago in Croatia.
- 45,000 years ago in Ust-Ishim Siberia.
- 50,000 years ago in Siberia.

I'm also very proud to have naturally tanned cousins presently living in central South Africa as linked in another DNA website.

In my FamilySearch.org (FSO) family tree my Great Grandparent (GG) ancestors include Attila the Hun as 45th and 47th GG and numerous Emperors of the Han Dynasty as 46th to 97th GGs. Other regions where my GG lived as natives include Assyria, Egypt, France, Greece, Israel, Palestine, Persia, Holy Roman Empire era Ggs, and a few Visigoth Kings in the 40th GG era. Also have three Catholic Pope's as Great Uncles.

Naturally the family tree is only as truthful as the participants and for sure there's a lot of wankers in cyberspace whose tiny brain tells them its funny to falsify family records for a complete stranger. This was demonstrated when I advertised innocently enough on my one person participating Facebook account with no actual "friends" — but for my family to see, the famous cousins FSO had linked to me. As FSO is USA based they're mostly from USA. I knew for some years (I had a dream) Martin Luther King was a cousin but when I posted it on my Facebook page (January 2023) someone got into my linked records on the FSO website and erased my family links. This is precisely what Freemasons in Australia have done in my real life to my family associations. They claim, they insist I'm not me but that I'm someone else. These are Government officials tasked with recording our history as fact. Clearly they are expert in recording fiction as true fact and won't let anyone challenge them in a court of law.

This is probably a good spot to state that recently (June 2024) I was on my mobile phone for the alleged lawyer I was talking to when I dialed the number for the State Government's free legal advise at the Legal Services Commission office in Adelaide. She kept going away and coming back several times in total I probably waited for 30 minutes for her to come back to the phone. After all that time she gave me no legal information at all. Before I rang I switched my phone to block my number. When I hung up I looked that the network service section to reconnect my number as visible to callers when I noted that it had already been unblocked. That means whomever I rang at the Legal Services Commission of the State of South Australia criminally hacked into my mobile phone to steal my private data on my 2024

15: Qld State website (childless) Aunt Ann HUSSEY married William SIMPSON

Reg #	Marriage Party Surname	Marriage Party Given Name(s)	Marriage Party Surname	Marriage Party Given Name(s)
1931/C2946	Simpson	William Henry	Hussey	Annie Jacobina

bdm.qld.gov.au https://www.bdm.qld.gov.au/IndexSearch/querySubmit.m?ReportName=MarriageSearch

1 Matches [1 page]

« Start | Prev | 1 | Next | End »   20 ⌄ Records per page

« Start | Prev | 1 | Next | End »

Copyright | Disclaimer | Privacy | Access keys | Other languages
© The State of Queensland (Department of Justice and Attorney-General) 2009.
Queensland Government

manufactured Motorola handset.

The reason I had to buy another phone is because I clicked on a link that told me I needed to perform a "network update" after I did that I was locked out of accessing the internet completely. I've had to toss that phone and buy a new one. So if you see an "Network update" request IGNORE it its hackers Australia's Government funded based intent on causing you grief.

Other tips:

- Reboot your phone after you access the internet and never leave the internet connected permanently. Use it then switch it off and reboot. You should NEVER pay bills on your phone and NEVER use a bank industry application to access your savings. Phones are too easily hacked and the Government public officers do it for entertainment and personal profit.

Use cash when possible. Don't use your debit or credit card to do regular shopping or any of those rewards cards, you can be stalked through your electronic shopping habits and stalkers will know where you are and how long you take, to get into your house to plant surveillance bugs in your computer or other surveillance devices in your rooms. They're minuscule and almost impossible to see amongst your stuff. I purchased a cheap 1080p audio CCTV camera that looks like a regular screw. The camera is a pin head dot in the middle of the screw head. You could buy pinhole matchbox sized cameras with microphones at Jaycar for under Au$50 in 1990s. I had 3 or 4 caught a few stupid Goulburn police on them in 2004. I went to Bowral NSW police station in 1990s to report finding a wired illegal surveillance device in my residence — the arrogant Freemason in police uniform said to me: *"How do I know you didn't plant it yourself"* then he refused to take my statement. I didn't have a criminal record or any issue with police. I didn't know they'd stolen my biometric identity then. I was at that time an elected member of my local council, a young mother with very small children. He and his mates probably planted it. Went back home ripped it out and threw it on the counter back at the station. That boys and girls is why you'll often hears people of varying ages and social status call police officers, "pigs".

I turn to my ancestry to ground me. According to FamilySearch.org the fella they call Viking King of France, Rollo ROGNVALDSSON of Normandy, is my 2nd cousin 28R (28 times removed)ther famous cousins include, authors authors Emily Dickinson, Robert Lewis Stevenson, George Bernard Shaw, singer/actor Bing Crosby and many more however, due to the propensity of people to be humongous wankers what's on the Internet family tree websites isn't necessarily accurate. I will say many decent hobby historians and professionals alike try to keep FamilySearch.org factual. When I see I'm 1st cousin 50R to Jesus of Nazareth Bible fame its a case of probable foul play. Although I do have ancient ancestors in the Gaza strip region so maybe. I am related to the STEWART (Scottish Royal) family through my proved descendancy from Rob Roy MacGREGOR. MyTrueAncestry.com confirmed my DNA relationship with the Neil Armstrong family and many other family groups represented in the FamilySearch.org database as my grandparents, cousins, aunts or uncles.

Some FamilySearch.org documented famous cousins include author Henry David THOREAU is my 7th Cousin 7R.

USA President James BUCHANAN my 8th cousin 5R.

USA President Benjamine HARRISON, inventor Samuel MORSE my 8th cousins 6R.

USA President Abraham LINCOLN 9th cousin 4R.

USA President Theodore ROOSEVELT, author Edgar Allen POE 9th Cousin 5R

Beetles musician John LENNON, filmmaker Walt Disney 10th cousin 2R.

Author Mark TWAIN 10th cousin 4R.

Artist Jackson POLLOCK my 11th cousin 1R.

USA President Harry TRUMAN, USA President Warren G HARDING, USA President William McKINLEY, inventor Thomas EDISON, aviator Charles LINDBERG my 11th cousin 3R.

Civil rights activists Martin Luther KING Jr, actors Lucille Ball, Katherine Hepburn, John Wayne MORRISON are my 12th proper cousins.

UK Princess Diana Spencer, Aviator Amelia Earhart, USA President Lyndon JOHNSON, singer actor Elvis Presley my 12th cousins 1R.

UK Prime Minister Winston CHURCHILL, USA to moon astronaut Neil ARMSTRONG my 12th cousins 2R.

Beetles musician George Harrison my 13th cousin.

Actor Marilyn Munroe (Norma Jean BAKER) my 14th cousin. ♉

T H A N K   Y O U

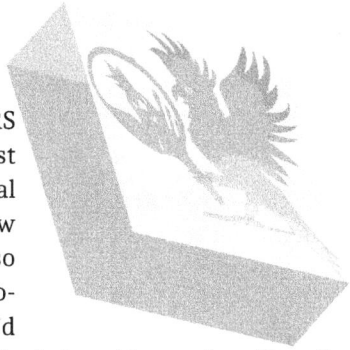

I acknowledge that the REX JOHN WALTERS family of Ingleburn NSW are recidivist terrorists whose ideological cause is financial reward and social status for all fellow FREEMASON terrorists. However, I want to also thank all those persons who without their co-operation and dedication to these crimes I'd never have been able to possess and republish their evidence they illegally manufactured to pass off as legal documents that prove irrefutable the criminal premeditated terrorist plan of a handful of State police as the instigating group, a terrorist plan that was brought to fruition by Australia's Freemason community and politically aligned State Government public officers. I'm eternally grateful that you're all so entertainingly stupid. Thank you also to your parents for their DNA.

This crime could not have happened at all if it didn't have official backing and participation by Australia's Labor and Liberal political parties controlling our Governments along with their Nazi styled police departments, funded by Australia's tax payers. They stole land from the original owners then sell it off to descendants of immigrants so they can steal it back and resell it to more immigrants, *a television personality said recently that about one in three people in Australia weren't born here* which makes what's happened to me a proper crisis for national security. This is Australia's Government historical *modus operandi.*

This evidence in these attached documents prove irrefutably that Australia's Freemasons and Australia's Labor and Liberal political party governments are an unincorporated Tripartizan political party who control all of Australia's parliaments and the largest terrorist organization in Australia. This major fraud by a criminal conspiracy and Government organized political terrorism directly fabricated a multiplicity of criminal defamation's most they secreted from me for many years, some are still a mystery to me.

This extensive multi-government multi-national terrorist family begun their criminal defamations with their 1989 copyright dated paperback[42]; swiftly followed by my surgical rape that begun to my knowledge when I was

---

[42] *1989 paperback in "Brothers In Arms The Inside Story of Two ... Gangs" by authors Sandra Harvey (aka Leanne WALTERS) and Lindsay Simpson (aka twin Sharon or Tamara UNWIN) published by Allen-Unwin-Hyman family internationally.*

mid-term pregnant in 1991 however evidence suggests it may have started as early as 1984. with secret criminally illegal injections of illegal silicone in my face to alter my bio-metric features, which is a major element in their initial defamation of me as someone else's daughter.

Once that had finished physically mutilating and deforming me they started on falsifying a criminal record and mental illness record to compliment their 1989 paperback they republished in 2001 and 2012 where two-governments[43] created a television mini series about the 1989 paperback they sold as "true crime" which reads like a verb rather than a noun.

I thank you as I'm certain all future generations of humans thank you. We all thank you so much to Australia's departments of the Attorney-Generals; departments of police; departments of health; and South Australia's department of transport. There are too many of you perfect idiots to name individually without your criminal involvement I simply would not have had any evidence against you. Thank you from the bottom of my heart. I love having impeccable integrity, to be able to prove government public officers and their Freemason comrades are eitherıcompulsive sycophantic liars, so psychopathically[44] amoral as expert corporate thieves and **trixie publisher hobbitses** and sneaky medical confidence tricksters, or perverting judicial Justice terrorist's plants, that they possess no fear whatsoever of criminal accountability for their acts of political or ideological terrorism for their causes, because Australia's police departments are among their numbers.

I'm an exact opposite. Perfectly mentally balanced, legally and ethically squeaky clean — always have been. Guess that's why this large family of terrorists have become fixated on me as their obsession. My proverbial shoulders are broad enough to take them all on according to Australian law. Like Mahatma Gandhi wrote in his autobiography: 'While they're picking on me they're leaving someone else alone.'

Don't be mistaken, don't be misled — this set of "**they**" are not your garden variety bullies. They're harboring something else fare more sinister. Their smear campaign isn't just targeted at me its a custom of practice that is an already established and recognizable state of mind that's been mildly described by Boston Globe in United States of America as a "phenomenon". It can't be said that cause and explanation of men raping children is in question. That's an absurd opinion based of no logic whatsoever. All through recorded time men have possessed the mental state of mind of a barbarian. A lustful

---

[43] *Two governments: Commonwealth of Australia and the State of New South Wales.*

[44] *Humans are humane; psychopaths are not humane therefore, not human.*

greedy person intent on gaining power and wealth by stealing everything that belongs to someone else. That's the root cause of pedophilia in this the 21st century. This matter is larger than the global rape cover-up by the Catholic Archdiocese. Its the global child rape cover-up by the terrorist network known as Freemasons and Governments who turn a blind eye to Freemason child rape and murder off police officers (plural) one when giving his eye-witness evidence of Freemason police child rape and murder.

People are still in the Barbarian Era where they will remain until they no longer desire to control someone else's child. Australian police are liars. Our parliaments expect them to lie. All of our government public officers are liars. Their documents prove that. Their police are armed terrorists. Our elected political-party parliaments and executive pretend they're running a lawful democracy when in reality they're secretly dismantling it slowly but surely enacting unconstitutional laws to nullify natural and legal rights of Australian citizens and residents not politically or Freemason associated naturally I refer to the Australia Act 1986 enacted by the 34th federal parliament which illegally altered our constitution without a referendum blocking our constitutional right of appeal the out British monarch from an illegal decision of our judiciary who are becoming increasingly overtly political terrorist aligned.

They openly went at so called "outlaw bikers' because they knew most public would be biased against that type of shabbily dressed fringe group, shielding well groomed Freemason terrorists in police departments from accountability for murder and child rape. Australia's political parties and global Freemasons network have always been more prevalently secretly criminal than any motorcycle club on this warring planet.

Only way to fight Terrorist Governments is by lawful use of a courtroom as opposed to the Star Chambers they lead me into as a self representing litigant, taxpayer funded terrorists. Evidently in Australia access to public services and your basic legal rights depends on your 'likability' — its a popularity contest run by pederasts, pedophiles, misogynists, and other psychopathic political activists. ♉

French Letters

These are evidence, letters, departmental and political being my attempts to resolve the matter of SIMPSON & HARVEY's 'Brothers In Arms' paperback when I realized it was still being published in 2001 with my biometric identity as fake dead fake Leanne. The letters end with Commissioner's office illegally outlawing me in 2003; my failed attempted to sue the department with either Sydney's terrorist sympathizers dominating our legal industry, or NSW police illegally intercepting my mail and telephone services to illegally (criminally) impersonating NSW lawyers so they could pervert the course of justice and due administration of law in the evidence of five murders:

1. My family friend and Freemason Jack BASSET (retired police officer.)

2. Olive BUNDOCH (my elderly maternal grandmother.)

3. The fake Leanne WALTERS.

4. Comanchero (Robert LANE my neighbour Bob MAHER The Oaks NSW.)

5. Bandido (Anthony SPENCER my de-facto Owen HALLThe Oaks NSW.)

Winter of 1994 three Campbelltown NSW police two in full uniform, had falsely imprisoned me (*at gunpoint*) in a public place (*Campbelltown Catholic Club during my Toastmaster's meeting*) to falsely accusing me of "*being*" Leanne WALTERS and "*faking my death on 2 September 1984*". The detective was waving a copy of SIMPSON & HARVEY's BIA paperback at me as his 'evidence in chief'. I grew up in Campbelltown from 1962, lived with my parents and siblings. I was East Campbelltown State Primary School student (1962 to 1968) I was Campbelltown State High School student (1969 to 1972) I was employed at Government Insurance Office of NSW in Elizabeth Street Sydney from November 1972. I was employed at the Carrington Street Sydney Department of Social Security office in 1973. I attained my Provisional Drivers License at Campbelltown RTA motor registry, corner of Lindsay and Sturt Streets in August 1973. My male parent was a Master Mason from 1973 all Campbelltown police knew me only because they were also Freemasons. Was obvious in winter of 1994 event that these three police officers were either incredibly stupid or intended to falsely defame me. I was led to believe they'd cause the withdrawal of SIMPSON & HARVEY's BIA. Evidently there was no intent for that. The detective in that winter of 1994 event is named in SIMPSON & HARVEY's BIA as **Detective Sergeant Paul**

SHIELDS from Bass Hill NSW police station.

OBSERVATION OF OUR MODERN ERA

In Australia on average people are by far wealthier than they were 400 years ago. When a community is mostly impoverished they band together to improve their conditions. When a community is mostly well off relatively speaking they band together to keep when they've gained. As it appears from these examples of politicians letters, the more illegal the situation the greater benefit is gained by the "team players" and the greedier they become. Recently a female Labor Party parliamentarian Fatima PAYMAN was *"indefinitely suspended from the Labor caucus*[45]*."* That situation proves that there is no democratic process in that parliament. Caucus by basic definition is totalitarian not democratic. Fatima PAYMAN was elected to represent the people in her area in parliament not the Labor party. If a political party is elected into parliament not the person, then the political party don't need any people in parliament they only need one Ficus tree for each political party and a telephone connection to the computer recording the political party's caucus decisions on issues before parliament put by the various political parties. *Interfering with any elected person's conscious decision is no different to witness tampering or industrial sabotage or brainwashing.* Where Parliament or Council caucus meetings exist under threat of retaliation by that organized caucus group for failure to agree to caucus decision/s — then democracy cannot exist. *Individuals give effect to democracy, groups give effect to mob rule.* Most obviously there is no democratic parliament in Australia — or anywhere else on this planet if there were we'd all be living in harmonious peace without need for police.

ISRAEL V PALESTINE OR AUSTRALIA V PALESTINE

For the record, I'm 100% against any war or warlike physical conflict.

I don't profess to 'know' anything about the conflict in the Gaza Strip region other than it has its roots in religion. I do know these set if facts:

★ BCE (before birth of Jesus) old Hebrew history text calls people descendent from Jacob, Israelites occupying ancient Israel.

★ Christian Bible originally Hebrew text translated to many languages.

★ Christian Bible says Jesus was a Jew.

★ For about 1K years we base our dates on birth of same Jewish Jesus.

★ Therefore logically Christianity is an arm of Judaism (Jewish).

---

[45] *www.smh.com.au 30 June 2024 (Palestine Australia crisis).*

BROTHERS IN ARMS BIKIE WARS SIMPSON & HARVEY FREEMASON LIES — ISBN 9780645597578

★ Britain's Australia begin with Christian laws.

★ Christian's Ten Commandments are basis of Australia's laws.

★ Many Freemasons claim to be Christian despite that Catholic Pope declared Freemasonry inconsistent with Christianity.

★ Christian allies went to war against Germany for Genocide of Jews.

★ Christian countries support Freemason cults despite that they're organized terrorists..

★ Israel is a Jewish State.

★ Israel's government won't recognize Palestine as a separate State.

★ Australia's government won't recognize Palestine as a State.

Therefore, logically, Christian Australia is also secretly a Freemason and a Jewish Australia — dominated or controlled by Freemasonry and Judaism.

What other reason is there that Australia's Labor and Liberal Party governments won't recognize Palestine in their own right? We're 21,458 kilometers apart[46]. Australia has no other causal link.

I don't think the majority of people in Australia believe they knew they had ever voted to be a part of a Freemason Jewish State.

Australia's Constitution says parliament can't legislate on religion[47]. The intent of that section is to prevent Parliament from making any decisions in parliament whatsoever (not limited to laws) based on any religion whatsoever. Refusing to acknowledge Siding with **intensely religious** Israel against Palestine is effectively making decision/s based on religion.

I might add that Australia's recent federal parliaments (plural) have infringed the federal Constitution more times than their parliamentarians have changed their underpants, not limited to **unconstitutional observance of Christmas and Easter** (s116) or their constitutional **Australia Act 1986**.

If there is to be national holiday for Christians then there is also to be national holiday for all religious events — or none at all. ☿

---

[46] *Google result by aeroplane British Australian, Airplane USA & others.*

[47] *Commonwealth of Australia Constitution Act. section 116. Commonwealth not to legislate in respect of religion: The Commonwealth shall not make any law for establishing any religion, or for imposing any religious observance, or for prohibiting the free exercise of any religion, and no religious test shall be required as a qualification for any office or public trust under the Commonwealth.*

1: Removed from the 2012 BIA BIKIE WARS reprint of SIMPSON & HARVEY's BIA these tweo matters: **First** reference to police necktie competition & formal dinner on anniversary of Milperra murders. I suggest "necktie" reference to faking 1985 Tony SPENCER Bandid prison hanging suicide. **Second** below, Kezra LORENZ's federal Arts grant 1999-2000 & film script BIA boasted she's written between 1984 & 1989. I'd made issue in my websites on both. My 'issue' Government happy to fund everything else about matter except my irrefutable proof potentially **3 were police falsified**. Disgusting disregard for human life when others had truly died.

Criminally Concealed Political Bribe

Right: 1989 and 2001 published Simpson & Harvey's Allen & Unwin paperback named "Brothers In Arms The Inside Story of Two Bikie Gangs" credited Kezra Lorenz for writing a screen play about her husbands crimes (proceeds of crime law prohibits profit from family crime).

Below: 1999 Federal government political entities pay Kezra Lorenz $2,000 for writing her 1980s screen play. Evidence it is a criminal bribe is gleaned from fact this detail was removed from the third publication in 2012 when Australia's Federal and NSW State governments joint funded a TV mini series about same 3 books, calling third book BIKIE WARS Brothers In Arms.

Comancheros Ian White and Glen Eaves are also appearing against their murder convictions and sentences. Their hearing is listed for March 1989.

Kezra Lorenz is divorced from Rick (Chewy) Lorenz and now lives in London where she has written a film script about her life with a Comanchero.

Chief Superintendent Ronald Harry Stephenson was awarded the Commissioner's commendation at the Goulburn Police Academy in NSW on 7 August 1987, in recognition of outstanding leadership and command of police resources concerned with the investigation of the Father's Day Massacre at Milperra on 2 September 1984. Detective Superintendent Stephenson showed ability in controlling and co-ordinating this inquiry, greatly contributing to the successful outcome of this matter which brought considerable merit to the NSW police force, the Commissioner said.

Same books the same governments knowingly falsely ID Janette Francis' 28 year old face as bikie gang murdered Leanne Walters aged 15

janettefraNCIS.com

Appendix 7

INDUSTRY ASSISTANCE

Australian Film Commission Annual Report 1999/2000

Title	Applicant	1999/2000	Future Years	Type*
FILM DEVELOPMENT				
FEATURES – PROJECT				
28 Stops At The Heartland	Andrew Bovell		30 000	I
Archangel	Roxy Films Pty Ltd	4 700		I
Bait	Jacquie Flecknoe-Brown	300		I
The Belly Of A Whale	RB Films Pty Ltd	10 000		I
Beneath Clouds	Teresa-Jayne Hanlon	14 000		I
Black Magic	Screentime Kuranya Pty Ltd	12 800		I
Blue Woman	Coalface Communications Pty Ltd and Jotz Productions Pty Ltd	16 400		I
Bright Futures	Huzzah Productions Pty Ltd	3 500		I
Brothers At War	Richard Bradley Productions Pty Ltd	4 200		I
Bugsly	Charles Doane and Fleur Films Pty Ltd	11 000	5 000	I
Cap N' Tag	CAAMA Productions Pty Ltd	10 000	4 000	I
Catching The Wind	Sasha Hadden	17 200	1 000	I
Caught In The Crossfire	**Kezra Southby-Lorenz**	**2 000**		I
Charging The Guns	December Films Pty Ltd	6 200		I
Chasing The Moon	Oracle Pictures Pty Ltd	2 800		I

*Note: Funding Types are I = Investments, L = Loans, G = Grants, S = Special AFC Initiative

Police keep watch as shoppers line up for toilet paper in a Sydney

2 – New South Wales police are budgeted to stand guard over rolls of toilet paper in Sydney supermarkets during early COVID pandemic panic buying but there's never been funds to investigate the brutal Freemason police murder by police, of senior retired (honest) police officer Jack BASSET in my presence, that police insist was suicide, and associated theft of my identity and my dozens of evidenced physical 'surgical rape mutilations' presently violently enforced on me by Australia's parliamentarians and their **Gestapo-styled Tripartizan** political party police and news industry.

3: **NEXT PAGE registered post receipt**: Sent to (above) SLOWMAN sisters UNWIN terrorist family publishing corporation which is a front for organized political & ideological terrorism in Australia. Date stamped August 8, 2001 registered mail receipt is evidence both were sent by Cessnock post office itself who used to take possession of all registered letters, to Allen and Unwin publishers and other NSW Ombudsman. **Out of pocket Au$18.20, before yellow post boxes.**

4: **August 7, 2001 first outgoing to** publishers **no response ever** received.

07–August–2001 {1}

J G Hall
Po Box 1163
NEWCASTLE NSW 2300
mob: 0401-223-661

Simone Ford
Allen & Unwin
83 Alexander St
CROWS NEST NSW 2065

FILE COPY

Dear Ms Ford,

RE: "Brothers In Arms" by Lindsay Simpson and Sandra Harvey, 1989 and 2001.

I write to confirm my initial contact with Claire Murdock last week and our brief meeting today. I note that I informed you a photograph of myself appears in the publication, claiming to be a photo of a deceased female, Leanne Walters and that you informed me that your inquiries with the author Ms Harvey revealed "the photograph was provided by the police and identified by the police" as being the deceased.

As per our discussion I request confirmation in writing by the author/s as to how the photograph came into their possession. I would also be interested in a meeting with Sandra and Lindsay to discuss the issue further.

Under the circumstances I also request that any further production of the book is ceased immediately and that all copies are recalled from sale.

An early response would be appreciated.

Yours sincerely,

Janette HALL

NB No reply was rec'd to this letter by 2.8.02

5: **August 7, 2001 first outgoing to Attorney-General Coroner p1 of 2.**

07-August-2001 {1} J G Hall
Po Box 1163
NEWCASTLE NSW 2300
mob: 0401-223-661

State Coroner
State Coroners Office
44 - 46 Parramatta Road
GLEBE NSW 2037

FILE COPY

URGENT ATTENTION

Dear Sir,

RE: Leanne Walters, (deceased, Milperra Sept 2, 1984) - request for an inquiry.

Recently I purchased a copy of a book titled Brothers In Arms. This regards the killing of seven people at the Viking Tavern at Milperra on Sunday 2nd September 1984.

Within this book is a photo which claims to be of Leanne Walters, one of the persons killed I contacted the publishers of the book, Allen & Unwin who have since advised me that the authors Ms Harvey claimed the photograph was supplied by the police and identified by the police as being Ms Leanne Walters.

My recent contact with police has resulted in verbal confirmation that the photo the police have on file is the same photo

However. **The photograph** is **NOT Leanne Walters** The photograph is actually of me. I have never had any involvement with any motorcycle group at any time The writing on the 'sex licence' attached to the photo is NOT my writing

Apart from the obvious damage this publication has caused me.
My very real concern is that there is a young woman lying in that grave who is *not* Ms Walters, and *her* family is desperately waiting for news of their missing daughter

I knew a Leanne Walters in 1984. I worked with her at the office of Visyboard Warwick Farm I recall the day that photo was taken, Leanne was with me. I was told by my co-

6: August 7, 2001 first outgoing to Attorney-General Coroner p2 of 2.

workers that Leanne was killed during this incident in 1984.

I recollect seeing a photo briefly on the TV claiming to be the deceased woman however I didn't recognise her as the Leanne I knew

However I thought they (co-workers) must have been mistaken as I had seen and spoken to the Leanne Walters I knew on 9th October 1984, after the incident

I went on with my life and gave the incident no further thought until recently when I came across a copy of the publication

Under the circumstances as I have briefly outlined I request an inquiry into the matter and would anticipate that you would order an exhumation and genetic test of the deceased There may also be a scientific method to measure my face to match the photo However, I still look the same, save the passage of time

The confusion surrounding my photo and the police identification of the deceased begs many questions. The family of the deceased has a right to know the truth.

Yours sincerely,

Janette HALL

7: **August 7, 2001 outgoing to Police Commissioner RYAN.**

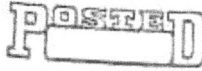

07-August-2001   {1}   J G Hall
                                                                      Po Box 1163
                                                               NEWCASTLE NSW 2300
                                                               mob: 0401-223-661

Peter Ryan
Commissioner of Police
Police Department Head Office   **FILE COPY**
College Street
SYDNEY NSW 2000

                              URGENT ATTENTION

Dear Commissioner Ryan,

RE: Fathers Day murders 2 September 1984 - Milperra - Leanne Walters

I believe there had been a mistake by the police in the identification of a deceased person, Leanne Walters, claimed to have been killed in the Viking Tavern shootings in Milperra on 2nd September, 1984.

Allen & Unwin have published a book "Brothers in Arms" in that book is a photo claiming to be Leanne Walters. **The photograph** is **NOT Leanne Walters**. The photo is of myself. I have never had any involvement with any motorcycle group at any time. The writing on the 'sex licence' attached to the photo is NOT my writing.

The publishers claim that the police provided them with the photo. My enquiries with police confirmed that the same photo is on police file as being Leanne Walters.

I request an urgent inquiry to determine the facts. I stress that this situation has caused me a great deal of distress and would appreciate full co-operation from you and your staff to resolve the matter without delay.

Yours sincerely,

J HALL

8: August 21, 2001 from Coroner's Court. Reasonable initial response.

WESTMEAD CORONER'S COURT

NSW ATTORNEY GENERAL'S DEPARTMENT

RECEIVED
2 1 AUG 2001

Institute Rd, Westmead NSW 2145
Box 106, Westmead NSW 2145

Tel: (02) 9633 8000 · Fax: (02) 9633 8080

Office Hours: 9.30am - 1.00pm and 2 00pm - 4 00pm

Ms J G Hall
PO Box 1163
NEWCASTLE 2300

Our ref: 893/1994

Dear Ms. Hall,

Death of Leanne Walters

I acknowledge receipt of your letter of 7th August, 2001 raising issues surrounding the death of Leanne Walters at Milperra on 2nd September, 1984. Your letter has been referred from the State Coroners Court to this office for attention.

I intend to discuss the contents of your letter with the Senior Deputy State Coroner to determine the nature of any further action that should be taken in relation to the issues raised by you. I will provide you with further advice as soon as possible.

Yours faithfully,

(Noel Drew)
Clerk of the Court
WESTMEAD
21st August, 2001

9: August 30, 2001 from Attorney-General Coroner's office. NSW State Parliament say there was an election on Thursday 6 Sept 2001 elections are never on a weekday. Therefore parliament are in a **state of perpetual lie.**

WESTMEAD CORONER'S COURT

NSW ATTORNEY GENERAL'S DEPARTMENT

Institute Rd, Westmead NSW 2145
Box 106, Westmead NSW 2145

Tel: (02) 9633 8000 · Fax: (02) 9633 8080

Office Hours: 9.30am - 1.00pm and 2.00pm - 4.00pm

Ms J Hall
PO Box 1163
NEWCASTLE 2300

Our ref: 893/1984

Dear Ms. Hall,

Death of Leanne Walters

I refer to our previous correspondence and advise that the Senior Deputy State Coroner has now directed police at Bass Hill to investigate the question of identification raised in your letter of 8th August, 2001 and advise this office of the results of that investigation.

I will advise you further when the police report has been received.

Yours faithfully,

(Noel Drew)
Clerk of the Court
WESTMEAD
30th August, 2001

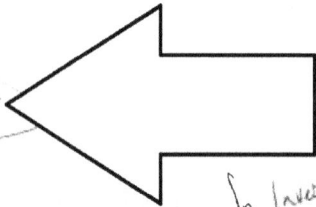

No Investigation was undertaken by the Bass Hill police. Police pulled the plug.

15.

10: **August 30, 2001 from police Commissioner's office**. NSW State Parliament say there was an election on Thursday 6 Sept 2001 elections are never on a weekday. Therefore parliament are in a **state of perpetual lie**.

NSW POLICE SERVICE

COMMISSIONER'S OFFICE

ABN 43 408 513 180

Police Headquarters
Avery Building
14-24 College Street
Darlinghurst NSW 20˙0
Box 45 GPO Sydney 2001

Ph: 9339 5011 / 5501˙
Fx: 9339 5471 / 5547˙
TTY: 9211 3776

Ref: NSWP/D/200./123640

30 August 2001

Mr/Ms J G Hall
P O Box 1163
NEWCASTLE NSW 2300

Dear Sir/Madam

On behalf of Commissioner Ryan, I am writing to acknowledge receipt of your recent letter concerning the death of Ms Leanne Walters, claimed to have been killed in the Viking Tavern shootings at Milperra in 1984.

The matters which you have raised are being examined As soon as the necessary enquiries are complete, a further communication will be sent to you

May I thank you for bringing your concerns under notice.

Yours sincerely

Terry O'Brien
Manager-Administration
Commissioner's Support Team
for Commissioner

Only enquiries was what the Coroner's Office had done – they pulled the plug on the Coroner's DIRECTION to Bass Hill police to investigate (Ref. Westmead Coroner 30/8/01)

19.

11: **February 11, 2002 outgoing to Police Commissioner RYAN's office.**

"I refer to your letter dated 30 August 2001. Almost 6 months has passed and as yet you have not forwarded a reply to my concerns. I note that you may have a busy work schedule, however I would appreciate a reply without any further delay."

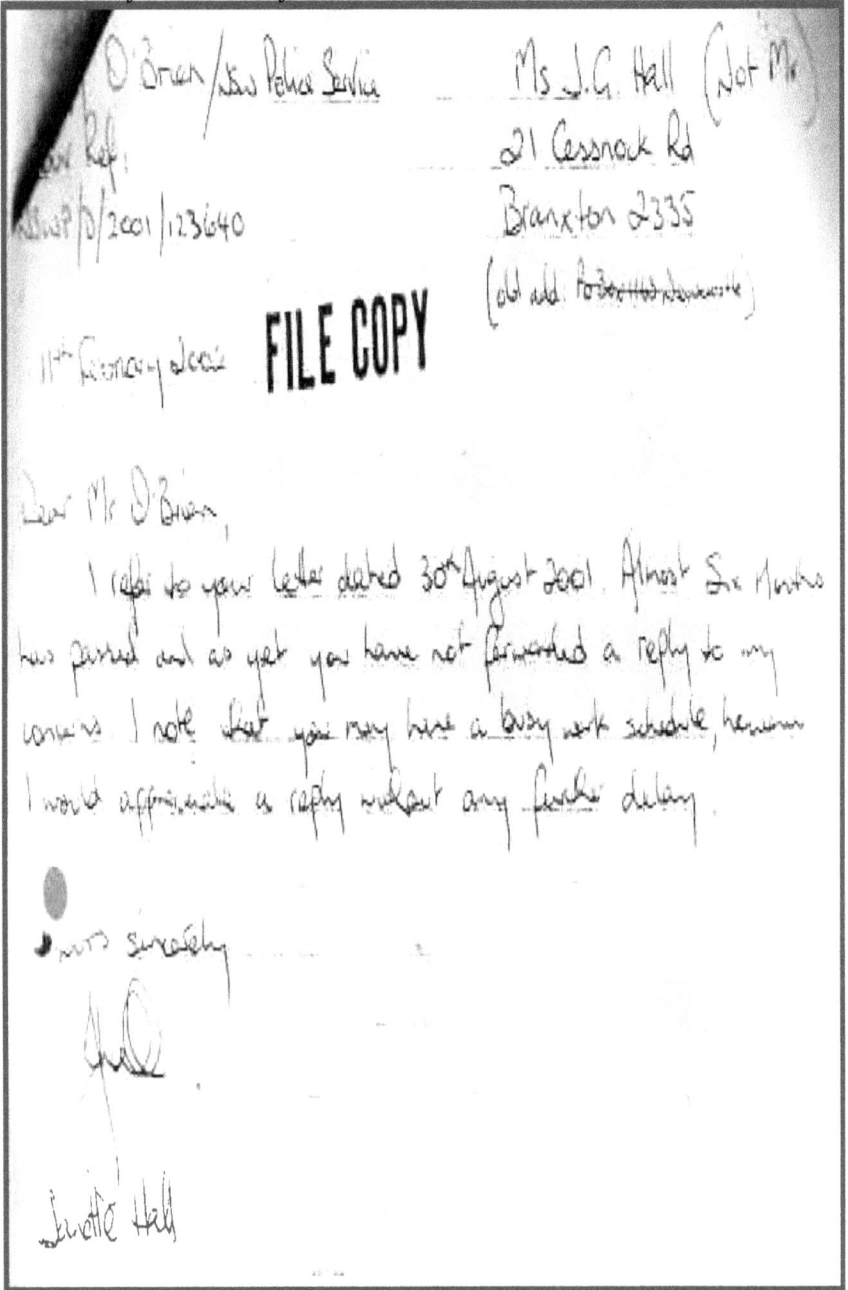

12: Feb 11, 2002 from Coroner. I wrote to police sent by snail mail from Cessnock NSW, Attorney-General's department in West Sydney supposedly receives police letter within two days and responded. As if. This is a false document probably intercepted illegally by AUSTRALIA POST FREEMASON. **Forged document from the police pursuant to ss 471.12, 143.2, 85T of The Criminal Code, Schedule, Criminal Code Act 1995 (Cth).**

WESTMEAD CORONER'S COURT

NSW ATTORNEY GENERAL'S DEPARTMENT

Institute Rd, Westmead NSW 2145
Box 106, Westmead NSW 2145

Tel: (02) 9633 8000 - Fax: (02) 9633 8080

Office Hours: 9.30am - 1.00pm and 2.00pm - 4.00pm

Ms J Hall
21 Cessnock Road   Our ref: 893/1984
BRANXTON NSW   2335

Dear Ms. Hall,

I refer to your letter of 11th February, 2002 and advise that I have not yet received a response from Bass Hill police in relation to the issues you raised in your letter of 7th August, 2001. I will send a reminder in an effort to determine if any action has been taken to clarify the issues raised by you.

I am in a position to inform you that the deceased girl, Leanne Walters (aged 14 years) was identified by a person who had known her for five years and that she had been residing at the premises of that person for at least three months. There does not appear to be any reason to believe that her body was incorrectly identified.

That being the case, it would appear that your concerns are matters to be addressed by the authors of the book you refer to, and by the police if the photograph they have on file is not of the deceased girl.

Yours faithfully,

(Noel Drew)
Clerk of the Court
WESTMEAD
13th February, 2002

13: February 22, 2001 from NSW police Commissioner's Office. Referring to the letter the Coroner answered mistakenly. **Another forged document from the police pursuant to ss 471.12, 143.2, 85T of The Criminal Code, Schedule, Criminal Code Act 1995 (Cth).**

NSW POLICE SERVICE

COMMISSIONER'S OFFICE

Police Headquarters
Avery Building
14-24 College Street
Darlinghurst NSW 2010
Box 45 GPO Sydney 2001

Tel: (02) 9339 5011 / 55011
Fax: (02) 9339 5471 / 55471

Ref: NSWP/D/2001/12 3640-002

22 February 2002

Ms J G Hall
21 Cessnock Road
BRANXTON NSW 2335

Dear Ms Hall

I have your recent letter concerning your previous correspondence pertaining to the Viking Tavern shootings at Milperra in 1984 and the death of Leanne Walters

May I apologise that you have not received a final response in regard to your concerns. I am arranging for an urgent follow up to be sent to the area of the Service concerned. As soon as this advice is received, a further communication will be forwarded to you

Thank you for writing and for the courtesy shown in your letter

Yours sincerely

Terry O'Brien
Executive Officer
Commissioner's Secretariat
for Commissioner Ryan

14: March 7, 2001 allegedly from Attorney-General's Coroner. Another forged document from the police pursuant to ss 471.12, 143.2, 85T of The Criminal Code, Schedule, Criminal Code Act 1995 (Cth).

WESTMEAD CORONER'S COURT

NSW ATTORNEY GENERAL'S DEPARTMENT

Institute Rd, Westmead NSW 2145
Box 106, Westmead NSW 2145

Tel: (02) 9633 8000 - Fax: (02) 9633 8080

Office Hours: 9 30am - 1 00pm and 2 00pm - 4 00pm

Ms J Hall
21 Cessnock Road
BRANXTON　NSW　2335

Our ref: 893/1984

Dear Ms. Hall,

I refer to your letter of 7th August, 2001 and subsequent correspondence in relation to issues raised in that letter and advise that inquiries relating to the identification of the body of a female person who died in a shooting incident that occurred at the Viking Tavern, Milperra on 2nd September, 1984 have been taken as far as they can be from this office.

I confirm advice provided in my letter of 13th February, 2002 that the deceased was identified as Leanne Walters (aged 14 years) by a person with whom she was residing and had known for five years. The postmortem report describes a "female child whose appearance is consistent with the stated age". Advice obtained from the Registrar of Births, Deaths & Marriages confirms that the informant for the registration of her death was her mother (Mrs P Walters).

I have not been able to identify any evidence which would raise concern that the identification of her body was flawed. Again, as I pointed out in my letter of 13th February, 2002, the use of a photograph which you believe is of yourself, is a matter you should take up with the publishers of the book in which it was reproducted.

Yours faithfully,

(Neal Drew)
Clerk of the Court
WESTMEAD
7th March, 2002

15: **March 12, 2001 from Commissioner's Office last before he resigned. Another** forged document from the police pursuant to ss 471.12, 143.2, 85T Criminal Code, Schedule, Criminal Code Act 1995 (Cth).

NSW POLICE SERVICE

COMMISSIONER'S OFFICE

ABN 43 408 613 180

12 March 2002

Mrs J G Hall
21 Cessnock Road
BRANXTON   NSW   2325

Police Headquarters
Avery Building
14-24 College Street
Darlinghurst NSW 2010
Box 45 GPO Sydney 2001

Ph: 9339 5011 / 55011
Fx: 9339 5471 / 55471
TTY: 9211 3776 (Hearing/Speech impaired only)

Ref: NSWP|D|2002|46024

Dear Mrs Hall

I refer to our previous correspondence regarding the Viking Tavern shootings at Milperra in 1984 and the death of Leanne Walters.

I followed up your concerns in respect of an aspect of this matter I am now advised that the matter was raised with the Coroner's Court at Westmead. I am informed that since then, the Westmead Coroner's Court has communicated with you advising its position in respect of the issue mentioned.

In light of the advice provided by the Coroner's Court, I believe that to be the final position and we have therefore closed our file on this matter

I trust that I have been of assistance to you in respect of your concerns

Yours sincerely

Terry O'Brien
Manager-Administration
Commissioner's Secretariat
for Commissioner of Police

16: RECAPPING I was living near Newcastle. Terrorist Michael COSTA is from Newcastle. As soon as he was elected in 2001 *after* I wrote to Police Commissioner he was appointed Police Minister with no experience in police operations (unless he's a convicted criminal.) Newcastle police refused to investigate my allegation of this matter as a crime. Evidence says terrorist Minister COSTA had Commissioner RYAN removed to silence me on this 1984 LABOR & FREEMASON *two parliament* organized crime.

PARLIAMENT OF
NEW SOUTH WALES

Enter Keyword(s) **Terrorist**   GO

Contact us

LIVE	LEGISLATIVE ASSEMBLY	LIVE	COMMITTEES	LIVE	LEGISLATIVE COUNCIL
ABOUT PARLIAMENT	MEMBERS	BILLS	HANSARD & HOUSE PAPERS	RESEARCH PAPERS	VISIT EDUCATION

Home > Members

Mr Michael COSTA (1956 -)
Place of Birth: Newcastle, NSW Australia

Position	Start	End	Period
Deputy Leader of the Government in the Legislative Council	30 Mar 2007	05 Sep 2008	1 year 5 months 7 days
Treasurer	17 Feb 2006	05 Sep 2008	2 years 6 months 20 days
Minister for Finance	03 Aug 2005	17 Feb 2006	6 months 15 days
Minister for Infrastructure	03 Aug 2005	05 Sep 2008	3 years 1 month 3 days
Minister for Ports and Waterways	03 Aug 2005	10 Aug 2005	8 days
Deputy Leader of the Government in the Legislative Council	01 Feb 2005	02 Mar 2007	2 years 1 month 2 days
Minister for Economic Reform	21 Jan 2005	03 Aug 2005	6 months 14 days
Minister for Ports	21 Jan 2005	03 Aug 2005	6 months 14 days
Minister for Roads	21 Jan 2005	03 Aug 2005	6 months 14 days
Minister Assisting the Minister for State Development	05 Aug 2004	21 Jan 2005	5 months 17 days
Minister Assisting the Minister for Natural Resources (Forests)	02 Apr 2003	01 Jul 2004	1 year 3 months
Minister for the Hunter	02 Apr 2003	05 Sep 2008	5 years 5 months 4 days
Minister for Transport Services	02 Apr 2003	21 Jan 2005	1 year 9 months 20 days
Minister for Police	21 Nov 2001	02 Apr 2003	1 year 4 months 13 days
Member of the NSW Legislative Council	06 Sep 2001	23 Sep 2008	7 years 18 days

ELECTED 6 SEP 2001
Police Minister
FROM 21 NOV 2001

17:'smoking gun' terrorist sisters authored this false document they claim is "true crime" the book is the true crime reinforcing the 1984 terrorist action

Lindsay Simpson and Sandra Harvey have written two other bestselling books, *My Husband, My Killer* (1992) and *The Killer Next Door* (1994). Lindsay is an ex-journalist and the author of *The Australian Geographic Guide to Tasmania* (1997) and *To Have and To Hold* with Walter Mikac (1997). She is currently the coordinator of Journalism and Media Studies at the University of Tasmania.

After collaborating with Lindsay, Sandra Harvey's first solo effort, *The Ghost of Ludwig Gertsch*, was published in 2000. Sandra is a former journalist for the *Sydney Morning Herald* and is currently senior media adviser to the NSW Minister for Police.

adviser to
NSW Minister
for Police

NSW Minister for Police.

18: Sue WILLIAMS another UK terrorist author imported for FREEMASON terrorist cause — book *published 3 months before* RYAN was squeezed out

Peter Ryan the Inside Story Paperback

by Sue Williams (Author)

5.0 ★★★★★   1 rating

— Import, January 1, 2002

Paperback
$18.42

Other Used from $14.43

Product details

Publisher : Viking, First Edition (January 1, 2002)
Language : English
Paperback : 356 pages
ISBN-10 : 0670040770
ISBN-13 : 978-0670040773
Item Weight : 1.15 pounds

Buy used: $18.42

$18.99 delivery April 4 - 16. Details

Deliver to Sweden

Used: Very Good | Details
Sold by Behamot Media

Length	Language	Publisher	Publication date	ISBN-10
356 Pages	EN English	Viking	2002 January 1	0670040770

Add to Cart

Add to List

Sue Williams

Sue Williams is an award-winning journalist and columnist who's written for all of Australia's leading newspapers and magazines, as well as having her own opinion segment on a TV show. Born in England, she has also worked in print and TV in the UK and New Zealand and spent many years travelling extensively around the world

She has written a number of best-selling biographies, including Mean Streets, Kind Heart; The Father Chris Riley Story, on the Catholic priest who's dedicated his life to helping streetkids, Peter Ryan: The Inside Story on the controversial former NSW Police Commissioner, and Father Bob about Australia's highest profile campaigner for social justice

Despite being a confirmed city-slicker, she's also written four immensely popular books about the Australian Outback. Her most recent is Heroines of the Outback, while the previous in the series was a travel book about her own personal adventures exploring the Outback, which included a fight in an Outback boxing tent, a cattle drive - her first time on horseback - and a trek through one of the most remote stretches of wilderness in the world.

Her first travel book was Getting There: Journeys of an Accidental Adventurer, about her time travelling the world alone with a backpack

Crime-writing is also a passion, and she wrote And Then The Darkness about the Peter Falconio killing, a book that was short-listed for the best true-crime book of the year in the international Gold Dagger Awards. In 2013, she wrote Left For Dead, about a policewoman's heart-wrenching fight for life after a brutal attack.

Other books include Love, Obsession, Secrets & Lies, Death of a Doctor, a motivational women's health guide, Powering Up, and Apartment Living: The Complete Guide to Buying, Renting, Surviving and Thriving in Apartments.

Used (3) from $14.43

amazon book clubs
early access

See Clubs

Not in a club? Learn more

© 1996-2024 Amazon.com, Inc. or its affiliates

Viking Press (formally **Viking Penguin**, also listed as **Viking Books**) is an American publishing company owned by Penguin Random House. It was founded in New York City on March 1, 1925, by Harold K. Guinzburg and George S. Oppenheimer[1] and then acquired by the Penguin Group in 1975.[2][3]

Imprints   [edit]

* Viking Kestrel
* Viking Adult, who got in legal trouble in 1946 due to John Steinbeck's bold eulogy, and fell out of public favor in 1947[clarification needed]
* Viking children's Books
* Viking Portable Library
* Pamela Dorman Books

WIKIPEDIA
The Free Encyclopedia

Viking Children's   [edit]

In 1933, Viking Press founded a department called Junior Books to publish children's books. The first book published was The Story About Ping in 1933 under editor May Massee. Junior Books was later renamed Viking Children's Books. Viking Kestrel was one of its imprints.

Its books have won the Newbery and Caldecott Medals, and include such books as The Twenty-One Balloons, written and illustrated by William Pene du Bois (1947, Newbery medal winner for 1948), Corduroy, Make Way for Ducklings, The Stinky Cheese Man by Jon Scieszka and Lane Smith (1993), The Outsiders, Pippi Longstocking, and The Story of Ferdinand. Its paperbacks are now published by Puffin Books, which includes the Speak and Firebird imprints. In 2023, Tamar Brazis was named v-p and publisher of Viking Children's Books.[4]

Viking Critical Library   [edit]

The **Viking Critical Library** offers academic editions of literary texts. Like W. W. Norton's Norton Critical Editions, all titles print the text alongside a selection of critical essays and contextual documents (including relevant extracts from the author's oeuvre). The series, which only saw sporadic publications in the late '70s and late '90s, has been dormant since 1998, with no new titles released since then. However, a number of existing titles remain in print.

Titles

Viking Press

Parent company	Penguin Random House
Status	Active
Founded	1925; 99 years ago
Founders	Harold K. Guinzburg, George Oppenheimer
Country of origin	United States
Headquarters location	New York City
Key people	President-Brian Tart, Children's publisher Kenneth Wright
Imprints	Viking Kestrel, Viking Adult, Viking Children's Books, Viking Portable Library
Official website	penguin.com/vikingbooks

19: Its no coincidence this "Sue Williams" Viking published her poison pen novel, secretly boasting Commissioner Peter Ryan was squeezed out because Freemason police falsified 1984 murder evidence in Viking Tavern car park for their Tripartizan cult (Freemasons Labor & Liberal).

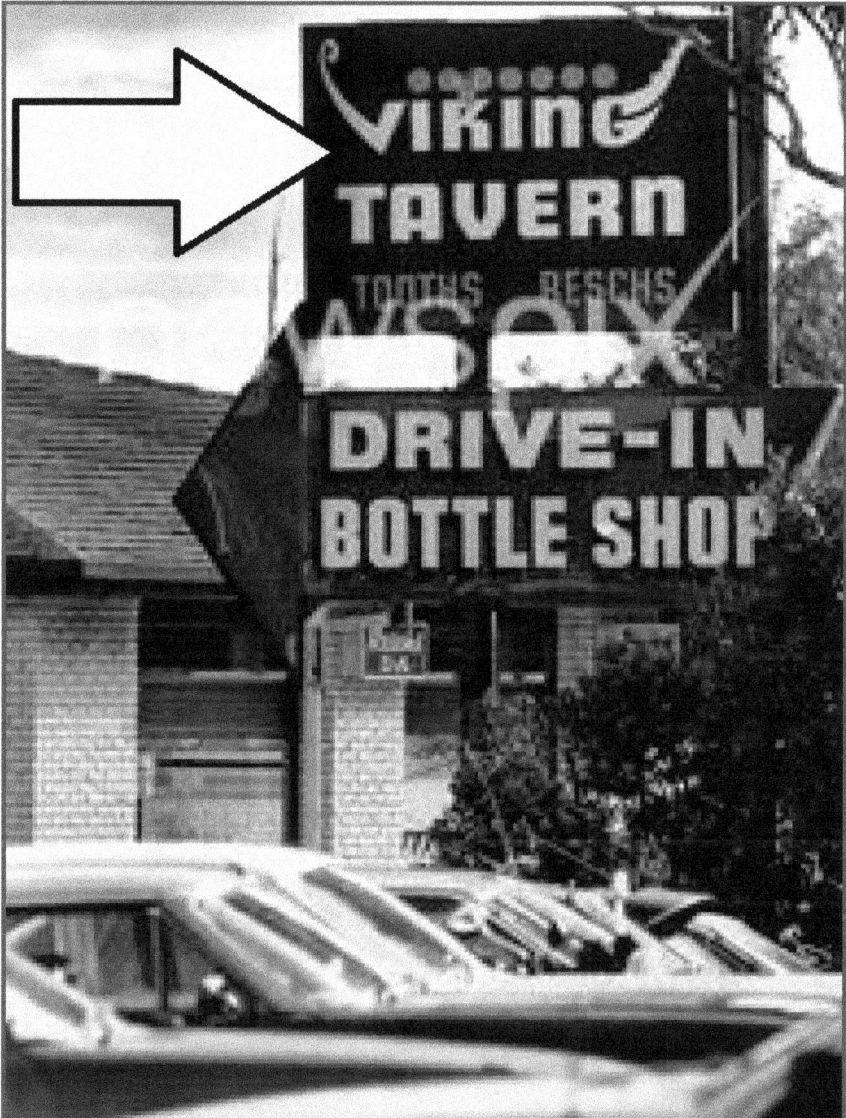

SEPTEMBER 2, 1984: SYDNEY, NSW.
SIGN FOR THE...
By News Ltd
02 September, 1984

20: **August 2, 2002 outgoing letter in person to Freemason police terrorist known as Rex John WALTERS of Ingleburn New South Wales.**

Friday, 2 August 2002   {1}   Mrs J Hall
                                                                 Po Box 1373
                                                      GOULBURN NSW 2580

Mr Rex Walters   *Delivered by hand*
44 Delaunay Street   *in person - He wrote his name +*
INGLEBURN NSW 2565   *phone number on the folder*
                                  I had with me.
                  WITHOUT PREJUDICE

Dear Mr Walters,

I do apologise for any distress this may cause you. I have a problem which surrounds the book, "Brothers in Arms" published by Allen & Unwin The need for me to ask you some questions makes this situation unavoidable

I came across this book only last year. The problem I have is with the photo that's labelled with Leanne's name. Its actually a photo of me. I had it taken when I was about 28. However, the handwriting on the document to which the photo is attached, isn't mine, nor did I attach the photo to the document I wasn't involved with any groups as described in the book

The publishers of the book claim that all the photos were provided by the NSW Police Department. However I have had conflicting versions from the police.

I hope you can assist me by letting me know when you first saw this photo, and if you know how the police came by this photo. Plus any further information you feel relevant. I would also appreciate a copy of, one of your photos of Leanne

I don't intend litigation against you or your family I do however hold the police responsible for not making every possible effort to absolutely ensure that they had the correct information, before releasing my photo as that of Leanne I hope you share this opinion and would appreciate your support and an early reply on this matter

Yours sincerely,

Janette\HALL

He couldn't remember when he 1st saw my photo (used in the book)
He said didn't knew how police got my photo
He didn't realise it (my photo) wasn't his daughters
He's a lying arsehole

1: Previous page: 2002-2007 Terrorist Kenny MORONEY another Police Commissioner rendered useless by terrorists culture in New South Wales police department heard about by Parliament one and all after the tabled documents from the Justice Wood Royal Commission into policing , parliament. Intentionally rendered toothless by the same culture of terrorism against citizens perpetrated by the **Tripartizan Party** Labor-Liberal-Freemason (single-minded[1]) unincorporated political Party terrorist organization of Australia. AUSSIE AUSSIE AUSSIE OUI OUI OUI for short. Means virtually same as the world war two Germany political Party, the **Nazi Party** salute to Adolph Hitler SEIG HEIL SEIG HEIL SEIG HEIL which is said by Collins Dictionary to mean "HAIL TO VICTORY". Australia's police departments nationally have even turned to black as their corporate color for police uniforms, same color that 20th century Nazi Germany's Gestapo police 'donned'.

ABC Online

Curfew for Goul

[This is the print version

Last Update: Sund

Ken Moroney says curfews will be rigorously policed. (ABC TV)

One officer has been charged with offensive behaviour and others are being investigated about an altercation.

The curfew comes amid claims of a culture of rampant sexual misconduct within the police force and at the academy.

http://www.abc.net.au/cgi-bin/common/printfriendly.pl?http://www.abc.net.au/news/newsitems/200608/s1707252.htm

---

[1] *Single-mindedness of the unincorporated Tripartizan Party if unjust enrichment of self by any illegal means at any cost to anyone else.*

21: June 13, 2002 letter from Mark STENBERG's legal firm.

MARK
STENBERG
& ASSOCIATES

S O L I C I T O R S

ABN 44 125 370 456

MARK STENBERG

OUR REF: MS\J202084

13 June, 2002

Ms J.G. Hall,
C/- P.O. Box 1373,
GOULBURN, NSW, 2580

Dear Janette,

RE: ADVICE PUBLISHER
_____

We refer to our telephone discussion with you this morning and confirm we have spoken to Mr. Michael Lee, Barrister who has perused the documentation provided by you.

Before Mr. Lee provides his written advice to you he wishes to hold a conference with you which will be held on **Friday the 5th July 2002 at 9.00am** at Mr. Lee's chambers which are located at:

Selborne Chambers,
Level 12, 174 Phillip Street,
SYDNEY, N.S.W, 2000
Tel: (02) 9232-7975

Following such consultation with Mr. Lees we would expect to receive his written advice and shall forward same as soon as it is to hand.

Yours faithfully

MARK STENBERG
& ASSOCIATES

Michael Lee
9 2327975.

FAX. (02) 9477 2485   225 PACIFIC HIGHWAY, HORNSBY, N S W. 2077 AUSTRALIA   **TELEPHONE: (02) 9477 1199**
Liability limited by the Solicitors   P.O. BOX 119, HORNSBY 1630   INTERNATIONAL: (61-2) 9477 1199
Scheme, approved under the   DX 9705 HORNSBY
Professional Standards Act 1994 (NSW)   EMAIL: lawstop@cherry.com.au

22: **July 5, 2002 from barrister Michael LEE to STENBERG** page 1of2.

MICHAEL LEE
12ᵀᴴ FLOOR
WENTWORTH CHAMBERS

5ᵗʰ July 2002

Mr. Mark Stenberg
Mark Stenberg & Associates
DX 9705 Hornsby

Dear Mr. Stenberg

~~JANETTE HALL~~

- 8 JUL 2002

I return my brief in the above matter.

As arranged I had the benefit of a lengthy conference with Mrs. Hall this morning.

It is fair to say that Mrs. Hall is agitated about a number of matters including her assertion that there has been some "conspiracy" resulting in Police inaction concerning her contention that Leanne Walters, who both the Police and the Coronial Court consider to have died in 1984, is still alive and that the publicity concerning the publication of "Brothers in Arms" had a causal effect in her being removed from public office as a Councillor.

I attempted to explain to Mrs. Hall the relevant issues, as I saw them, in considering whether the publication of which she complains is defamatory and whether any defences would be available to the publisher. Mrs. Hall was informed that not only was I required to satisfy myself that reasonable prospects existed in order to advance her case, my assessment of her case (and an forensic difficulties it presented) was relevant to a determination as to whether I would be prepared to accept it on a "speculative" basis.

180 Phillip Street Sydney NSW 2000
Phone: 9232 7975 Mobile: 0418 406 938 Fax: 9223 3710
Dx 389 Email: michaellee@12thfloor.com.au

24 : **July 5, 2002 from barrister Michael LEE to STENBERG** page 2of2.

COPY

I am afraid that I cannot reach that conclusion and return the papers. I am more than happy to expand on the reasons if you require clarification. Thank you for sending the brief and I regret being unable to assist.

Yours Sincerely

MICHAEL LEE

23: I fo=irst met these SLOWMAN FAMILY terrorist sisters when I was a computer data entry clerk (1981—1985) in the upstairs office of Richard PRATT's Visyboard, in Scrivener Street Warwick Farm NSW.

25: **July 16, 2002 outgoing about LEE to STENBERG** page 1 of 2.

16-July-2002   {1}   J G Hall
                                                          Po Box 1373
                                                   GOULBURN NSW 2580
                                                   mob: 0403-788-462

Mark Stenberg
Mark Stenberg & Associates
Po Box 119
HORNSBY NSW 1630

FAX : 02 9477 2485

Dear Mr Stenberg,

RE: MS/J202084

In response to your letter dated 11 July 2002 I am unclear as to how Mr Lee perceived that I was determined that there was a "conspiracy" regarding the police etc. I indicated that I was confused as to how the police had come to the conclusion that a photo of me was the deceased person. The police stated that they indeed have my photo on file (flagged with the deceased person's name). The book has the same photo of me and the publisher claim to have been given that by the police. It's all that simple.

What precipitated these events is very unclear. I knew a Leanne Walters, whom I saw after the event. After my consultation with Mr Lee I took the opportunity to peruse the newspaper archives at the State Library. Therein I discovered a photo of another person identified as Leanne Walters, (not my photo, not a photo of the Leanne Walters I knew) I can only presume that this is indeed the deceased person. I gave a copy to the receptionist at the office of Mr Lee and asked him to call me. He didn't

The fact remains my photo has been published in a book and identified as another. The police admit to me that they gave the photo to the publisher. The publisher state clearly in the book the police gave the photo to them. I am not the person that is identified in the book.

I want something done about this. On the whole I want a public retraction as this was aired in the public arena. Defamation laws as I understand it provided that. Quote from "The Law Handbook - 7th Edition," Redfern Legal Centre, 1999. pp280-281.

> "Anyone identified as the subject of a defamatory statement can sue over it."
> "A person may be identified by their ... photograph ..."
> "A publication may be ... written or communicated in any form including photograph ..."
> "Anyone involved in , or authorising, a defamatory publication may be sued. This could include the author, editor, publisher and the source"
> "A defamatory publication tends to lower a person's reputation in the eyes of the community, making others think less of them"
> "Defamatory imputations (the 'sting of the story) can arise not only on the literal meaning ... or the colloquial meaning of words, but from reading between the lines."

The use of my photograph in the publication, the description of the character of the person identified by my photograph, and the admission of the source of the provision of my

16-July-2002   {2}   J G Hall
                                                                    Po Box 1373
                                                            GOULBURN NSW 2580
                                                            mob: 0403-788-462

photograph, and events which have effected me since the publication of the book in question,
all fit into the above definitions of the Defamation (Act) law.

What I need to know is are you willing to help me achieve justice in this matter?

Yours sincerely,

Janette HALL.

27: **July 16, 2002 outgoing about LEE to STENBERG** page 2 of 2.

26: **July 16, 2002 outgoing to STENBERG fax confirmation**.

TRANSMISSION VERIFICATION REPORT

                                            TIME : 16/07/2002 14:38
                                            NAME :
                                            FAX :
                                            TEL :

DATE,TIME   16/07 14:37
FAX NO./NAME   0294772485
DURATION   00:01:15
PAGE(S)   02
RESULT   OK
MODE   STANDARD

28: **July 17, 2002 from Mark STENBERG** legal firm to me.

MARK
STENBERG
& ASSOCIATES

LAWSTOP

S O L I C I T O R S

MARK STENBERG

ABN 44 123 370 456

OUR REF: MS\J202084

17 July, 2002

Ms J.G. Hall,
C/- P.O. Box 1373,
GOULBURN, NSW, 2580

Dear Janette,

RE: ADVICE PUBLISHER

Reference is made to previous correspondence in this matter.

As requested we now enclose all original documents held by us.

We wish you all the best for the future.

Yours faithfully

**MARK STENBERG
& ASSOCIATES**

encl

FAX: (02) 9477 2485   225 PACIFIC HIGHWAY, HORNSBY, N.S.W. 2077 AUSTRALIA   **TELEPHONE: (02) 9477 1199**
Liability limited by the Solicitors   P.O. BOX 119, HORNSBY 1630   INTERNATIONAL: (61-2) 9477 1199
Scheme, approved under the   DX 9705 HORNSBY
Professional Standards Act 1994 (NSW)   EMAIL: lawstop@cherry.com.au

29: **July 30, 2002 outgoing to STENBERG** to return the paperback.

30-July-2002   {1}   **J G Hall**
                                                                                         Po Box 1373
                                                                              GOULBURN NSW 2580
                                                                              mob: 0403-788-462

Mark Stenberg
Mark Stenberg & Associates Solicitors
PO Box 119
HORNSBY NSW 1630

FAXED to: 9477 2485

Dear Mr Stenberg,

RE: MS/J202084

Thank you for the recent return of my documents. I would appreciate it if you would also return the paperback titled 'Brothers In Arms' (relating to the documents) which I also left with you to consider.

Yours sincerely,

Janette HALL

No Response
Book never returned house

```
CONFIRMATION REPORT           30-JUL-02 11:54 pm

PHONE NUMBER    :   94772485
PAGES           :   01
START TIME      :   30-JUL 11:53 pm
ELAPSED TIME    :   00'45"
MODE            :   9600/STANDARD/MR
RESULTS         :   OK
```

30: **July 31, 2002 from Mark STENBERG** silent refusal to return my copy of the SIMPSON & HARVEY paperback. Obvious Tripartizan cultist.

MARK
STENBERG
& ASSOCIATES

LAWSTOP   S O L I C I T O R S   MARK STENBERG
ABN 44 125 370 456

OUR REF: MS\J202084A

July 31, 2002

Ms. J.G. Hall,
P.O. Box 1373,
GOULBURN,   NSW,   2580

Dear Janette,

RE: ADVICE PUBLISHER

We thank you for your facsimile of the 16th July 2002 and note the contents thereof.

Whilst we would normally be delighted to assist you in this matter we are unable to take on your file due to time constraints and its size and complexity and therefore feel you should consult a local Solicitor.

We wish you all the very best with the matter.

Whilst we have not personally used the services of other Solicitors in Sydney we believe the following firms may be able to assist you in this matter:

Messrs Carroll & Associates   Maurice Blackburn Cashman
Solicitors,   Solicitors
Level 7, 77 Castlereagh Street,   269 Sussex Street,
SYDNEY,   NSW,   2000   SYDNEY,   NSW,   2000
Tel: (02) 9231-2244   Tel free call 1800 810 812

Should we be able to assist you with any other matter please do not hesitate in contacting the writer.

Yours faithfully

MARK STENBERG
& ASSOCIATES

FAX: (02) 9477 2485   225 PACIFIC HIGHWAY, HORNSBY, N.S.W. 2077 AUSTRALIA   **TELEPHONE: (02) 9477 1199**
Liability limited by the Solicitors   P.O. BOX 119, HORNSBY 1630   INTERNATIONAL: (61-2) 9477 1199
Scheme, approved under the   DX 9705 HORNSBY
Professional Standards Act 1994 (NSW)   EMAIL: lawstop@cherry.com.au

31: **August 5, 2002 from terrorist Labor Party Minister** —consistently criminally unconstitutional willful ignorance on Australian law with same content sent 21 AUG to his fellow parliamentarian, K HODGKINSON MP. Its Criminal harassment & False Document: *section 471.12 Using a postal or similar service to menace, harass or cause offence (max 2 years imprisonment) and* **section 143.2 "make" False documents** *(offense is forgery)* **section 144.1 forgery** *(max 10 years imprisonment).* *See Criminal Code Act 1995 (Cth), Schedule, The Criminal Code.* Not "information released" is **"reporting serious crime of terrorism"**.

Office of the Minister for Police

RML 177789

5 August 2002

C 9 AUG 2002

Ms Katrina Hodgkinson MP
Member for Burrinjuck
PO Box 600
YASS NSW 2582

Dear Ms Hodgkinson

The Minister for Police, Michael Costa has asked me to acknowledge your further correspondence on behalf of Ms Janette Hall of PO Box 1373, Goulburn concerning the release of information by NSW Police.

The matters raised are currently being examined and a reply will be forwarded to you as soon as enquiries are completed.

Yours sincerely

Jocelyn Kirkwood
Assistant Private Secretary to
MICHAEL COSTA
MINISTER FOR POLICE

MLU24568 DOC

45.

LEVEL 36, GOVERNOR MACQUARIE TOWER, 1 FARRER PLACE, SYDNEY NSW 2000   TEL: (02) 9228 5665   FAX: (02) 9228 5699

32: **August 21, 2002 from terrorist Labor Party Minister** — consistently criminally unconstitutional willful ignorance on Australian law with same content sent 5 AUG to his fellow parliamentarian, K HODGKINSON MP. Its Criminal harassment & False Document: **section 471.12 Using a postal or similar service to menace, harass or cause offence** (max 2 years imprisonment) and section 143.2 "make" False documents (offense is forgery) section 144.1 forgery (max 10 years imprisonment). See Criminal Code Act 1995 (Cth), Schedule, The Criminal Code. .**Not "information released"** is "reporting serious crime of terrorism".

Office of the Minister for Police

RML 176428

21 August 2002

Ms Katrina Hodgkinson MP
Member for Burrinjuck
PO Box 600
YASS NSW 2582

Dear Ms Hodgkinson

The Minister for Police, Michael Costa has asked me to acknowledge your further correspondence on behalf of Ms Janette Hall of PO Box 1373, Goulburn concerning information released by NSW Police.

The matters raised are currently being examined and a reply will be forwarded to you as soon as enquiries are completed.

Yours sincerely

Jocelyn Kirkwood
Assistant Private Secretary to
MICHAEL COSTA
MINISTER FOR POLICE

MLU24883.DOC

LEVEL 36, GOVERNOR MACQUARIE TOWER, 1 FARRER PLACE, SYDNEY NSW 2000   TEL: (02) 9228 5665   FAX: (02) 9228 5699

33:September 3, 2002 Sydney Sun-Herald propaganda.

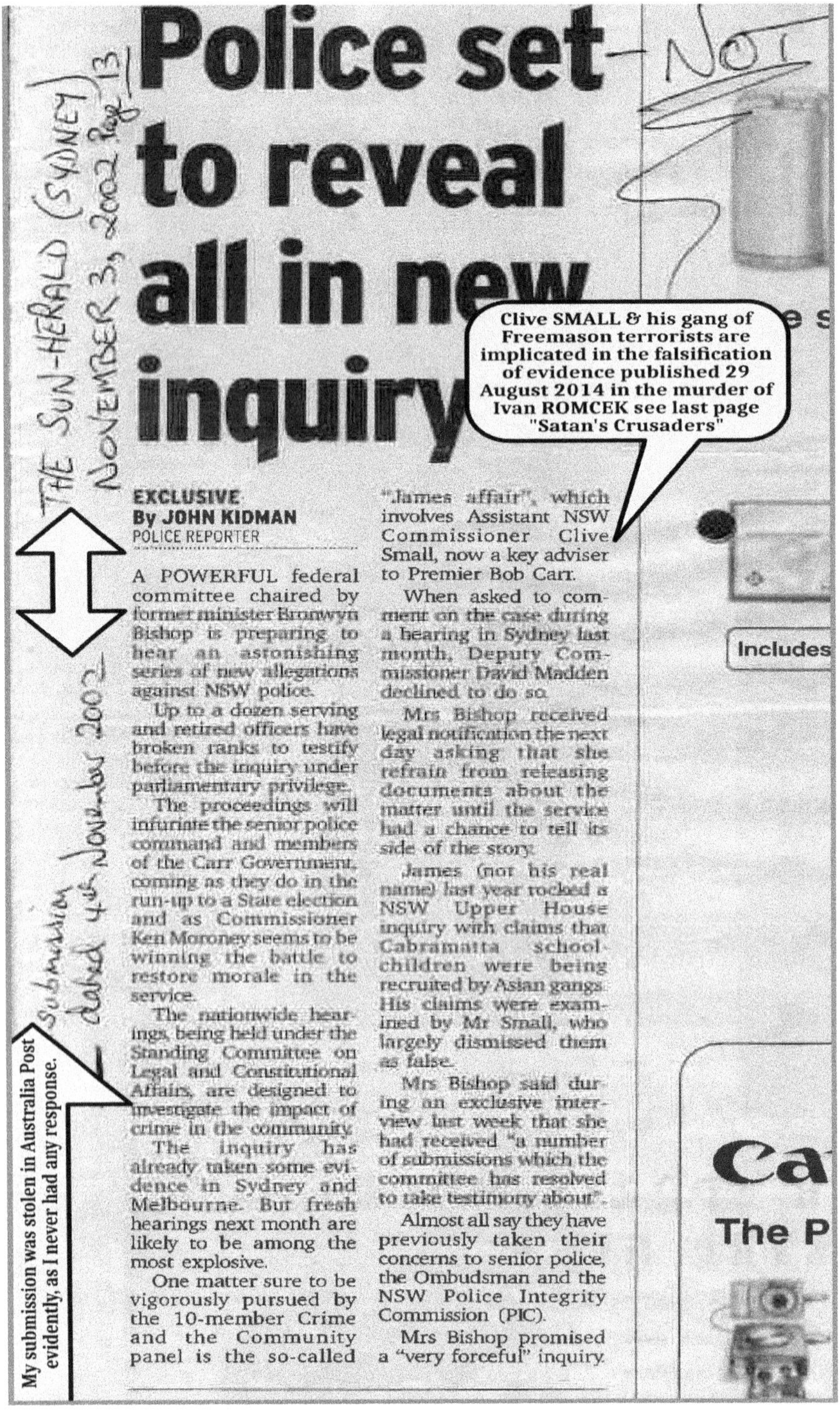

Police set to reveal all in new inquiry

EXCLUSIVE
By JOHN KIDMAN
POLICE REPORTER

A POWERFUL federal committee chaired by former minister Bronwyn Bishop is preparing to hear an astonishing series of new allegations against NSW police.

Up to a dozen serving and retired officers have broken ranks to testify before the inquiry under parliamentary privilege.

The proceedings will infuriate the senior police command and members of the Carr Government, coming as they do in the run-up to a State election and as Commissioner Ken Moroney seems to be winning the battle to restore morale in the service.

The nationwide hearings, being held under the Standing Committee on Legal and Constitutional Affairs, are designed to investigate the impact of crime in the community.

The inquiry has already taken some evidence in Sydney and Melbourne. But fresh hearings next month are likely to be among the most explosive.

One matter sure to be vigorously pursued by the 10-member Crime and the Community panel is the so-called "James affair", which involves Assistant NSW Commissioner Clive Small, now a key adviser to Premier Bob Carr.

When asked to comment on the case during a hearing in Sydney last month, Deputy Commissioner David Madden declined to do so.

Mrs Bishop received legal notification the next day asking that she refrain from releasing documents about the matter until the service had a chance to tell its side of the story.

James (not his real name) last year rocked a NSW Upper House inquiry with claims that Cabramatta schoolchildren were being recruited by Asian gangs. His claims were examined by Mr Small, who largely dismissed them as false.

Mrs Bishop said during an exclusive interview last week that she had received "a number of submissions which the committee has resolved to take testimony about".

Almost all say they have previously taken their concerns to senior police, the Ombudsman and the NSW Police Integrity Commission (PIC).

Mrs Bishop promised a "very forceful" inquiry.

THE SUN-HERALD (SYDNEY)
NOVEMBER 3, 2002 Page 13
NOT
Clive SMALL & his gang of Freemason terrorists are implicated in the falsification of evidence published 29 August 2014 in the murder of Ivan ROMCEK see last page "Satan's Crusaders"
Submission dated 4th November 2002
My submission was stolen in Australia Post evidently, as I never had any response.
Includes
The P

34: January 7, 2003 outgoing to my State MP page 1 of 2.

J. Hall
Po Box 1373
Goulburn 2580
7/1/2003

Dear Ms Hodgkinson,

Following please find copy of letter I received today from Supt. Rattenbury of Camden Local Area Command.

Apart from the fact this man was a customer at my retail computer shop in Camden between 1989 - 1995 I have had no communications with him.

The only letter I sent, dated Nov 29, 2002 was the one sent to you + three others (copy following). I didn't send him a copy, nor would it have been appropriate for anyone else to. The Camden L.A.C. doesn't extend to Goulburn, which is covered by the Southern Region L.A.C. Why would he get copy of my letter?

This individual — as well as being one of my customers also knew my then husband Mr Owen Hall, who is the person I make reference to in my letter to you (+ others) — pg 2 — point 8.

If I don't blame you for this Camden police officer's possession of the letter, I don't know who is responsible. However, I hope you can take a closer look at this incident and my original complaint. Why is nothing being done to investigate this by the police. I have given copious amounts of documents to the Goulburn

4S.

35: **January 7, 2003 outgoing to my State MP** page 2 of 2.

Police - including original copies of photographs.

I read in the Sunday paper that Customs is trialing computer identification software – for Passport Recognition etc. (Sun Herald pg 5, Jan 5, 2003) Would you please approach the Minister, Chris Ellison, on my behalf to request the possibility of using this software to match my face with the photograph the police have on file (as in the book, 'Brothers in Arms') labelled with the incorrect name "Leanne Walters"?

I would truely appreciate your valued assistance in this matter.

Sincerely

Janette Hall (Jenny) 7/1/03

Mob.
0408 788 462

> Box 1373
Goulburn 2580

49.

36: **January 20, 2003 from my State Member in parliament.**

Katrina Hodgkinson, MP

Ref: 03A037/VF

NSW Nationals

2 0

20 JAN 2003

Ms Janette Hall
PO Box 1373
Goulburn NSW 2580

Dear Ms Hall

Thank you for your recent enquiry concerning the letter you received from
Superintendent Rattenbury, of the Camden Local Area Command.

I have made representations on your behalf to the Minister for Police, the Hon
M Costa MLC.

When I receive a reply from the Minister, I will contact you again

Once again, thank you for bringing this matter to my attention.

Yours sincerely

KATRINA HODGKINSON MP

Member for Burrinjuck

Opposition Spokesman for Energy in the Legislative Assembly
NSW Public Accounts Committee Member

52

133 Comur St · (PO Box 600) Yass · NSW 2582 · Ph: (02) 6226 3311 · Fax: (02) 6226 3345
Freecall: 1800 00 2580 · Website: www.burrinjuck.com · Email: Burrinjuck@parliament.nsw.gov.au

37: Jan 23, 2003 from Federal MP & dedicated Freemason terrorist.

Alby
Schultz MP
MEMBER FOR HUME

of Australia
Representatives

23 January 2003

Ms J Hall
PO Box 1373
GOULBURN NSW 2580

Dear Ms Hall

I have received correspondence from Ms Katrina Hodgkinson MP dated 20th January 2003 regarding your *incorrect identification* as stated in your letter of 7th January 2003.

Further to receiving Ms Hodgkinson's correspondence I have taken the liberty of forwarding a copy of your letter to Senator The Hon Christopher Ellison Minister for Justice and Customs for his attention and consideration to the matters you have raised.

Please be assured that as soon as a response is received from Senator Ellison that I will contact you again.

Yours sincerely

ALBY SCHULTZ MP
Federal Member for Hume

AJS:KC

110.

PO BOX 700 GOULBURN NSW 2580
77 • FAX: (02) 4822 1029 • FREECALL: 1800 806 525
EMAIL: alby.schultz.mp@aph.gov.au
PO BOX 637 COOTAMUNDRA NSW 2590
• TEL/FAX: (02) 6942 4650
PARLIAMENT HOUSE
• TEL: (02) 6277 4386 • FAX: (02) 6277 8482

01.03.doc

38: Below "INCONVENIENT TRUTH of GOVERNMENT CRIME one of many photo groups with explanation I've published on my websites since c2005. its irrefutable evidence my 1980s face was altered to mistake me for (left) female alias Lynette SLOWMAN, Joanne SLOWMAN, Leanne SLOWMAN, Leanne WALTERS, Lorraine WALTERS, Pamela WALTERS, Karen BRENNAN, Sandra HARVEY, Camilla UNWIN, Camilla CORGY & Kerry telephone reception staff at Labor police Minister Michael COSTA's office.

I don't mind being naturally ugly but I do strongly object to having *someone else's fugly face features staring back at me from the mirror.*

FAR LEFT: **1985** bridesmaid to author Jennifer COOKE called herself Lorraine. I suspect she's Camilla UNWIN the others in the group called Lorraine WALTERS step-mother of the fake dead and fake person Leanne.

SECOND LEFT: **Camilla** (Mrs Corbin) **UNWIN** in brown top photo copyright to "Daily Mail UK Australia indicating she's presently resident in Australia criminally stalking me still. internet published headline *"A house fit for a hobbit: Home of Tolkien publisher goes on sale"* 26 August 2012.

CENTRE: **Janette Gail FRANCIS**. In blue top demonstrates Janette's face after her surgical rape and illegal silicone injections to her face to look like Camilla UNWIN snapped for Wollondilly Council 1997-1998 annual report as councillor HALL.

SECOND RIGHT: **Janette Gail FRANCIS** as she should look circa 1982 with her naturally sunken chieeks and dominent Scandinavian DNA.

FAR RIGHT: **Janette Gail FRANCIS**, in her stolen grey-scale of herself criminally reproduced in UNWIN HYMAN 1989 book "Brothers In Arms"

www.WitchHunted.com

39: March 5, 2003 file note of outgoing phone call to terrorist police Minister Michael COSTA's office — the Labor Party Union delegate who boasted his greatest achievement in parliament was to "block" things which includes to block my right to have police investigate any crime perpetrated against me since 24 April 1988. I was refused an appointment to see him. Probably blocked in Australia Post or by author Sandra HARVEY & her friends employed in Minister COSTA's office.

40: **March 5, 2003 outgoing FAXED to NSW police Minister COSTA**'s office so I knew he got it unless terrorist police officers were illegally rerouting all my outgoing phone/fax calls. Never bothered to responded the staff ignored my rep[eat calls asking for acknowledgement — exactly the same as '*modus operandi*' as demonstrated by staff at Sydney publishers Allen & Unwin for SIMPSON & HARVEY paperback.

Michael Costa MP

Minister for Police

Fax 9228 5699

Ms Janette Hall

Po Box 1373

Goulburn 2580

5/3/03

0403 788 462

Dear Sir,

Re: your response ref RML 176423/177789 17/Oct/02 Incorrect Identification of my photo by NSW Police I request an appointment to see the Minister regarding this matter + to provide proof of possible untoward matters, which need police investigation; which has been refused by police department.

Regards

Mob 0403 788 462

This letter NOT ACKNOWLEDGED

```
CONFIRMATION REPORT          05-MAR-03 12:03

PHONE NUMBER    :   92285699
PAGES           :   01
START TIME      :   05-MAR 12:02
ELAPSED TIME    :   00'56"
MODE            :   9600/FINE/MR
RESULTS         :   OK
```

41: **March 7, 2003 AUSTRALIA POST FORGERY** allegedly from police Commissioner MORONEY's office, however the enveloped had obviously been opened and resealed.

NSW Police
www.police.nsw.gov.au ABN 43 408 613 180

COMMISSIONER'S OFFICE

Police Headquarters
Avery Building
14-24 College Street
Darlinghurst NSW 2010
Box 45 GPO Sydney 2001
Ph: 9339 5011 / 55011
Fx: 9339 5471 / 55471
TTY: 9211 3776 (Hearing/Speech impaired only)

EDMS/2003/1319

Ms J Hall
PO Box 1373
GOULBURN NSW 2580

Dear Ms Hall,

On behalf of Commissioner Moroney I acknowledge the receipt of your recent letter and the CD.

The letter has been referred for further attention and reply will be forwarded to you in due course

Yours faithfully,

[signature] 7/3/03

Coordinator,
Commissioner's Secretariat.

[handwritten annotations:] Body of deceased facially mutilated

Points

Re family of claimed deceased put forward

3 different photos of three different women elder + still

as their daughter - all women alive after claimed death

The CD is the letter proof

The envelope containing this letter had been opened + resealed prior to me receiving in the mail

42: Mar 19. 2003 Police Minister letter to State Parliament Member.
More evidence of AUSTRALIA POST FORGERY (26-11-2002) *as I'd not sent any letter as claimed in this letter.* It would appear that the letter writer had been criminally impersonating me in that letter. I asked for copy of that alleged letter (26 November 2002) but never got one. Obviously the forgers had written more than one letter criminally impersonating me.

---

*Parliamentary Secretary to
the Minister for Police*

NEW SOUTH WALES

Ms Katrina Hodgkinson MP
Member for Burrinjuck
PO Box 600
YASS NSW 2582

Our Ref: RML 18/886
Your Ref: 03A037/VFM

1 9 MAR 2003

Dear Ms Hodgkinson

Thank you for your further letter on behalf of Ms Janette Hall of PO Box 1373, Goulburn, regarding correspondence she received from Superintendent Mark Rattenbury, Camden Local Area Commander. The Minister for Police, Michael Costa, has asked me to reply.

I understand the letter to which Superintendent Rattenbury refers in his communication to Ms Hall is her letter to the Commissioner of Police dated 26 November 2002, which was referred to the Camden Local Area Command for action.

NSW Police informs me, Ms Hall's concerns about police conduct were assessed in accordance with section 141 of the *Police Act* 1990 as disclosing no complaint about the conduct of any police officer.

The New South Wales Ombudsman oversees the manner in which NSW Police investigates and resolves complaints about the conduct of police officers. If Ms Hall has further concerns about the manner in which her complaint was dealt with, she may contact the Ombudsman's Office on telephone number (02) 9286 1000.

I regret the Minister can be of no further assistance to Ms Hall in relation to this matter.

Yours sincerely

BRYCE GAUDRY MP
PARLIAMENTARY SECRETARY

MLU27327.doc

56.

LEVEL 31, GOVERNOR MACQUARIE TOWER, 1 FARRER PLACE, SYDNEY NSW 2000
TEL: (02) 9228 5665 - (02) 9228 5608   FAX: (02) 9228 5699

43: April 8, 2003 from Sen ELLISON via Federal MP. Interesting that this Senator see "his" Federal *"customs and justice"* department as completely and corporately separate from law enforcement responsibilities of a State police department & evidence this Christopher ELLISON is indeed **another in a long list of terrorist enemies of Australia undermining Australian law by politically motivated abuse of public office & misfeasant refusal to act in the public interest when its in his power as a Minister.**

SENATOR THE HON. CHRISTOPHER ELLISON

Minister for Justice and Customs

Senator for Western Australia

Ministerial No: 81521 / 227039

The Hon Alby Schultz MP
Member for Hume
PO Box 700
GOULBURN NSW 2580

Dear Mr Schultz

Thank you for your letter of 23 January 2003 concerning correspondence you received from Ms Katrina Hodgkinson MP on behalf of Ms Janette Hall. In her letter Ms Hall raises the possibility of using photo-matching identification software reported in *The Sun Herald* on 5 January 2003 to resolve an 'incorrect identification' issue.

The software is currently being used in the Australian Customs Service's SmartGate system to automate the movement of aircrew across the Australian border at Sydney International Airport. SmartGate confirms that the aircrew person is the passport holder and has the authority to enter Australia, it cannot be used to identify an individual.

By law, Customs is required to adhere to the Information Privacy Principles set out in the *Privacy Act 1988*. Among other things this means that Customs must only obtain data required to process persons across the border and use or disclose the data only for the purpose for which it was collected or as otherwise required or authorised by law.

Consequently the SmartGate system is not available for use by Customs in non-border crossing applications.

I regret that Customs is unable to assist Ms Hall with her request.

Yours sincerely

CHRIS ELLISON
Senator for Western Australia

- 8 APR 2003

Telephone (02) 6277 7260   Parliament House Canberra ACT 2600   Facsimile (02) 6273 7098

BROTHERS IN ARMS BIKIE WARS SIMPSON & HARVEY FREEMASON LIES — ISBN 9780645597578

44: April 9, 2003 from evasive Federal Liberal Alby SCHULTZ MP parliamentarian, another in a long list of alcoholic-Freemason nodding Party-puppets. Why he sent the CD to the Minister for communications is a mystery. Within nine years the Minister with this ARTS portfolio approved $MILLIONS to fund a TV miniseries to further conceal this 1984 Freemason terrorist crime.

Parliament of Australia
House of Representatives

Alby Schultz MP

MEMBER FOR HUME

April 9, 2003

Ms J Hall
PO Box 1373
GOULBURN NSW 2580

Dear Ms Hall

Thank you for your correspondence dated 24th March and for forwarding a copy of the CD.

I have taken the liberty of forwarding your CD and correspondence to Senator the Hon. Richard Alston Minister for Communications, Information Technology and the Arts requesting his response to the matters you have raised.

Please be assured that as soon as a response is received from the Senator I will contact you again

Yours sincerely

ALBY SCHULTZ MP
Federal Member for Hume

No Response by 21/05/03

115.

PO BOX 700 GOULBURN NSW 2580
77 • FAX: (02) 4822 1029 • FREECALL: 1800 806 525
EMAIL alby.schultz.mp@aph.gov.au
PO BOX 637 COOTAMUNDRA NSW 2590
• TEL/FAX: (02) 6942 4650
PARLIAMENT HOUSE
• TEL: (02) 6277 4386 • FAX: (02) 6277 8482

45: April 14, 2003 from the evasive Federal Liberal parliamentarian, all he did was forward my letters to him — no parliamentary representation which PROVES they never intend to represent the PUBLIC INTEREST they only intend to represent their own interest and the Party of their favor.

Parliament of Australia
House of Representatives

Alby Schultz MP

MEMBER FOR HUME

14th April 2003

Ms J Hall
PO Box 1373
GOULBURN NSW 2580

Dear Ms Hall

I refer to representation made on your behalf dated 23rd January 2003 to The Minister for Justice and Customs, Senator the Hon Christopher Ellison regarding your incorrect identification as stated in your letter of 7th January 2003.

A response to those representations, a copy of which is attached for your attention and information, has been received from Senator Ellison.

I trust that the information provided by Senator Ellison will be of help to you and I thank you for seeking my assistance on this occasion.

Yours sincerely

ALBY SCHULTZ MP
Federal Member for Hume

AJS:FB

113.

PO BOX 700 GOULBURN NSW 2580
77 • FAX: (02) 4822 1029 • FREECALL: 1800 806 525
EMAIL: alby.schultz.mp@aph.gov.au
PO BOX 637 COOTAMUNDRA NSW 2590
• TEL/FAX: (02) 6942 4650
PARLIAMENT HOUSE
• TEL: (02) 6277 4386 • FAX: (02) 6277 8482

46: **May 7, 2003 from Consumer Affairs watchdog.** Which is a gross waste of State resources. This crime was & is also a consumer matter of *"false advertising – not of stated quality and not fit for purpose"* see chapter *"Fail of Two Cities"*. No idea where he got idea I'd seen a lawyer. What is clear is that the pretend Government services to act as 'watchdogs' over legislation to alleviate pressure ion the court system are a haven for terrorists and other politically minded creeps.

OFFICE OF **FAIR TRADING**
NSW Consumer Protection Agency
Department of Commerce

Ms Jeanette Hall
53 Gibson St
GOULBURN   NSW   2580

Our Ref   CWO03/504
Your Ref
Contact   Paul Humble
Telephone 4254 3401
Facsimile 4229 3929
Email   phumble@fairtrading.nsw.gov.au

Dear Ms Hall

I refer to your complaint regarding Allen & Unwin and the publication of a photograph in a book published by them

I advise that I have carefully reviewed the documentation supplied by you, however regret to advise that the issues you have raised do not fall within the jurisdiction of the Office of Fair Trading. This Office is not in a position to compel the publisher or author to withdraw the book or cease publication nor investigate the circumstances behind the publishing of the book

It appears that you have already had legal advice and written to the Commissioner of Police concerning the matter and it appears that these avenues would be the most appropriate methods of pursuing the matter. Whilst I appreciate that the above may not be all that you would have hoped I trust that the above actions will resolve the matter.

Your documentation is returned herewith

Yours sincerely

Paul Humble
Fair Trading Centre Manager
for Commissioner
7 May 2003 .

Fair Trading Centre Ground Floor, 63 Market Street, PO Box 5275, Wollongong NSW 2520 Australia
Tel (02) 4254 3433   Fax (02) 4229 3929   TTY (02) 9338 4943
http://www.fairtrading.nsw.gov.au

47: May 7, 2003 from Police Commissioner. I knew if I kept pumping out letters sooner or later some poor fool would send me a 'smoking gun' This is a f. Don't matter if a "deputy commissioner" penned it himself, its a forged letter — the main task for police is to ADDRESS crime and PREVENT ongoing crime, not ignore it because its political terrorism. Lets look at *federal Criminal Code Act 1995, schedule* 143.2 "make" False documents, the offense is forgery s144.1 (*10 yrs*) 145.5 Giving information derived from false or misleading documents (*7 years*) 471.12 Using a postal or similar service to menace, harass or cause offence (*2 years*) that's *19 years* for *each* letter.

NSW Police

www.police.nsw.gov.au ABN 43 408 613 180

COMMISSIONER'S OFFICE

Police Headquarters
Avery Building
14-24 College Street
Darlinghurst NSW 2010
Ph: 9339 5011 / 55011
Fx: 9339 5471 / 55471

TTY: 9211 3776 (Hearing/Speech impaired only)

7 May 2003

Ms J Hall
PO Box 1373
GOULBURN NSW 2580

Dear Ms Hall,

The Commissioner of Police, Mr Moroney has asked me to reply to your letter regarding the publication of your photograph in a book entitled "Brothers in Arms" concerning the 1984 Milperra Fathers Day "shootout" between rival "bikie" gangs.

Police inquiries have been made in the matter and I can assure you no photographs of yourself or the late Leanne Walters have been provided by NSW Police to the publishers of "Brothers in Arms".

In the circumstances, it is suggested you direct your inquiries to the publishers of the book with a view to having the situation rectified.

In view of the considerable amount of police resources expended in pursuing this issue, I do not propose to undertake further inquiries in the matter. Any further correspondence from you on this subject will not be acknowledged and simply filed with departmental papers.

Yours sincerely

D B Madden
Deputy Commissioner Operations

48: May 9, 2003 from Freemason brother Schultz p1, its now offensive to cry in presence of parliament electorate staff. I haven't cried since.

Alby
Schultz MP

Parliament of Australia
House of Representatives

MEMBER FOR HUME

9th May, 2003.

Ms Jeanette Hall
53 Gibson Street
Goulburn NSW 2580

Dear Ms Hall,

I have been advised by my staff member Kathleen that you attended my office today in relation to your concerns about your mail deliveries to your post office box

and politicians

I understand that you must suffer severe frustration through your dealings with the police, courts and solicitors, and at best, this can be unnerving. However, when there are such difficult times upon us, it is always best to focus on remaining calm and allowing people such as ourselves to help you as opposed to becoming irritated and venting at those who are only trying to help or advise you of the best way to go about doing things.

Lying
CRAP I was
crying not angry

In urgent response to your request to have "something done" about your mailbox, I have taken the liberty of writing the attached letter to the Manager of Australia Post in Goulburn, making the following requests:

- That your mail be monitored for a period of one month. This ensures that none of your mail is opened when it is placed in your mailbox. This is a discreet act carried out by the Manager of the Post Office.
- That there will be "test mail" placed in your mail stream for the period of two weeks. This will ensure that as these "test letters" are randomly placed, that none of your mail is being opened, and is also carried out by the Manager of the Post Office.

116.

PO BOX 700 GOULBURN NSW 2580
77 • FAX: (02) 4822 1029 • FREECALL: 1800 806 525
EMAIL: alby.schultz.mp@aph.gov.au
PO BOX 637 COOTAMUNDRA NSW 2590
• TEL/FAX: (02) 6942 4650
PARLIAMENT HOUSE
• TEL: (02) 6277 4386 • FAX: (02) 6277 8482

I trust that this will adequately address your issues and that if there is anything else which I can help you with, then please do not hesitate to contact my office

not by a longshot

Yours sincerely,

ALBY SCHULTZ MP
Federal Member for Hume.

Kathleen informed me that the police can intercept anyone's mail and telephone calls whenever they want to and we — meaning no — can't do anything about it.

117

49: May 9, 2003 from Freemason brother Schultz p1 about the note Katrina Hodgkinson told me they didn't need any grounds to eavesdrop — evidently police and their family do it for entertainment — obviously a forerunner to BigBrother TV and the GoggleBox because its voyeuristic and predatory sex perverts who actually have control over our parliaments and Government departments.

50: **May 25, 2003 from** someone else's State representative in parliament, **she faxed advise everyone is "*looking*" we know what that means.** No person has done the job taxpayers expected. To understand extent of this terrorist cancer I sent over 100 faxes and many more letters across entire country to politicians, leading newspapers, television networks, wherever. Nothing more than handful of replies came from broader community. No news industry response. Evidently police have me in an illegal "information" censorship "bubble" as verbally threatened.

Judy Hopwood MP

Member for Hornsby

2. May 2003

Ms J Hall
PO Box 1373
GOULBURN NSW 2580

Dear Ms Hall

Thank you for your recent correspondence in relation to your concerns about issues concerning yourself and police allegations.

I would like to advise you that Ms Katrina Hodgkinson and the Shadow Min s to Police are looking into these allegations

Once again thank you for making me aware of your concerns

Yours sincerely

Judy Hopwood MP
Member for Hornsby
Parliamentary Secretary to the Leader of the Opposition

Post-it Fax Note 7671 Date 30/5/03 To Lords Assemb Co./Dept Browder From J. Hall Fax # 48220740

No — see following letter from Katrina. After I sent her a copy of the letter on CD to Commissioner Moroney — dated 20th Feb 2003 — I haven't been able to get appointment. Per Vanessa, her office. This may well be a tough one. But ignoring it won't make it go away. Esp. when you look below the surface — it is a filthy mess.

Hornsby Electorate Office: First Floor 30 Florence Street, Hornsby NSW
Mail: PO Box 1587 Hornsby Westfield NSW 1635   Phone: 02   Fax
House Macquarie Street Sydney NSW 2000   Phone   Fax
Email: judy.hopwood@parliament.nsw

51: **May 26, 2003 from federal Attorney-General** who wasn't and still isn't interested in addressing homeland terrorism within their parliament or departments — by 2012 federal Arts Department funded the multi-million dollar television miniseries to further cover up this 1984 crime and refuse to acknowledge the 2014 Federal Court ruling on the photos in the paperback not matching the photos in the 1984 newspapers — See *"Satan's Crusaders"* and *"Alice in Peasant Toes"*.

ATTORNEY-
GENERAL'S
DEPARTMENT

Corporate Services

230626:sk

2 6 MAY 2003

Ms Janette Hall
53 Gibson Street
GOULBURN NSW 2580

Dear Ms Hall

I refer to your facsimile of 15 May 2003, to the Attorney-General, the Hon Daryl Williams AM QC MP, regarding the alleged death of a girl during the 'Milperra massacre'.

The matters raised in your letter come within the responsibilities of the New South Wales Attorney-General. Accordingly, I have now referred your letter to the Hon R J Debus MP, for consideration.

Yours sincerely

(L A Watson)
Director
Ministerial and Parliamentary
Services

Robert Garran Offices, National Circuit, Barton ACT 2600 Telephone (02) 6250 6666 Fax (02) 6250 5900 www.ag.gov.au ABN 92 661 124 436

52: **May 28, 2003 from** someone else's State representative in parliament, **you have to wonder what was said around parliament corridors** on this because no person acted as they should have — as they're paid to act — the whole SURGICAL RAPE and WITNESSING MURDER of a retired police officer INSIDE A POLICE STATION has never been heard inside a court room — they'd be spreading rumors of me being a couple of slices short of a loaf I'd say. That's democracy, so long as its a majority doing crime its ok.

PARLIAMENT OF NEW SOUTH WALES
LEGISLATIVE ASSEMBLY

DON PAGE, M.P.
MEMBER FOR BALLINA

OFFICE: Shop 1
           7 Moon Street
           Ballina NSW 2478

PHONE: (02) 6686 7522

FACSIMILE: (02) 6686 7470

MAIL: PO Box 1018
           BALLINA NSW 2478

WEBSITE: www.donpage.com.au

28 May 2003

Ms Janette Hall
PO Box 1373
GOULBURN   NSW   2580

Dear Ms Hall

I wish to acknowledge receipt of your facsimile regarding the book 'Brothers In Arms' published in 1989.

Thank you for bringing your concerns in this matter to my attention.

I am aware Ms Hodgkinson MP, Member for Burrinjuck has made representations on your behalf in this matter and no doubt she will contact you when further information comes to hand.

Yours faithfully

Don Page MP
MEMBER FOR BALLINA

DP:tg

53: **May 29, 2003 from** federal Ombudsman made a big enquiry into whether funding for the TV miniseries to cover up this crime was lawful — he/she decided it was. The person on the street must be fully aware of the legal aspect of the problem is before they make a complaint, the receiving 'watchdog' doesn't have to be intelligent enough to work that out for you, you must tell them else they can't help you. **In 2003 I'd no idea this was a three parliament terrorist conspiracy. What's a bet BARBOUR did.**

EIVED
3 JUN 2003

NSW Ombudsman

Our reference: C/2001/6378
Your reference:

Level 24 580 George Street
Sydney NSW 2000

Phone 02 9286 1000
Fax   02 9283 2911

Tollfree 1800 451 524
TTY   02 9264 8050

Ms J Hall
PO Box 1373
Goulburn NSW 2580

FILE COPY

Web   www.ombo.nsw.gov.au

Dear Ms Hall

Re: Your complaint about police

I refer to your letter dated 15ᵗʰ May 2003 concerning the 1984 Milperra bikie shootings.

This matter was previously dealt with by my Office and has been subject to a review. Previously you were advised that no further action would be taken and the file closed.

This Office is not able to provide the specific information you request in your letter and I do not intend to take any further action.

I wasn't advised this at all. Until now.

I wish to reiterate my earlier advice and advise that any further correspondence in relation to this matter will be read and filed, but will not be acknowledged unless it raises new issues which in my opinion warrant fresh action. I take this last step reluctantly, but to act differently would be to rob other meritorious complaints of the resources to which they are entitled.

I have enclosed a copy of my earlier advice for your records. *Their letter dated 26 Sept 2003*

Yours sincerely

B. A Blomm

Bruce Barbour
Ombudsman   29/5/03

BROTHERS IN ARMS BIKIE WARS SIMPSON & HARVEY FREEMASON LIES — ISBN 9780645597578

54: **November 10, 2010 from Federal Ombudsman their story.**

Ombudsman delivers ruling on Screen Australia's Brothers at War as

http://if.com.au/2010/11/10/article/DQUONZSKFF.html

Ombudsman delivers ruling on Screen Australia's Brothers at War assessment

[Wed 10/11/2010 11:11:29]

By Brendan Swift

The Commonwealth Ombudsman has ruled that Screen Australia did not breach its own conflict of interest guidelines when assessing the funding application for the $6.5 million feature film *Brothers At War*.

The dispute, centred on producer Scott Meeks' dual role as evaluation manager of *Brothers At War* as well as executive producer of a competing feature, *Griff the Invisible*, prompted the producers to lodge a complaint with the Ombudsman, which handed down its decision after a six-month investigation.

"Screen Australia advised, and we have accepted, that when Mr Meek initially assessed your project, he was not aware of its potential to be in competition with his own project," the Ombudsman told the *Brothers at War* producers Wayne Groom and Richard Bradley.

The issue, which resulted in the government funding agency overhauling its conflict of interest policies earlier this year, was originally raised in the Senate by Liberal Senator Simon Birmingham.

Meek accepted the role of executive producer on the $2.7 million *Griff the Invisible* – which included just over $1 million in Screen Australia funding – after he was involved in assessing the project through the IndiVision scheme. Screen Australia approved his appointment.

But Groom and Bradley raised concerns that Meek did not tell them he was involved in *Griff the Invisible* despite their initial plans to also cast Ryan Kwanten and shoot at the same time of year in late 2009.

Brothers at War was rejected for funding by Screen Australia.

However, Screen Australia rejected Groom and Bradley's claims on two grounds: Meek was not aware of the proposed casting conflict, while the potential scheduling conflict was removed when *Brothers at War* shoot date was delayed to 2010 after director Peter Andrikidis became attached to another project, *Kings of Mykonos: Wog Boy 2*, in the second half of 2009.

The Ombudsman said if Meek had been aware of the casting of Kwanten in *Griff the Invisible* while assessing *Brothers at War*, Screen Australia would have been required to declare that information to Groom and Bradley.

The producers of *Brothers At War* argued that it was "highly unusual" for an executive producer to not have been aware of, or involved in the casting of, the main actor. However, they said they have accepted the Ombudsman's ruling based on the evidence presented to them by Screen Australia.

Screen Australia's new conflict of interest guidelines ban contractors (other than casual assessors) from becoming professionally involved with any production they have worked on through their employment with Screen Australia.

Meek and fellow assessor Tristram Miall finished their tenure at Screen Australia last Christmas and were replaced by Victoria Treole and Matthew Dabner. Meek remains a feature film consultant to Screen Australia.

Griff the Invisible stars Ryan Kwanten and Maeve Dermody and marks the feature film directorial debut of Leon Ford. The film is scheduled to be released in March 2011.

Brothers At War remains in development. It previously had an Australian/New Zealand distribution deal with Paramount Pictures, a world sales agreement with Arclight Films International, production funding from the South Australian Film Corporation and private investment of over $1 million.

[Wed 10/11/2010 11:11:29]

Tags:
brothers-at-war griff-the-invisible maeve-dermody peter-andrikidis ryan-kwanten screen-australia

55: **June 20, 2003 from** State Independent Commissioner Against Corruption won't investigate corrupt conduct of investigative process of the **Police Integrity Commission** illegally investigating police — no one does because Parliament is delighted to have corrupt police in their proverbial pocket and covering up for political terrorist attacks on Australian citizens. They just get their mates to import some more terrorists to replace honest citizens they've murdered, like Jack BASSET.

ICAC

INDEPENDENT COMMISSION AGAINST CORRUPTION

Janette Hall
53 Gibson Street
GOULBURN NSW 2580

Our Ref: E03/0878
Contact: Tania Caldwell
Telephone: 8281 5807

IN CONFIDENCE — I *was wasn't*.

Dear Ms Hall

I refer to your correspondence of 2 and 8 June 2003 regarding officers of the NSW Police Service.

As you may be aware, the Police Integrity Commission was established in 1997 to investigate serious allegations of suspected corrupt conduct involving police officers. As such, the ICAC no longer deals with allegations of corrupt conduct involving police officers. The NSW Police Service and the Office of the Ombudsman also investigate complaints about police officers. I understand that you have already raised your concerns with the Police Integrity Commission and the NSW Ombudsman, which seems appropriate.

Thank you for contacting the ICAC.

Yours sincerely

Caldwell

Tania Caldwell
Assessment Officer
20 June 2003

he name reminds me of Caldwell, Martin + Cox Solicitors of Camden — used by Wollondilly Council

ALL CORRESPONDENCE TO GPO BOX 500 SYDNEY NSW 2001
TELEPHONE (02) 8281 5999 FACSIMILE (02) 9264 5364
www.icac.nsw.gov.au

56: **June 20, 2003 from Geoff CORRIGAN** was a fellow elected member of council in nearby Camden when I was abducted from patio Council Chamber before a MacArthur Region Organization Of Councils meeting & surgically raped to my head — I was to chair but due to surgery terrorist attack I was unable to talk or move. *They all knew what happened.* Before he was elected onto Camden Council Geoff was a struggling used car salesman in north Camden when he'd been headhunted by Labor Party. We were both members of same Chamber of Commerce when I was vice president of Camden Chamber of commerce. Isn't that right Geoff! Members of parliament (as members of Council) are *representatives* of the people in parliament or council meetings, not act as a *referral* service.

PARLIAMENT OF NEW SOUTH WALES
LEGISLATIVE ASSEMBLY
MEMBER FOR CAMDEN

Electorate Office
66 John Street
Camden 2570
Tel: (02) 4655 3333
Fax: (02) 4655 3325

20 June 2003

Ms Janette Hall
53 Gibson Street
GOULBURN NSW 2580

Dear Janette, ~~Jenn~~

Thank you for your fax dated 29th May 2003 regarding the book "Brothers In Arms".

I have carefully read the material provided by you and thank you for giving me the opportunity to read it.

Unfortunately I am unable to assist you in this matter, as the avenues that I would have normally suggested have been pursued by you.

I would suggest that you contact your State Member of Parliament, Ms Katrina Hodgkinson, who may be able to assist you further with any future enquiries.

Yours sincerely

Geoff Corrigan MP
MEMBER FOR CAMDEN

Geoff had been involved with Wollondilly Council Before he was elected as Camden's State Member (also was Ex mayor of Camden)

57: Fast forward six months — it appears they broke into my house (criminally) to steal my documents whoch were not inside my residence when they arrived to steal them. I'd informed the manager at the Housing office I was relocating to Adelaide. In retrospect it was a combined Government sting that involved the Child Support Agency illegally withholding my pau=yments causing me & children to be stranded in Adelaide unable to return however, I was still making advance payments on the rent.

March 22, 2004 from New South Wales State housing a bill for their criminally organized conspiracy to break into my rental residence when I was away from it. The State forced me to pay bill after they illegally imprisoned me for complaining about being sent the bill and expecting damages for the associated theft and out of pocket expenses over $1,000.00 story for another paperback — sentenced me to 5 year Apprehended Violence Order& 2 BONDS for my lawfully written complaint to police Department & others.

I Reported my house broken into the police attended but didn't give me a report number — card — Nothing

⟶ All I got was this

NSW DEPARTMENT OF **HOUSING**

Janette Hall
53 Gibson St
Goulburn, Nsw
  2580

PAY REF NO : 786659310

REQUEST FOR REIMBURSEMENT   DATE : 22 March 2004

REFERENCE : 53 Gibson St Goulburn NSW 2580

Dear Janette Hall

The Department of Housing has undertaken the following repairs
and you are responsible for the cost as indicated :

ORDER NO.	ITEM DESCRIPTION	COST
3037945/1	MIN03350 - Drill out cylinder of lock to gain entry to dwelling	85.64
	TOTAL COST :	85.64

Please present your rent card with your payment to an Australia
Post outlet or discuss with your local Client Service Team
about repaying it through the Department's Rent Deduction
Scheme.

If the cost of the repairs is not paid within (21) days of the
date of this letter, the Department will apply to the Consumer
Trader and Tenancy Tribunal for a Money Order. The Tribunal
will notify you of the date and place of the hearing.

If you are on a renewable tenancy, part or all of this amount
may be placed on your renewable tenancy debt account. This
will happen only if the start date for the amount was before
the beginning of your current renewable tenancy.

For more information concerning this request for recovery of
Repairs costs, please contact your Client Service Officer, contact
phone number: 02 48230555.

58: April 13, 2004 - The criminal breakin which cost me over AU$1,000 in theft and damage itemized to the Tribunal. The legislation allowed me to claim damages in the Tribunal but because we're a totalitarian regime and not a democracy my legal rights are extinguished against criminals in Government. As seen on page "6" of her "reasons" Rieteke CHENOWETH made an admission by inference that I had shown her evidence of this crime, apparently in her mind the civil "test" is fah greater a burden on the accuser than the criminal test. Which is the opposite in a democracy. There is no legal reason why "the Department" should not bear the burdon of damages for the illegal actions of their staff" None whatsoever.

CONSUMER, TRADER & TENANCY TRIBUNAL
Tenancy Division

APPLICATION NO: RT 04/14258

APPLICANT: Janette Hall

RESPONDENT: Department of Housing

APPLICATION:
1. Reversal of Debit raised by Dept of Housing on 4 March 2004 of $216.60 for costs.
2. Compensation of $5,000 for damage to personal property after 4 March 2004 and removalist costs.

APPEARANCES: The Applicant appeared in person
Mr R Weeks appeared on behalf of the Respondent

HEARING: The matter was heard on 13 April at Goulburn

LEGISLATION: *Residential Tenancies Act* 1987

ISSUES: Whether the Department of Housing correctly charged $216.60 for costs incurred in taking possession of the property.
Whether the Respondents are liable for the costs of the damage to the Applicant's possessions as well as removal costs incurred by the Applicant.

ORDERS

On 13 April 2004 the application was dismissed because having considered the material placed before it, the Tribunal is not satisfied (at the civil standard of proof) that the grounds required to make the costs orders sought have been established.

CTTT-COMMON\REASONS\2004\RT\04-14258.rtf   1

6

a matter which can be taken up with the police although I acknowledge that it will be difficult to obtain satisfaction in regard to this at this late stage. It is not a cost that should be born by the Department. I note that the Applicant's tenancy in the house at 53 Gibson St. Goulburn is continuing. Accordingly I dismiss the Application.

(Signed)

Rieteke Chenoweth
Member
Consumer, Trader & Tenancy Tribunal

19 July 2004

CTTT-COMMON\REASONS\2004\RT\04-14258.rtf   6

59: May 18, 2004 as vendetta for me applying to Tribunal the respondent staff applied to Tribunal to have me evicted for causing their staff undue duress by my lawful and peaceful and legal civil litigation. That's my addition, typed "wrong 14258" Government employ staff who are mentally deficient as they're more malleable than intelligent honest ones. Obviously all those involved enforcing this farce are malleable political terrorists.

File Number: RT 04/24160

Lodgement Reference No: 20000019784

Date Lodged: 18/05/2004

Applicant Details (Landlord)

Related Files: 414258   wrong 14258

Contact Email: t408@housing.nsw.gov.au
Contact Phone: 48230555

N S W Land and   c/-: T408
Housing Corporation   Ground Floor, Shops 5-8 Huntley   GOULBURN 2580 NSW Australia
ACN: 45754121940   Arcade 153 Auburn STREET

Residential Premises

53 Gibson STREET GOULBURN 2580 NSW Australia

Respondent Details (Tenant)

Janette Hall   53 Gibson STREET GOULBURN 2580 NSW Australia

Order/s Sought

An order ending the Tenancy Agreement ? Other

Reasons for the Order/s

The Applicant landlord applies for an order under Section 69 of the Residential Tenancies Act terminating the Residential Tenancy Agreement of the Respondent tenant as the landlord is in the special circumstances of this case suffering undue hardship. On 13 April, 2004 in proceedings RT 04/14258 heard at Goulburn an application by the tenant Janette Hall against the Department of Housing, was dismissed because ?having considered the material placed before it, the Tribunal is not satisfied at the civil standard of proof, that the grounds required to make the Order sought have been established.? The claim involved a compensation claim by the tenant. Since that decision was made the tenant has placed notices in the rear windscreen and on the front dashboard of the vehicle of her motor vehicle XAF-987 stating as follows: BRAIN CHILL - NSW - 2004 LEISA BRADBURY PIG BITCH from GOULBURN BROKE INTO MY HOME SHE HAD LOCKS CHANGED TOOK PHOTO - INVENTORY of MY THINGS. LEFT DOOR OPEN SHE WORKS 4 DEPT. HOUSING. meanwhile__ME on SOJOURN in S.A. no $ TO GET HOME. R.CHENOWETH - BITCH 4 FAIR TRADING TRIBUNAL RULED IT s O.K. AS MY NEIGHBOUR TOLD BRADBURY I DROVE OFF WITH TRAILER $1,000 VALUE BROKEN STOLEN ADROIT? DUTY COP THINKS NO LAWS BROKEN - MUST B THE COLD AIR - The aforesaid notices are displayed to cause and have caused distress,anxiety,discomfort and inconvenience to the landlord s officer named The landlord has suffered inconvenience, loss in administrative time and future adjustment of work functions in steps taken for the occupational health and safety principles The continuation of the present landlord/tenant relationship would be to inflict an injustice on the landlord

Special Needs

Unavailability Days: Wednesday   REC'D Mon 24/5/c4

---

60 June 28, 2004 this two page statement Stephen SHANAHAN signed his office is located at Queanbeyan NSW — only15 kilometers from our nations federal parliament in Canberra ACT. These are his legally prohibited reasons for seeking my eviction because Goulburn Housing department employee **Leisa Maree BRADBURY** allegedly masterminded the criminal break-in of my public housing residence "allegedly" as I suggest her dad, police officer **Peter Robert BRADBURY** had attempted to break in via back (laundry) door however, he was unable despite bending the security door back quite a way in the bottom opening corner.

IN THE PUBLIC

STATEMENT

274

Postmark 30/6/4 6pm

I STEPHEN SHANAHAN c/- Department of Housing state as follows:-

1. _____ I am an Area Manager with the Department of Housing.

2. _____ I am responsible for overall management of a number of areas within the Department of Housing and one of those areas includes Goulburn. The Department of Housing manages approximately 730 residences in the general Goulburn area.

3. _____ I was informed by staff at the Goulburn office that consequent to the hearing of Consumer Trader and Tenancy Tribunal proceedings RTO4/14258 Ms Janette Hall of 53 Gibson Street, Goulburn, the tenant in those proceedings, placed a sign on her motor vehicle referring to Ms Leisa Bradbury, an employee of the Department of Housing at Goulburn.

4. _____ The initial notice annexure "A" hereto placed on the motor vehicle by Ms Hall is abusive, offensive and unfair to the employee concerned. .

5. _____ As a supervisor I have an obligation to consider the interests of an employee and to provide a safe system of work.

6. The notice has caused distress, anxiety, discomfort and inconvenience to the staff of the landlord. Counselling is ongoing. That counselling represents a cost to the New South Wales Land and Housing Corporation. Further there is and has been a loss of administrative time in dealing with the actions of the tenant. This has involved consultation and telephone calls with numerous staff, including legal staff, as well as contact with the Police. This has diverted staff and management form their normal duties and created a backlog in some areas of operation.

7. _____ The Police have instituted on behalf of the employee concerned an Application seeking an Apprehended Violence Order. Personnel from the Department attended at the Local Court on 2 June 2004 when an interim order was granted and further staff will be required to assist the employee at the hearing on 15 July next.

8. _____ Internal changes in the office at Goulburn have been required to be made to ensure a safe system of work which relates to any contact by any employee with the tenant Ms Hall..

{20032067 \ MAC \ 00028215}

61: June 28, 2004 Stephen SHANAHAN statement. So they planned the department's front door lock drilling exercise to mask their illegal back door attempt. I have very thin wrists and relatively strong finger muscles. I'd installed a floor padlock far enough away that I could just reach with my wrist through the diamonds of the security door and awkward enough so my dexterous fingers to easily (for me) unlock with the key. On order of the Tribunal, I gave evidence to Crown Solicitor's lawyer Michael CALLEN that **Leisa Maree BRADBURY** was 'family' associated with **Peter Robert BRADBURY** the police detective I saw murder retired senior police officer Jack BASSET then stole the photo of me printed in the SIMPSON & HARVEY BIA paperback both in 1988 when we were neighbours at The Oaks NSW. Next time I saw CALLEN his face was bloodied & beaten up & his hands had evidence of defensive injuries, he declined to respond to my questions.

9.____There are further long term issues for the Department as to how to organise personnel in order to avoid any personal vilification being made against them for any reason by this tenant.

10.____Goulburn is a town of approximately 20,000 people. It is a close community and the notice singling out of an employee has caused extreme emotional discomfort to staff at the Goulburn office.

11. The actions of the tenant continue and result from a decision of an independent tribunal ie the Consumer Trader and Tenancy Tribunal.

12.____Annexed hereto and marked with the letter "B" is a copy of a letter sent by Michael Callen, Solicitor, to Ms Hall which was displayed on Ms Hall's car as at 8 June, 2004.

13.____Annexed hereto and marked with the letter "C" is a copy of the Application filed in these proceedings which was displayed on Ms Hall's car as at 8 June, 2004.

14.)____Annexed hereto and marked with the letter "D" is a copy of the Application in respect of Apprehended Violence Order which was displayed on Ms Hall's car as at 8 June, 2004.

15. Annexed hereto and marked "E" is a ten page document given to Michael Callen solicitor for the Department by Ms Hall at the initial hearing of these proceedings on 8 June 2004

DATED   day of   June   2004

[handwritten margin notes: giving Solicitor Lawyers this document claimed Goulburn police A.V.O. (breached) I'd breached Bond (sentence) I got 12 mth Bond for punishment.]

STEPHEN SHANAHAN

MEGHAN
HIBBERT
JP
980693

62: **July 5, 2004 PERVERTING JUSTICE.** Stephen SHANAHAN & his fellow Freemason terrorists illegally used their Tribunal application to falsify evidence to fabricate a application to criminal court with intent of (long-term) attempting to cause my (unlawful) incarceration by breach of an Apprended Violence Order. I'd not had a criminal record then (child or adult) this is the only criminal record I have since. I was illegally penalized for legally passing document evidence to the lawyer, they claimed I caused that evidence to be sent to Leisa Maree BRADBURY thereby breaching the AVO they arrested after storming my single parent residence, menaced me and my children withy their handguns threating to shoot dead our equally terrified kelpie pup & kept me over night in Goulburn police cells leaving my young children alone. *That's the face of terrorists not lawful police.*

IN THE PUBLIC INTEREST   5/7/4

COURT ATTENDANCE NOTICE
(DEFENDANT COPY)

HALL
H 21328158

List No. _____

You are required to attend the GOULBURN LOCAL Court on Thursday 15th July, 2004 at 9:30 am

DEFENDANT DETAILS

HALL, Jeanette Gail	CNI Number : 688865714
01/05/1956	Licence details :
53 GIBSON ST	Sex : Female
GOULBURN, NSW, 2580	ATSI Status : Unknown

PROSECUTOR (NSW POLICE) DETAILS

OIC (Prosecutor) : CON ADAM FITZGIBBON, Goulburn Target Action Group
CAN Created by : CON ADAM FITZGIBBON, 12:20 pm 05/07/2004
CAN Accepted by : SENCON PAUL GOODWIN
Apprehended : 10:50 am on 05/07/2004   Charging station : Goulburn
Apprehended by : CON ADAM FITZGIBBON, Goulburn Target Action Group

DETAILS OF OFFENCE/S

001	Crimes Act 1900, Section 562I(1)	Law Part Code 1208
	Contravene apprehended violence order	
	between 4:30 pm and 4:40 pm on 30/06/2004 at Goulburn.	
	did knowingly contravene a restriction specified in a non-domestic apprehended violence order.	

Doc sent from Shanahan I'd given to Callen on his request.

D.O.H.

Stephen Shanahan Statement 28 June 2004
2) point "8"
"Internal changes in the office at Goulburn have been required to be made to ensure a safe system of work which relates to any contact by any employee with the tenant Ms Hall."

D.O.H. Tribunal Appl'n 4 Ms Hall's Eviction 19 May 04
(then INTERUM AVO - 2 June 04)
cause I'm threatening apparently.
4) "...The landlord has suffered inconvience, ..."

INFORMATION FOR DEFENDANT

1. You should obtain legal advice immediately about your rights regarding this Court Attendance Notice. You may wish to contact a legal practitioner, LawAccess (1300 888 529), the Legal Aid Commission or a Chamber Magistrate at a Local Court if you require assistance. On your first date of appearance at Court, you should be in a positon to advise the court, if required, whether you wish to plead guilty or not guilty to the alleged offence/s.
2. If you have a physical impairment, or require an interpreter to assist you at Court, please advise the Local Court at which you are to appear as soon as possible.
3. If you have been charged by the Police, then the Police Officer responsible for investigating the alleged offence/s will, on request, make arrangement for a language interpreter to assist you at Court
4. Failure to appear may result in your arrest or in the matter being dealt with in your absence

Printed at 1:11 pm on 05/07/2004

in steps taken for the occupational health and saftey principals ..."

63: July 5, 2004 PERVERTING JUSTICE. All the police at Goulburn police station were involved in this premeditated crime for the Freemason political cause of falsifying the life & murder of the Fictitious LEANNE Walters. Goulburn is where the police training Academy is located. Note they mispely my first name & claimed not to know I was born down the road in Cooma NSW. They claim to have six witnesses to prove I committed an act they define as a crime that could never be in mind of a sane person.

New South Wales Police

FACTS SHEET

H 21328158
BAIL CAN

Offender	: HALL, Jeanette Gail			
Address	: 53 GIBSON ST : GOULBURN, NSW, 2580			
Nationality	: Unknown	**D.O.B**	:	01/05/1956
Occupation	: Computer Operator	**CNI No.**	:	688865714

Seq. No.	Offences	
1. Act Section	Contravene apprehended violence order Crimes Act 1900 562i(1)	Law Part : 1208

ARRESTING OFFICER

Name : CON ADAM FITZGIBBON
Station : GOULBURN TARGET ACTION GROUP

INFORMANT

Name : CON ADAM FITZGIBBON
Station : GOULBURN TARGET ACTION GROUP

ACCEPTING OFFICER

Name : SENCON PAUL GOODWIN
Station : Goulburn
Date : 05/07/2004

COURT

Court Name : Goulburn Local Court
Court Date : 15/07/2004

WITNESSES

Police Witnesses : 4
Civilian Witnesses : 2

BAIL

Bail Type : Bail Conditional

ANTECEDENT

The defendant is currently unemployed and is the mother of two.

page 1   05.07.04 13:11

BROTHERS IN ARMS BIKIE WARS SIMPSON & HARVEY FREEMASON LIES — ISBN 9780645597578

64: July 5, 2004 PERVERTING JUSTICE. Evidently I hit my target. In a style befitting the Government men of the USA fiction film *"Pelican Brief"* they came at me from all sides illegally & vigorously targeting me to cover up their prior Government made crimes they need to keep secret from the public. Evidently in public housing you must never leave house unoccupied to vacation or shop, else you risk Government taking possession. Leisa Maree BRADBURY didn't seek the AVO, *Goulburn police were the only applicant.* That speaks of their criminal intent & Freemason involvement.

New South Wales Police

H 21328158
BAIL CAN

FACTS SHEET Cont'd
Defendant : HALL, Jeanette Gail

FULL FACTS

Accused: Janette HALL, DOB: 01/05/1956. 53 Gibson Street, Goulburn.

BRADBURY works at the department of housing in Auburn Street Goulburn and has the portfolio of placing and evicting tennants from government owned premises. The accused has taken a personal vendetta and dislike to BRADBURY after the accused left for South Australia leaving 53 GibsonStreet unattended. After neighbours had reported the accused leaving Goulburn BRADBURY followed procedure in having the locks changed to make the premises available for new tennants. After the locks were changed the accused returned to Goulburn wanting to move back into the house. The accused has since taken BRADBURY to the departmentof fair trading where it was found BRADBURY acted directly in accordance with the housing departments policy and procedure. The accused complaint was dismissed accordingly. Since this event the accused has decorated her vehicle with offensive and degrading comments directed at BRADBURY. One of the signs placed on the rear of the accused vehicle read, "Leisa BRADBURY Pig Bitch from Goulburn broke into my home she had locks changed took photo 4 Dept of housing meanwhile me on so journ in SA. No $ to get home CHENOWERTH bitch 4 fair trading tribunal ruled its ok as my neighbour told BRADBURY I drove off with trailer $1000.00 broken stolen. Adroid? Duty cop things no laws broken Must be the cold air". Since reading this sign BRADBURY has been approached by friends and work colleagues who have been asking her what the sign is about. . On 2nd June 2004 BRADBURY attended the Goulburn Local Court where she was granted an Interim Apprehended Violence Order against the accused. the conditions on the order states:- The defendant must not assault, molest, harass, threaten or otherwise interfere with the protected person.

About 4:30pm on 30th June 2004 BRADBURY was at work when she received some mail through the internal mail system which was addressed from the area manager. Upon opening the envelope BRADBURY discovered it was some more paper work from the accused regarding another tribunal. BRADBURY read the report until she came across a hand typed article which was prepared and signed by the accused. The last page of the article read:- "From what I've discovered Ms BRADBURY is associated with Rex and Loraine WALTERS. I saw the man who calls himself Rex WALTERS enter and stay for extended periods, the home of family with the surname BRADBURY who moved after me to the OAKS. I also saw regularly at this home, the woman known to me as Rose, (who moved to the

Margin annotations:
A

(A)
Not
so
1) No name
2) not estab.

(B)
No Defence allowed

(C)
Fitz
"FAX"
taped
1 view

L8
L19

page 2

05.07.04 13:11

65: July 5, 2004 PERVERTING JUSTICE. This sage begun because I asked police to investigate Rex John WALTERS and Peter Robert BRADBURY in association with my biometric theft of identity in the SIMPSON & HARVEY paperback. ts easy to lose sight of the start when the criminals (Freemason police) start spot fires to attract your attention away from their crimes. Here they accuse me of accusing the BRADBURY police family of being associated with motorcycle clubs which is what they accused me of the the SIMPSON & HARVEY book. Prosecutor Mr WINTER claimed in face of Goulburn court, my "Club" brand steering wheel lock sticker was proof I am motorcycle club associate, the Freemason magistrate agreed with WINTER.

New South Wales Police

H 21328158
BAIL CAN

FACTS SHEET Cont'd
Defendant : HALL, Jeanette Gail

FULL FACTS Cont'd.

house across the road from me in Goulburn NSW). Mr BRADBURY was a policeman. I got a letter from Camden Centrelink NSW signed by Ms BRADBURY, during the time when my Centrelink file was stolen and replaced with incorrect and misleading data. I'm not related to the WALTERS, I've never been involved with motorbke riders of any kind. After reading this BRADBURY has felt very stressed and upset. BRADBURY is concerned that HALL is associating her with an Outlaw Motor Cycle Gang and the WALTERS family. BRADBURY is very scared and feels very intimidated and defensive.

About 3:00pm on Friday 2nd July 2004, the accused vehilce was observed parked in Auburn Street. Upon inspection of the vehicle it was found that the accused had placed a section of the document she had created on the rear of her vehicle which referred that Ms BRADBURY has having an association with Lorraine and Rex WALTERS. About 10:30am on Monday 5th July 2004, the accused attended the Goulburn Police station whereshe was placed into custody and informed of her rights under part 10a of the crimes act. The Accused then participated in an electronically recorded interview. During the interview the accused was presented with a document that she had created and had placed on full display on the side of her vehicle. The accused gave Police a version that the Ms BRADBURY she had referred to as being associated with Rex and Lorraine WALTERS was a different Ms BRADBURY that worked for the Department of housing. Although the accused referred to the two Ms BRADBURY's as different people they were both mentioned on the same page in two different paragraphs. The interview was completed was the accused was charged with the matters now before the court.

Facts Created by : CON ADAM FITZGIBBON

Date : 05/07/2004

page 3

05.07.04 13:11

66: Over one year out of order - *dated 24 March 2003 - addressed to my evasive Federal Liberal representative in Parliament, Freemason terrorist Alby SHCULTZ MP.* The intent of writing this letter was to convey my natural feelings as objectively as possible. Having now read the response of police you can tell they mimicked my reasonable outrage in the words they put in the mouth of theur terrorist puppet, Freemason terrorist supporter Leisa Maree BRADBURY of Goulburn, NSW State Housing public officer.

Monday, 24 March 2003

FILE COPY

Ms J G HALL
PO Box 137?
GOULBURN NSW 2580

Alby Schultz MP
Federal Member For Hume
Auburn St
GOULBURN NSW 2580

Dear Sir,:

I refer to your letter dated 23 January 2003, and thank you for any representations you have made on my behalf. It's been a shock to realise that I had become associated with such a set of circumstances, not having been knowingly associated with any of the people involved Equally, it has been difficult to understand the reasoning behind barriers that are placed before me when I have attempted to clarify this matter. The only conclusion I am able to draw is the probable embarrassment of the Police when confronted with proof of a procedural error.

Considering the massive cost of the investigation etc to the government of the day, and the media frenzy that ensued after the incident in which it is claimed seven lives were lost, to be now faced with the proof that someone in the department made a big mistake – I can empathise with such fears – but to be ignored as I have, well that's not very decent at all is it

I've enclosed a CD which contains an, as yet unacknowledged, letter to the NSW **Police Commissioner**, Ken Moroney, dated 20 February 2003 (sent by overnight express post). It is contained in internet hyperlink format, due to the inclusion of a great deal of scanned picture files. It can be accessed by an internet file reader such as 'Microsoft Internet Explorer' the file is named "**MsJ_Hall.html**"

The situation I now find myself in, in relation to the difficulty of getting any action whatsoever by Police, may be compounded by the possibility that Federal Police were involved in the original investigation in the 1980's That being the case I would greatly appreciate your assistance in forcing the present relevant authority to take responsibility for this obvious mistake. The letter to Commissioner Moroney is fairly self explanatory. However I will briefly explain the situation

67: *24 March 2003 page 2*. I treat everyone in Government as if they know nothing of this crime that just about everyone their age in 1984 Sydney had been bombarded with in TV news. I usually only address logic of a situation. My verbal discussions no different in context or tone to my written words. I'm not an overly emotional person, I'm an INTJ I've never over reacted to anything, unless I'm searching for evidence. Unlike Rex John WALTERS when I confronted him personally c2003. He has a well rehearsed duologue & fake tears.

– 2 –   March 24, 2003

During a violent altercation on September 2, 1984, it is claimed six adult males and one female minor, were killed. The female was facially mutilated There is a contradiction of the stated age of the female minor between the family and the Coroner. At least three photographs have been publically identified as the deceased, by the female's family. One of these is my photograph I have photographic evidence that the three photographs are indeed three different people I defiantly know two are still alive, if my evidence and firm belief is proven, the third is also alive too

The family, according to police, still insist that the photo of me is their daughter They have deceived the police by this false claim, we are very dissimilar in physical appearance The female minor had a criminal record, complete with official Police photo The Police used a private photo, and not the Police file photo, to identify this person to the public

Due to Police refusal to investigate their blatant error, I have been forced to take steps in order to prevent further physical attacks on my person This includes the necessity to make a visual statement on my car. Something that a citizen should not have to do in Australia I have been refused due process of law. This was my only means of protection from further physical recriminations by persons who have incorrectly maintained I had conned the public and faked my death Persons which include certain members of the NSW Police force, which I can only presume is fuelled by the family of the claimed deceased female I've been followed, only recently in Goulburn, by persons vocalising such accusations

Members of this family relocated to a house in close proximity to my current residence, and have vocalised this connection, and appear to have access to information I have given to Police The fact I no longer have an extended family, assists the claimed deceased's family, to maintain their abhorrent lies

I truly appreciate any action you may be able to take on my behalf to resolve this matter as soon as humanly possible I thank you in anticipation

Yours sincerely,

FILE COPY

Janette Hall

112

68: **June 2004,** below top, steps of Goulburn NSW Local Court. Freemason terrorist supporters demanding I'm punished because I dared complain about *'my stuff'* being illegally ransacked by terrorists @Goulburn's NSW State Housing office. *Cow dung'd be inhabited by lifeforms of higher moral integrity* — left their alleged Goulburn office manager, centre their Leisa Maree BRADBURY, probably Freemason Stephen SHANHAN far right.

Meanwhile question of criminal accountability for cold blooded sadistic murder of retired senior police officer Jack BASSET before me as he gave police (my) supporting evidence of Freemason child rape & ritualistic Freemason murders during Freemason meetings, that constitutional atrocity remains outside budget of abysmal State of New South Wales Tripartizan Terrorist's police department — 30 years after his Sunday murder, early evening 24 April 1988 inside Camden NSW police station's detective area back room.

69: April 8, 2004 my fax to the Law Society seeking legal referral and legal assistance in 'these trying times'. I got an answer almost instantly.

Ms Janette Gail Hall
53 Gibson Street
Goulburn NSW 2580
8th April 2004.

LAW SOCIETY of NSW   FAX 02 9231 5809
SYDNEY
Att: The MOST RESPONSIBLE OFFICER

COPY

To Whom It May Concern,
Dear Sir/Ms,

I have a situation which I hope no other Australian has to go through, however with the innate stupidity of the NSW govt. some other is most probably.

I've been identified as a deceased person by a group of people who claim I'm of their family. I tried to get the Police to investigate, however the commissioner claims that the NSW Govt. doesn't have any money to do that.

I had asked you some time ago for names of solicitors who might take up this matter, but all three firms you gave me the names of said they couldn't as they also rep. govt. departments.

I have tried many solicitors the last two are the norm <u>to me</u> of the caliber of legal people in NSW ie. "I've never heard of police harassment" said one, the other cross examined me as if he was against me rather than ready to represent me.

Do I have to go overseas to find a legal firm to represent me or is there a single legal firm in NSW with the guts to do the job? - <u>PROPERLY</u>

I've been trying for two and half years now in NSW and I've yet to come across <u>ANY</u> decent, fair-minded, democratic Australians in the NSW legal system. So where are they all hiding? Don't tell me the same cupboard as the NSW Legislative Assembly there wouldn't be enough room.

Regards

Janette Hall.

70: **April 8, 2004** faxed back same day from Law Society, *Manager Of Dispute Resolution*, who by inference *told me to drop dead*. She's since been rewarded in Australia's legal industry for her terrorist attitude.

You'll note that I reduce empty space in some documents like PDF compression software. ☿

The Law Society of New South Wales

Our Ref: CRS:
Direct Line: 9926 0367

8 April 2004

Ms Janette Gail Hall
53 Gibson Street
Goulburn NSW 2580

170 Phillip Street
Sydney NSW 2000
DX 362 Sydney
Phone (02) 9926 0333
Fax (02) 9231 5809

ACN 000 000 699

Dear Ms Hall,

Re: Your enquiry

We acknowledge your letter received at The Law Society of NSW on 8 April 2004.

Kindly note we no longer provide legal advice or assistance. For legal information and assistance, you may contact LawAccess NSW, a telephone service provided by the Attorney General's Department of NSW.

Please note that LawAccess NSW cannot respond to written requests for legal assistance and advice except where demonstrated exceptional circumstances exist. You can contact LawAccess NSW during business hours on 1300 888 529. TTY enquiries : 1300 889 529.

Postal address:
PO Box 620
PARRAMATTA NSW 2124

You can also visit their website at www.lawaccess.nsw.gov.au for a range of plain language legal information resources.

We have also enclosed for your interest a copy of the Accredited Specialists in Wills & Estates.

Yours faithfully,

BRIDGET SORDO
Manager, Dispute Resolution &
Community Referral Service

Quality
Endorsed
Company

Fail of Two Cities

SYDNEY & ADELAIDE. IN REALITY AUSTRALIA
HAS NO CITIES THEY'RE ALL CONTROLLED LIKE
COMMUNES, IF YOU KNOW THE COMMUNE
LEADER YOU'VE IMPUNITY FOR ANYTHING.

"Quantum theory" scientists say if you can't see it it ceases to exist. Ergo: if you're stabbed in the back it didn't happen or if you wear clothes you only have the bits poking from the clothes the rest of you doesn't exist, they magically become real when you take your clothes off. So that means when a man rapes someone and their penis disappears inside the victim they're not really raping the victim because the alleged rapist has no penis. This insanity was funded by taxes at "Australia's National University" in Canberra1. This 'special people' insanity contributes to the mindset that covers up a very long history of very real Freemason child rape.

I started reading the original Tale of Two Cities when my male parent was in the 1960s. He put it down so I picked it up to read. Never finished it I just wanted to know his mind. It was circa 1967, soon after I'd witnessed he and his Freemason Brothers rape two boys and murder one of them. I was about eleven or twelve. At this point in time I started riding my older sister's bicycle to the local library after I got Mum to give me permission to open a Campbelltown library account in my name. The 1960s librarian was of the same mindset as my male parent — psychopathic. She recommended I read "The Moon is Blue" by Edgar Allen POE which even I knew was totally unsuitable for a child my age. Psychopaths can't help themselves tell you they're psychopaths they tell you with their eyes. Don't be mistake psychopaths are not human they're psychopathic mutants of humans. Sure they're people like us humans but only humane people are human.

What I'm leading onto, my segway, is that Tale of Two Cities is reported to have about 139,000 words. I've published easily three times that number of words on my websites and attempting to write this book so you can understand it since the evolution of my I realization begun circa 2003 that New South Wales police are the original terrorist enemies of Australia accompanied in that diabolical crime are every individual member of the

1 2015, May 27 https://www.anu.edu.au/news/all-news/experiment-confirms-quantum-theory-weirdness (accessed 8/Oct/2021)

1: Australian National University (hopefully inadvertently) aid all of government cover up of any and all government crimes – not observed. Its childish absurdity, someone's screwing with their head.

Experiment confirms quantum theory weirdness   1

Australian
National
University

Search ANU web staff & maps

Newsroom Events Safety Maps Services Library Jobs Directories

ABOUT   STUDY   RESEARCH   GIVING   ALUMNI   CURRENT STUDENTS   STRATEGIC INITIATIVES

Newsroom » All news » Experiment confirms quantum theory weirdness

Experiment confirms quantum theory weirdness

27 MAY 2015

Associate Professor Andrew Truscott (L) with PhD student Roman Khakimov

The bizarre nature of reality as laid out by quantum theory has survived another test, with scientists performing a famous experiment and proving that reality does not exist until it is measured.

Physicists at The Australian National University (ANU) have conducted John Wheeler's delayed-choice thought experiment, which involves a moving object that is given the choice to act like a particle or a wave. Wheeler's experiment then asks - at which point does the object decide?

Common sense says the object is either wave-like or particle-like, independent of how we measure it. But quantum physics predicts that whether you observe wave like behavior (interference) or particle behavior (no interference) depends only on how it is actually measured at the end of its journey. This is exactly what the ANU team found.

"It proves that measurement is everything. At the quantum level, reality does not exist if you are not looking at it," said Associate Professor Andrew Truscott from the ANU Research School of Physics and Engineering.

Despite the apparent weirdness, the results confirm the validity of quantum theory, which governs the world of the very small, and has enabled the development of many technologies such as LEDs, lasers and computer chips.

https://www.anu.edu.au/news/all-news/experiment-confirms-quantum-theory-weirdness

global terrorist cult that call themselves the Freemasons — and their friendly DNA family members or workmates in Government and private enterprise.

Like Justice Katzmann wrote:

> **"This is, however, no bare assertion. Contrary to the assertion in the respondents' submissions, there is evidence to support it."**

So lets look at the evidence that the resources of Australia, the country, the Government, the political parties, the Freemasons and all their sycophantically psychopathic members and supporters continue to cover up a very long history of Freemason child rape that begun from the time British invaders and convicts set foot on terra firma of "terra australis incognita" second century Latin for"unknown southern Land[2]". Obviously Matthew Flinders wasn't the first explorer to Australia. Just as obvious the current indigenous population now mixed predominately with Scandinavian Germanic East Europe DNA, they too "invaded" Australia from somewhere else potentially wiping out the original inhabitants they potentially errantly claim as their ancestors.

News flash people. Ancient DNA excavated in Hungry Siberia Russia and China and other coldish regions where DNA was preserved proves we're all mixed races. The basic difference between us people is not the color of our skin its between your ears, our only measurable difference is whether you're psychopathic or human. That's what drives skin and eye color prejudices. Brown are the most dominant eye color, I've experienced prejudice from brown eyed people because my eyes are blue. Prejudice I call a jealous fixation just as brown skin is for the majority of white people who'll risk death on the beaches or in tanning coffins to make their skin darker. Prejudice envy and jealousy is like beauty, its in the mind of the beholder.

This is my interpretation of the evidence in Australia's Freemason child rape cover up from my beholding 'law centric' mind told in their documents (even without my words) that prove irrefutably — **there're no clinically sane persons employed, elected or tenured** in a senior position, in Australian Government or News industry outlet.

None people, none.

Naturally that's my personal opinion based on my research compared to my knowledge of Australian law, having studied it extensively personally and successfully completed half of a Bachelor of Laws Honors degree I don't

---

[2]   *Source: https://byjus.com/question-answer/the-word-australia-is-derived-from-the-atin-word-australis-what-could-australis-mean-northernsouthernpacificaboriginal/*

2: *FRANCIS V ALLEN & UNWIN PTY LTD ORS* [2014] FCA 1027

IN THE FEDERAL COURT OF AUSTRALIA
NEW SOUTH WALES DISTRICT REGISTRY
GENERAL DIVISION   NSD 339 of 2014

BETWEEN: JANETTE GAIL FRANCIS
                    Applicant

AND: ALLEN & UNWIN PTY LIMITED
                    First Respondent

                    LINDSAY SIMPSON
                    Second Respondent

                    PAMELA WALTERS
                    Fourth Respondent

                    REX WALTERS
                    Fifth Respondent

                    LORRAINE WALTERS
                    Sixth Respondent

JUDGE: KATZMANN J
DATE OF ORDER: 22 SEPTEMBER 2014
WHERE MADE: SYDNEY

THE COURT ORDERS THAT:

1.   The interlocutory application filed by the first, second, fifth and sixth respondents on
        18 July 2014 be dismissed with costs.

Note: Entry of orders is dealt with in Rule 39.32 of the *Federal Court Rules 2011*.

intend on completing due to them farcical nature of Australia's State University's scoring system intended to politically score down selected individuals and score up those in political favor.

Everything Australia the advertised and combined country of people does, is a blatant lie. Now I've waffled on long enough to preach my version of Armageddon here are the documents that prove the seven alleged violent deaths on Fathers Day 1984 broadcasted globally by out global Freemason propaganda network is a lie.

Its true the judge doesn't say that the Fathers Day 1984 murders were a Freemason lie, what proves Australia the country lied about the seven 1984 deaths and the evidence of thereof was falsified by Sydney's Freemason police is that despite its historical significance this Federal Court of Australia ruling was not Sydney news or National news or Global political news despite that the first story of it has been a political sensation for weeks, months and years costing Australian taxpayers billions of dollars.

All 1984 Sydney police were Freemasons as was my male parent and Jack Basset who was also a Cooma New South Wales police officer when my male parent raped me when I was 2 years 11 months old, on 3 March 1959.

This is Australia's inconvenient truth.

2014 ORDER OF THE FEDERAL COURT OF AUSTRALIA FRANCIS V ALLEN&UNWIN ORS

This previous page order was in response to an interlocutory application filed on 18 July 2018 well before Sydney's national Network Nine 60 Minutes (fake) news program using the images from the paperback the subject to the documentary and the subject to the 2012 two-Government funded television miniseries involving Network Nine's alleged rival Network 10 — the absence of an exposure on this cover up indicates inter television network collusion or 'fake news'.

What may bind the Sydney television networks to act as one? Ownership? Politics? Freemason family membership?

Network Ten also defended foul mouthed Mick MOLLOY for his 2011 indecency slur by defamatory statement about a specific woman whose husband was a high profile sports person. Which means they paid thousands to court defend and appeal a televised misogynistic slur, against one woman that equates to their feelings about all women generally. So who else were best suited to publish a six part mini series based on the paperbak that stole

3: 2014 Sept 22, cover letter for Federal Court order "reasons".

FEDERAL COURT OF AUSTRALIA

Chambers of Justice Anna Katzmann
Level 19
Law Courts Building
Queens Square, Sydney 2000
DX 613 Sydney

Phone: (02) 9230-8474
Fax: (02) 9230-8361

22 September 2014

Janette Gail Francis
34 Whitestone Crescent
Seaford Rise SA 5169

Dear Ms Francis

Janette Gail Francis v Allen & Unwin
NSD 339 of 2014

I refer to the judgment of Justice Anna Katzmann, delivered on 22 September 2014 and now enclose a certified copy of the reasons for your records.

Yours sincerely

Fiona Chong
Associate to the Honourable Justice Anna Katzmann

my biometric identity since 1989 and called the person who owned my face when aged fifteen:

"A cheap little slut" and *"bikie moll"*

I bring to light that in 1971 when I was really fifteen years old I was statutory raped by the children of Campbelltown High school Freemason police in New South Wales, who were never charged with my statutory rape. Right there we have motive to criminally defame me with the Allen and Unwin SIMPSON and HARVEY paperback, funded by Freemasons called "Brothers In Arms".

In 2014 Network Nine published their television and youtube.com (terrorist) documentary to perpetuate the cover up the then, 30 year NSW Freemason police crime its been 40 years now in 2024. The order like so many other court orders, in itself is nothing without the judges "reasons for judgment".

Its a **Copyright Act** infringement claim I've been unable to finish because of the strong terrorism undercurrent that ravages Australia's secret Freemason centric legal system. My evidence based allegation is that my photo of my adult face was stolen by the publishers and authors and Walters family as their third representation of their fake dead fake person Leanne Walters. The falsely alleged "innocent bystander" that fed the anti motorcycle club frenzy since the 1980s.

Freemason police alleged a female child was murdered by 'warring outlaw bikies' when caught in the crossfire of their gunfight. Obviously a psychologically trick, intended to fabricate public rage with the eyes focused on the motorcycle clubs as the offenders when in reality they were the targeted victims of Freemasons. They generated the 'mob mentality' to cover up their own crimes and the people globally acted like imbeciles believing the terrorist's spin year after decade despite the evidence to the contrary the terrorists are still elected back into parliament in all of the ensuing 40 years.

In reality "Leanne Walters" was an elaborate mannequin toss after undercover Freemason police cold bloodedly murdered an unknown number of the actual dead. The facts of that is evidenced in the photos published amongst the three versions of the SIMPSON & HARVEY paperback.

Evidently the secret Freemason ambush was elaborately planned to dispose of adults who had been child witnesses to Freemason child rape, as I was throughout my unenviable childhood with psychopathic male parent.

The documents themselves don't prove the cover up in those words. That conspiracy is proved irrefutably by the Government's 100% lack of lawful action (demanded by statute) and the news industry's absence of ethical news reporting in response to the matters defined by the photographs in the first SIMPSON & HARVEY paperback document — first copyright or

FEDERAL COURT OF AUSTRALIA

Francis v Allen & Unwin [2014] FCA 1027

Citation:	Francis v Allen & Unwin [2014] FCA 1027
Parties:	**JANETTE GAIL FRANCIS v ALLEN & UNWIN PTY LIMITED, LINDSAY SIMPSON, PAMELA WALTERS, REX WALTERS and LORRAINE WALTERS**
File number:	NSD 339 of 2014
Judge:	**KATZMANN J**
Date of judgment:	22 September 2014
Catchwords:	**PRACTICE AND PROCEDURE** – application by respondents for summary judgment – whether applicant has reasonable prospect of successfully prosecuting the proceeding – claim of infringement of copyright and moral rights in artistic work – photograph – photograph alleged to be a self-portrait of the applicant – factual dispute about the identity of the subject – whether real issue of fact to be tried – whether applicant's case that she is the subject of the photograph fanciful, frivolous, vexatious or an abuse of process – *Federal Court of Australia Act 1976* (Cth), s 31A(2)
Legislation:	*Copyright Act 1968* (Cth) ss 10, 31, 31A, 35 , 36, 115, 189, 195AC, 195AI, 195AK, Division 6 of Part IX *Evidence Act 1995* (Cth), s 75 *Federal Court of Australia Act 1976* (Cth) s 31A(2)
Cases cited:	*Australian Securities and Investments Commission v Cassimatis* (2013) 220 FCR 256 *Cachia v Hanes* (1994) 179 CLR 403 *George v Fletcher (Trustee) (No 2)* [2010] FCAFC 71 *George v Fletcher (Trustee)* [2010] FCAFC 53 *Jefferson Ford Pty Ltd v Ford Motor Company of Australia Ltd* (2008) 167 FCR 372 *Spencer v Commonwealth of Australia* (2010) 241 CLR 118 *Visscher v Teekay Shipping (Australia) Pty Limited (No 3)* [2012] FCA 212
Date of hearing:	18 September 2014

4 Citation page 1 of 2 *Francis v Allen & Unwin* [2014] FCA 1027

published globally in 1989.

My evidence is in addition to that already existing irrefutable "pictorial" evidence.

Then my documented evidence since 1989 establishing what Governments have done to me without lawful authority — unconstitutionally, compared to my verbal evidence that my male parent was imprisoned for my rape in 1959 and since I became an adult Freemasons claim his imprisonment never happened and verbally claim to my face my 1959 ripped vaginal skin, scars, happened because my nappy wearing crutch fell on something else that extensively tore my skin without having any evidence of that allegation.

Freemason government officials had evidently destroyed my male parent's conviction to pervert the course of justice. One cog in nation-wide Australian Freemason child rape *quantum* cover up.

The pivotal finding that should have been plastered globally across newspapers was on page "-8-*" of the 'reasons for judgment' thus:

> *"While the quality of the copies in evidence is admittedly poor, I am not presently persuaded by the respondents' submission that the photographs published in the newspaper are of the same person depicted in the photographs in the book. The photograph published in the book appears to be of an older woman with different facial features. There is no evidence to suggest that any member of the Walters family supplied the photograph to either the authors or the publisher. The book contains a statement to the effect that the photograph was supplied by the NSW Police Department, although the NSW Police Department wrote to Ms Francis denying that they were the source of the photograph.*

This spells out in no uncertain terms by inference that the 2012 multipart television series funded by two Government taxpayer Arts grants[3] was in reality criminal misappropriation of government resources that kept feeding the child rape cover up Freemason propaganda machine. That Screen Australia, Screen New South Wales and Screentime Australia[4], the private

---

[3] *Grants from Commonwealth and State of New South Wales.*

[4]

5: Citation page 1 of 2 *FRANCIS V ALLEN & UNWIN* [2014] FCA 1027

- 2 -

Place:	Sydney
Division:	GENERAL
Category:	Catchwords
Number of paragraphs:	28
Counsel for the Applicant:	The Applicant appeared in person.
Counsel for the First, Second, Fifth and Sixth Respondents:	Mr D Thomas
Solicitor for the First, Second, Fifth and Sixth Respondents:	Banki Haddock Fiora
Counsel for the Fourth Respondent:	No appearance.

venture, along with the original publishing company Unwin Hyman Limited (Scotland) and Allen and Unwin Pty Ltd (Australia & NZ) author Lindsay SIMPSON[5] and author Sandra HARVEY[6], and all the kings men including HARVEY's real mother author Lynette STYLES[7], director Peter ANDRIKIDIS, writers Greg HADRICK, Josephine MARTINO, Roger SIMPSON, producer Roger SIMPSON, Louisa Kors (or Cors) , executive producers Gred HADDRICK, Rick MAIER and Des MONAGHAN — they were all involved in this terrorist crime as enemies of Australia. They would have reasonably known there was an ulterior reason to fake the identity of the fake LEANNE WALTERS whether or not they knew it was to cover up Freemason history of child rape is inconsequential in the totality of their despicable crime.

Instead of the breaking news hitting the printing presses and radio airwaves there was silence.

Back in 2002 New South Wales police Commissioner's office wrote to me dated 2002 May 7 to inform me they intended to undermine Australian law, the Commonwealth Constitution and my statutory rights not to be criminally assaulted by Australia's Freemasons or anyone in relation to my identity theft if this criminal Copyright theft/ Alleged assistant commissioner too spineless to give their full name wrote the details of their personal terrorist plan decided in a criminal conspiracy with the actual Commissioner of police and and the Minister of police in 2003. Their only expenditure in "this" my issue was opening the file and remembering the crime and refusing to correct the 1989 terrorist act, their terrorist plan thus:

> *"In view of the considerable amount of police resources expended in pursuing this issue, I do not propose to undertake further inquiries in the matter. Any further correspondence from you on the subject will not be acknowledged and simply filed away with departmental papers."*

That means I've been officially outlawed by police which has the effect of not protecting my statutory right not to be criminally defamed as a "cheap little slut" and "bikie moll".

Police are tasked to investigate crime — this is a crime, its called perverting the course of justice since the Commonwealth & State funded the TV miniseries they describe the miniseries as *"based on the paperback"* not based on the true facts of the alleged crimes.

---

[5] *Raynor UNWIN's daughter, either Camilla, Sharon or Tamara Unwin.*

[6] *Leanne SLOWMAN.*

[7] *Mother Elaine SLOWMAN alleged wife of the company secretary, Duggy.*

6: Reasons for Judgment, page 1 of 10 *FRANCIS V ALLEN & UNWIN* ORS.

IN THE FEDERAL COURT OF AUSTRALIA

NEW SOUTH WALES DISTRICT REGISTRY

GENERAL DIVISION   NSD 339 of 2014

BETWEEN: JANETTE GAIL FRANCIS
                Applicant

AND: ALLEN & UNWIN PTY LIMITED
                First Respondent

                LINDSAY SIMPSON
                Second Respondent

                PAMELA WALTERS
                Fourth Respondent

                REX WALTERS
                Fifth Respondent

                LORRAINE WALTERS
                Sixth Respondent

JUDGE: KATZMANN J
DATE: 22 SEPTEMBER 2014
PLACE: SYDNEY

REASONS FOR JUDGMENT

1. On the first Sunday in September 1984 seven people were killed in a notorious shootout between two rival motorcycle gangs in the southwest of Sydney in what came to be known as the Milperra massacre. One of the victims was Leanne Walters, then aged 15, who was caught in the crossfire.

2. Two journalists, Lindsay Simpson and Sandra Harvey, wrote a book about the event entitled "Brothers in Arms: The Inside Story of Two Bikie Gangs". The book was published by Allen & Unwin. The first edition appeared in 1989. The book includes two copies of a photograph of a young woman, who is named as Leanne Walters ("the photograph"). In this proceeding the applicant, Janette Francis (formerly Hall), insists the photograph does not depict Ms Walters but is a photograph of her at the age of 27. She pleads that she took the photograph herself in a photo booth in Liverpool and that it is an artistic work showing her smoothing her lips inside the booth. She alleges that the photograph was reproduced in the

Sure I can take civil action — if I can find a lawyer not aligned with the Tripartizan terrorist organization in Australia in the past decades on this issue that hasn't happened.

Effectively anonymous author DB MADDEN claimed to be deputy Commissioner operations NSW police department. The actual police Commissioner was Kenneth MORONEY was/is a Campbelltown NSW resident.

MINISTERS FOR TERRORIST POLICE AT MATERIAL TIMES[8]

LABOR Peter Thomas ANDERSON, 26 May 1982-6 Feb 1986.

LABOR George PACIULLO, 6 Feb 1986 - 21 Mar 1988.

LIBERAL Edward (Ted) Philip PICKERING, 25 Mar 1988 - 23 Sep 1992.

LIBERAL Terry Griffiths, 23 Sep 1992 - 27 Jun 1994.

NATIONAL Garry West, 27 Jun 1994 - 4 Apr 1995.

LABOR Paul Francis Patrick WHELAN, 4 Apr 1995 - 21 Nov 2001. WHELAN the longest serving NSW POLICE MINISTER evidently because he was a die-hard terrorist, he employed author Sandra HARVEY as his news media "spin doctor" evidently because she'd proven herself to hold her nerve as a compulsive liar despite evidence that proved her wrong. LABOR Michael COSTA, 21 Nov 2001 - 2 Apr 2003.

LABOR John WATKINS, 2 Apr 2003 - 21 Jan 2005.

LABOR Carl SCULLY, 21 Jan 2005 - 26 Oct 2006.

LABOR John WATKINS, 26 Oct 2006 - 2 Apr 2007.

LABOR David CAMPBELL, 2 Apr 2007 - 5 Sep 2008.

LABOR Matt BROWN, 8 Sep 2008 - 11 Sep 2008.

LABOR Tony KELLY, 11 Sep 2008 - 14 Sep 2009.

LABOR Michael DALEY, 14 Sep 2009 - 28 Mar 2011.

LIBERAL Mike GALLACHER, 4 Apr 2011 - 2 May 2014.

LIBERAL Stuart AYRES, 6 May 2014 - 1 Apr 2015.

NATIONAL Troy GRANT, 2 Apr 2015 -23 Mar 2019.

LIBERAL David ELLIOTT, 2 Apr 2019 - 21 Dec 2021.

---

[8] *https://en.wikipedia.org/wiki/Minister_for_Police_(New_South_Wales)3 (accessed 7 Feb 2024)*

7: Reasons for Judgment, page 2 of 10 *FRANCIS v ALLEN & UNWIN* ORS.

- 2 -

book without her permission, and that, by reason of the publication, each of the respondents has infringed her copyright and also her moral rights in the photograph.

3   Rex Walters is Leanne's father, Pamela Walters is her mother, and Lorraine Walters is Rex Walters's wife. Their involvement, if any, in the alleged infringement is presently obscure.

4   The *Copyright Act 1968* (Cth) permits the owner of a copyright to bring an action for an infringement of the copyright (s 115). Subject to s 35 of the Act, the author of a literary, dramatic, musical or artistic work is the owner of any copyright subsisting in the work (s 35). A photograph is an artistic work, regardless of whether it is of artistic quality (s 10). For the purposes of the Act, unless the contrary intention appears, copyright, in relation to an artistic work is the exclusive right to reproduce the work in a material form, to publish the work and to communicate the work to the public (s 31). Subject to the Act, the copyright in an artistic work is infringed if a person who is not the owner of the copyright or who does not have the licence of the owner does or authorises to be done in Australia any act comprised in the copyright (s 36). Since 2000, "moral rights" have also been protected by the Copyright Act. A "moral right" in relation to an author is a right of attribution of authorship, a right not to have authorship falsely attributed or a right of integrity of authorship (s 189). Section 195AC provides that the author of a work has a right not to have authorship of the work falsely attributed. Section 195AI provides that the author of a work has the right not to have the work subjected to derogatory treatment (defined in s 195AK in relation to an artistic work to include the doing of anything in relation to the work that is prejudicial to the author's honour or reputation). The circumstances in which infringement of moral rights may occur are set out in Division 6 of Part IX of the Act.

5   No defence has been filed. Rather, on 18 July 2014 the first, second, fifth and sixth respondents ("the respondents") filed an application for summary judgment or, alternatively, an order striking out the substance of the statement of claim. The application is supported by three affidavits from Peter Christopher Banki, the solicitor for the respondents. The basis of the application, as it was outlined in the respondents' written submissions, is that the proceeding enjoys no reasonable prospect of success because:

> the allegation that the Photograph depicts [Ms Francis] is fanciful, implausible and improbable and contrary to all available material. The likelihood of [Ms Francis] proving the contention on the balance of probabilities at trial is non-existent. In the absence of the allegation, [Ms Francis's] pleaded case falls away.

National Paul TOOLE, 21 Dec 2021 - 28 Mar 2023.

Labor Yasmin CATLEY, 5 Apr 2023 - publication.

Minister for Counter Terrorism Exempting Terrorist Police[9]

Liberal David ELLIOTT, 30 Jan 2017 - 2 Apr 2019.

Anthony ROBERTS, 2 Apr 2019 - 21 Dec 2021.

Labor Yasmin CATLEY, 5 Apr 2023 -publication.

Lot of money pumped into ministerial appointments but no action to stop perpetuation and proliferation of terrorist crimes from within the rank and file of "Party faithful" being paid by taxpayers to act within Australian official law in government or at large infiltrating the community in their search for indentured apprentices for future government public office terrorism. ♉

---

[9] *https://en.wikipedia.org/wiki/Minister_for_Police_(New_South_Wales)3 (accessed 7 Feb 2024)*

8: Reasons for Judgment, page 3 of 10 *FRANCIS V ALLEN & UNWIN* ORS.

- 3 -

6   The respondents contend that there is no "real question of fact" as to whether Ms Francis was the person in the photograph (*Australian Securities and Investments Commission v Cassimatis* (2013) 220 FCR 256 at [47]). The respondents also contend that the allegation that the photograph depicts Ms Francis, rather than Ms Walters, is "frivolous" and "vexatious" and that there is no evidence of it. The evidence they rely on to support their contentions is essentially contained in Mr Banki's affidavit of 18 July 2014 and a signed copy of the first edition of the book, which they tendered. Errors in the 18 July 2014 affidavit are corrected in Mr Banki's second affidavit, affirmed on 23 July 2014.

7   The evidence establishes, relevantly, that the photograph in issue appears in the book in the top left hand corner of page ix and the fourth page of photographs between pages 132 and 133. Under the copy of the photograph on page ix the words "Leanne Walters, shot dead" appear. The source of the photograph, along with all the accompanying photographs, is said to be the NSW Police Department. Rex Walters told Mr Banki (when, where and in what circumstances Mr Banki does not say) that he (Mr Walters) was certain the photograph was a photograph of his daughter, Leanne. The other photograph (which is identical to the first) appears as part of a "Sex License" and bears the name in handwriting "Leanne Walters" which Mr Walters told Mr Banki he was certain was his daughter's signature. Mr Walters attended the launch of the book and the authors gave him the copy of the book that was tendered in evidence. It is inscribed by the authors with messages of gratitude to Mr Walters for his assistance.

8   Mr Banki's evidence also demonstrates that Allen & Unwin is a reputable publisher, that Ms Simpson is a former journalist for the *Sydney Morning Herald* and the author and co-author of six works of non-fiction, and that Ms Harvey is dead. I interpolate that Ms Harvey was named as the third respondent but was later removed as a party. Mr Banki stated that he was told by Mr Walters that Leanne's mother, Pamela Walters, is also dead. At this stage, however, she remains a party. Over Ms Francis's objection and in the absence of a death certificate, death or funeral notice or an obituary or, indeed, anything more than the bare assertion, I decline to make a similar order in her case.

9: Reasons for Judgment, page 4 of 10 *FRANCIS V ALLEN & UNWIN* ORS.

- 4 -

9   The rest of Mr Banki's evidence consists of:

- references to websites operated by Ms Francis;

- a hearsay account of Ms Francis driving a vehicle in the streets of Campbelltown painted with the words "Walters is a liar", which was apparently reported to the police;

- a reference to an action brought by Ms Francis in the Equal Opportunity Tribunal of South Australia against Christies Beach Medical Centre, the relevance of which is opaque; and

- a reference to a proceeding in the Supreme Court of South Australia in which Ms Francis sued Allen & Unwin over its use of the photograph, in which she maintained it was a photograph of her.

10   The Supreme Court of South Australia struck out Ms Francis's statement of claim and dismissed her action with costs when she failed to appear at a directions hearing. According to an account of what occurred from the lawyers who appeared, presumably as agents for Allen & Unwin's solicitors, the orders were made because the statement of claim did not disclose a reasonable cause of action and was "vexatious" and because the court considered that Ms Francis was unable to plead "a cause of action known to law on which there could be a fair trial". The respondents drew particular attention to the following two orders Ms Francis sought in that proceeding:

> 13   Urgently, I want the foreign objects of technological advancement hindering me and hurting me internally and externally, removed by qualified medical personnel not affiliated with any person involved with the 1984 murders of the seven people in Milperra as previously stated, and to be funded by Defendants.
>
> 14   I want the Allen & Unwin Pty Ltd directors' to experience exactly what they have caused me, I want them bankrupt, penniless, with no future, lousy health, and no help, and no support, and tortured for at least 22 uninterrupted years, and a criminal record.

11   Mr Banki's affidavit of 18 July 2014 also refers to a large number of documents, few of which ultimately made their way into evidence. Those that did include statements made on websites operated by Ms Francis in which she claimed, amongst other things, that:

10: Reasons for Judgment, p 5 of 10 *FRANCIS V ALLEN & UNWIN* ORS.

- 5 -

- • Allen & Unwin, the Walters family, the NSW Government, the Commonwealth Government, the Australian Labor Party and the Liberal Party of Australia are engaged in a criminal partnership by using her photograph and causing the book to be published.

- • Allen & Unwin had "totally offended [her] and was allowed to get off without any penalty whatsoever after they breached all the Australian laws of copyright and libel" and that it was "[her] turn to display photographs of the types of people who do this in Australia and are able to pay the Judge enough cold hard rewards to successfully buy their way out of being sued in court using diversionary tactics".

12   The substance of the respondents' case is that Ms Francis's claim should not be accepted over the evidence of Mr Banki about what he was told by Mr Walters because it is Mr Walters who is best placed to give evidence as to the identity of the subject of the photograph. The respondents argued that it was implausible that Mr Walters would attend the book launch, keep a copy of the book containing the photograph and instruct lawyers to prosecute this interlocutory application if it were not a photograph of his daughter. They also submitted that it was implausible that the inscriptions of gratitude in the book would have been made if the photograph were not of his daughter. They urged the Court to look critically at Ms Francis's evidence and weigh it against the other evidence. They submitted that Ms Francis's statements (made on her websites and in the statement of claim that was struck out) showed that the evidence of Ms Francis ought to be given less weight than that of the respondents. They submitted that the material posted on Ms Francis's websites was "ridiculous" and contained "outlandish, highly extravagant and unfounded allegations" against Allen & Unwin. They submitted that Ms Francis's statements showed that she was a vindictive person who had conducted a campaign against the publisher since at least 2006 (when the South Australian proceeding was filed). On this basis, they submitted that the Court could not be confident that the allegations made by Ms Francis were sensibly made and invited the Court to find that Ms Francis's application was "frivolous or vexatious or an abuse of process" (*Spencer v Commonwealth of Australia* (2010) 241 CLR 118 ("*Spencer*") at [22]).

13   For the reasons that follow these contentions must be rejected.

11: Reasons for Judgment, p 6 of 10 *FRANCIS V ALLEN & UNWIN* ORS.

- 6 -

14   Section 31A(2) of the *Federal Court of Australia Act 1976* (Cth) confers upon the Court the power in a civil action to give judgment for one party against another in relation to the whole or any part of a proceeding if the Court is satisfied that the other party has no reasonable prospect of successfully prosecuting the proceeding or that part of the proceeding. For the purpose of the section, subs (3) relevantly provides that the proceeding or part thereof need not be hopeless or bound to fail for it to have no reasonable prospects of success.

15   There is no doubt, as the respondents submitted, that the terms of s 31A demonstrate that Parliament's intention was to "relax" the requirements for obtaining summary judgment or dismissal. In *Spencer* at [53] Hayne, Crennan, Kiefel and Bell JJ described the test in s 31A as a radical departure from the provisions it replaced, which required "demonstrated certainty of outcome", rather than an assessment of the prospects of success (at [53]–[56]). I also accept that in *George v Fletcher (Trustee)* [2010] FCAFC 53 the Full Court said at [75] that the mere existence of a factual controversy, "however trifling, implausible, tenuous or tangentially relevant" does not preclude the Court from exercising the power in s 31A.

16   The respondents relied on the following remarks of Finkelstein J in *Jefferson Ford Pty Ltd v Ford Motor Company of Australia Ltd* (2008) 167 FCR 372 at [23]:

> [T]he section requires the judge to conduct what might loosely be described as a preliminary trial and look more closely than he would under an O 14 application to a party's assertion that there is a real question of law or fact to be decided. Such an assertion is to be examined with a critical eye. The judge is to decide whether the opposing party has evidence of sufficient quality and weight to be able to succeed at trial. There will be cases where the asserted facts appear to be so improbable that there is no point in allowing them to go to trial.

17   I accept that a party's assertion that there is a real question of fact to be decided should be examined critically. Still, the power remains draconian. As Allen & Unwin acknowledge, it must be applied with caution and is not to be exercised lightly: *Spencer* at [60]. In *Spencer* French CJ and Gummow J observed at [25] that s 31A(2) requires a practical judgment as to whether the applicant has more than a fanciful prospect of success. Nevertheless, their Honours continued:

> Where there are factual issues capable of being disputed and in dispute, summary dismissal should not be awarded to the respondent simply because the Court has formed the view that the applicant is unlikely to succeed on the factual issue.

12: Reasons for Judgment, p 7 of 10 *Francis v Allen & Unwin* ORS.

- 7 -

18   In my opinion this is such a case. Here there is a factual issue capable of being disputed and in dispute. Ms Francis asserts that it is she who is depicted in the photograph. Mr Banki's affidavit includes a statement to the effect that Mr Walters is certain that the photograph published in the book is a photograph of his daughter and that the signature on the so-called "Sex License" is his daughter's signature. Ultimately, whether Ms Francis's assertion is made good will depend on whether she can satisfy the Court on the balance of probabilities that she is, indeed, the subject of the photograph. If she gives evidence to support her assertion, the Court will need to evaluate the strengths and weaknesses of that evidence against all the other evidence. That will include an assessment of her honesty and reliability and, if Mr Walters gives evidence, his honesty and reliability also. Neither exercise can be undertaken at this early stage.

19   The respondents bear the onus of proof on the present application. Having cast a critical eye over the evidence, I do not consider they have discharged it. I am unable to accept the submission that Ms Francis's allegation is fanciful, even if it might be improbable. More particularly, I am not satisfied that there are no reasonable prospects Ms Francis will succeed. Nor am I satisfied that her action is frivolous or vexatious.

20   By her statement of claim Ms Francis alleges that the photograph is her self-portrait. She is capable of giving evidence to that effect. This is, however, no bare assertion. Contrary to the assertion in the respondents' submissions, there is evidence to support it. In her affidavit of 4 August 2014 Ms Francis states that the photographs in the book purporting to be photographs of Leanne Walters are in fact photographs of her at the age of 27. Her case does not rest there. She has demonstrated that there is evidence capable of corroborating her assertion. Annexed to her affidavit of 6 August 2014 is a handwritten statement dated 6 July 2002 from William Peters to whom Ms Francis says she was married for 13 years and to whom she would have been married when she was 27 years old. In that statement Mr Peters refers directly to the photograph appearing on page ix of the book. He states that the photograph said to be of Leanne Walters is, in his opinion, that of "Jenette Gail Hall" with whom he lived from 1974 to 1984. In the affidavit Ms Francis states that she was known as Ms Hall "due to a defacto (*sic*) relationship after [her] marriage" and Mr Peters has spelled her Christian name incorrectly.

13: Reasons for Judgment, p 8 of 10 FRANCIS V ALLEN & UNWIN ORS paragraphs 21 & 22 disclose the historical judicial decision Sydney's news industry chose to unethically suppress to this day ten years later in 2024..

- 8 -

21   In addition, annexed to Ms Francis's affidavit of 4 August 2014 are copies of newspaper articles about the death of Ms Walters published in the *Sun* newspaper on 3 and 4 September 1984, and in the *Daily Mirror* on 6 September 1984. The two articles in the *Sun* are accompanied by a photograph purportedly of Ms Walters. In the article in the *Daily Mirror*, there is a photograph of Rex Walters, shown holding that photograph of Ms Walters, which is described as "a cherished photo of Leanne". While the quality of the copies in evidence is admittedly poor, I am not presently persuaded by the respondents' submission that the photographs published in the newspaper are of the same person depicted in the photographs in the book. The photograph published in the book appears to be of an older woman with different facial features. There is no evidence to suggest that any member of the Walters family supplied the photograph to either the authors or the publisher. The book contains a statement to the effect that the photograph was supplied by the NSW Police Department, although the NSW Police Department wrote to Ms Francis denying that they were the source of the photograph.

22   Against that, all the respondents offer is hearsay and innuendo. While hearsay evidence is admissible on an interlocutory application (*Evidence Act 1995* (Cth), s 75), it is generally entitled to less weight than direct evidence. It was open to the respondents to proffer sworn evidence from Mr Walters but they elected, without explanation, not to do so. I do not doubt for present purposes that Mr Walters honestly believes that the photograph is a photograph of his daughter but the statement attributed to Mr Walters is a bare assertion. Without more, it is insufficient to persuade me that it renders Ms Francis's case fanciful, frivolous or vexatious. The fact that he instructed lawyers to bring this application may speak to the genuineness of his belief but no more than that. That the authors of the book expressed gratitude for Mr Walters's assistance tells us nothing about the subject matter of the photograph. The source of the photograph is not said to be Mr Walters. That Mr Walters attended the launch of the book and kept a copy of it sheds no further light on the matter.

23   In any event, the proposition that Mr Walters is best placed to identify the subject of the photograph is open to question. Buried within it is an assumption, yet to be proved, that the photograph is indeed a photograph of his daughter. If Ms Francis took the photograph, however, and if the photograph is of her, then surely she is best placed to identify its subject. The evidence relating to either the pleading in, or the disposition of, the South Australian proceedings does not support the conclusion that the proceeding in this Court is vexatious. In contrast to that case, the relief sought in the present case is orthodox. Moreover, in the South

14: Reasons for Judgment, p 9 of 10 *FRANCIS V ALLEN & UNWIN* ORS.

- 9 -

Australian case Ms Francis raised no claim of copyright infringement. Plainly, the possibility of such a claim had not at that time occurred to Ms Francis.

24　The subtext of the respondents' case is that Ms Francis is delusional and/or deceitful, actuated by some ulterior purpose, although they stopped short of making such a submission. The wild and outlandish statements upon which the respondents relied were made after Ms Francis became aware of the publication. If she is to be believed, she was deeply offended by the association of her image with statements in the book which, because of the use of her image, she regarded as highly defamatory. That is not implausible. She said in her affidavit of 17 September that the websites were "a form of defence of [her] good character". She stated:

> I was and am infuriated by the theft of my visual identity, the websites were a direct result of being ignored by the respondents I was thereby provoked into believing all my complaints had been linked to a common cause; to discredit my reputation.

25　While her response to the publication of the photographs might be regarded as an overreaction, even irrational in some respects, and while many of the statements, on their face, appear to lack credibility, I am not persuaded on the whole of the evidence that the case she wishes to make should not proceed to trial. Questions of credibility are quintessentially unsuitable for summary resolution.

26　Of course, the real question is not who is depicted in the photograph but who took it. The respondents offered no evidence touching on this question. Nor did they offer any evidence as to the circumstances in which the photograph was taken. The statement of claim pleads that it was Ms Francis who took the photograph and outlines the circumstances in which it was taken. There is nothing implausible in that allegation. For present purposes, at least, the respondents apparently accept that, if the photograph is in fact of Ms Francis, then she is the artist who owns the copyright. Whether or not that allegation is made out should be determined at trial.

27　In these circumstances the motion for summary judgment must be rejected. No submissions were directed to the alternative relief.

28　Accordingly, the respondents' application should be dismissed. Costs should follow the event. I note that as a litigant in person Ms Francis is not entitled to recover costs for the time and effort she spent in preparing her case or for presenting it in court (*Cachia v Hanes* (1994) 179 CLR 403; *George v Fletcher (Trustee) (No 2)* [2010] FCAFC 71), but she may

15: Reasons for Judgment, p 10 of 10 *Francis v Allen & Unwin* ORS.

- 10 -

recover her out-of-pocket expenses, such as filing fees and photocopying expenses (*George v Fletcher (Trustee) (No 2)* at [17]; *Visscher v Teekay Shipping (Australia) Pty Limited (No 3)* [2012] FCA 212 at [9]).

I certify that the preceding twenty-eight (28) numbered paragraphs are a true copy of the Reasons for Judgment herein of the Honourable Justice Katzmann.

Associate:

Dated: 22 September 2014

It'll never be over until these Tripartizan terrorists are in prison where they belong and barbarism is 100% outlawed.

Your 'fake' democratic constitution governments are subsidizing and encouraging community standard hate.

This is 'culture' is best personified by the answer to a reasonable question I saw video recorded on television recently. I suspect its an old interview involving a 'celebrity' chef who in reality should never have be banned from national television at the first signs of his bully-boy personality involving news industry applauded, psychopathically narcissistic tantrums, broadcast on television to let the viewers know this is what's expected of Australians if they want to be a stand-out "celebrity".

The person asking the question of TV tantrum chef sounded male. Evidently he'd been a paying customer in tantrum chef's restaurant where he asked for a type of meat cooked "well done" — the photo showed a crispy burnt piece of rotting flesh that not even you dog would want to chew on. The response from tantrum chef was effectively:

'if you don't like what I want you to like then you have no value as a person'.

Yes that's the non-verbal message oozing from this TV tantrum chef and by default, that's the message the television network want to send to you. The same corporate entity censuring all your daily news to ensuring your fake democracy government look perfect, like Jesus 'imself. Which government? The government who by refusing to allow poor or anti fake democracy persons their right to competently sue their own country's terrorist governments in Australia's public legal system are sending you this message:

"If you're not like us then you're not welcome in this country, fukoff and die somewhere we don't have to see you."

☿

www.ingramcontent.com/pod-product-compliance
Lightning Source LLC
Chambersburg PA
CBHW060233050426
42448CB00009B/1426